Washington Irving

Salmagundi

Washington Irving

Salmagundi

ISBN/EAN: 9783337174514

Printed in Europe, USA, Canada, Australia, Japan

Cover: Foto ©ninafisch / pixelio.de

More available books at **www.hansebooks.com**

BY

WASHINGTON IRVING.

NEW YORK:
JOHN W. LOVELL COMPANY,
14 AND 16 VESEY STREET.

SALMAGUNDI.

CONTENTS.

VOLUME I.

No.		PAGE
I.	SATURDAY, JANUARY 24, 1807	5
	Publisher's Notice. Shakespeare Gallery, New York	6
	From the Elbow-Chair of Launcelot Langstaff, Esq.	7
	Theatrics—Containing the Quintessence of Modern Criticism. By William Wizard, Esq	12
	New York Assembly. By Anthony Evergreen, Gent.	14
II.	WEDNESDAY, FEBRUARY 4, 1807.—From the Elbow-Chair of Launcelot Langstaff, Esq.	18
	Mr. Wilson's Concert. By Anthony Evergreen, Gent.	22
	Cockloft Family	24
	To Launcelot Langstaff, Esq.	27
	Advertisement	29
III.	FRIDAY, FEBRUARY 13, 1807.—From my Elbow-Chair	31
	Letter from Mustapha Rub-A-Dub Keli Kahn, Captain of a Ketch, to Asem Hacchem, Principal Slave-Driver to his Highness, the Bashaw of Tripoli	33
	Fashions. By Anthony Evergreen, Gent.	36
	Proclamation from the Mill of Pindar Cockloft, Esq.	41
IV.	TUESDAY, FEBRUARY 24, 1807.—From my Elbow-Chair	44
	Memorandums for a Tour to be entitled, "The Stranger in New Jersey; or, Cockney Travelling." By Jeremy Cockloft, the Younger	46
V.	SATURDAY, MARCH 7, 1807.—From my Elbow-Chair	51
	Letter from Mustapha Rub-A-Dub Keli Khan to Abdallah Eb'n Al Rahab, surnamed the Snorer, Military Sentinel at the Gate of his Highness's Palace	51
	By Anthony Evergreen, Gent.	59
	To the Ladies. From the Mill of Pindar Cockloft, Esq.	63
VI.	FRIDAY, MARCH 20, 1807.—From my Elbow-Chair	66
	Theatrics. By William Wizard, Esq	74
VII.	SATURDAY, APRIL 4, 1807.—Letter from Mustapha Rub-A-Dub Keli Khan, to Asem Hacchem, Principal Slave-Driver to his Highness, the Bashaw of Tripoli	80
	From the Mill of Pindar Cockloft, Esq. Notes by William Wizard, Esq.	87
VIII.	SATURDAY, APRIL 18, 1807.—By Anthony Evergreen, Gent.	91
	On Style. By William Wizard, Esq.	97
	To Correspondents	102

CONTENTS.

No.	PAGE
IX. SATURDAY, APRIL 25, 1807.—From my Elbow-Chair.	105
From my Elbow-Chair	110
Letter from Mustapha Rub-A-Dub Keli Khan, Captain of a Ketch, to Asem Hacchem, Principal Slave-Driver to his Highness, the Bashaw of Tripoli	111
From the Mill of Pindar Cockloft, Esq.	117
X. SATURDAY, MAY 16, 1807.—From my Elbow-Chair	122
To Launcelot Langstaff, Esq.	123

VOLUME II.

Note	129
XI. TUESDAY, JUNE 2, 1807.—Letter from Mustapha Rub-A-Dub Keli Khan, Captain of a Ketch, to Asem Hacchem, Principal Slave-Driver to his Highness, the Bashaw of Tripoli	131
From my Elbow-Chair. Mine Uncle John	138
XII. SATURDAY, JUNE 27, 1807.—From my Elbow-Chair	144
The Stranger at Home; or, A Tour in Broadway. By Jeremy Cockloft, the Younger	150
From my Elbow-Chair	156
From the Mill of Pindar Cockloft, Esq.	157
XIII. FRIDAY, AUGUST 14, 1807.—From my Elbow-Chair	161
Plans for Defending our Harbor. By William Wizard, Esq	164
From my Elbow Chair. A Retrospect; or, "What you Will"	169
To Readers and Correspondents	177
XIV. SATURDAY, SEPTEMBER 16, 1807.—Letter from Mustapha Rub-A-Dub Keli Khan to Asem Hacchem, Principal Slave-Driver to his Highness, the Bashaw of Tripoli	179
Cockloft Hall. By Launcelot Langstaff, Esq.	186
Theatrical Intelligence. By William Wizard, Esq.	193
XV. THURSDAY, OCTOBER 1, 1807.—Sketches from Nature. By Anthony Evergreen, Gent	197
On Greatness. By Launcelot Langstaff, Esq.	202
XVI. THURSDAY, OCTOBER 15, 1807.—Style at Ballston. By William Wizard, Esq.	209
Letter from Mustapha Rub-A-Dub Keli Khan, to Asem Hacchem, Principal Slave-Driver to his Highness, the Bashaw of Tripoli	214
XVII. WEDNESDAY, NOVEMBER 11, 1807.—Autumnal Reflections. By Launcelot Langstaff, Esq.	221
By Launcelot Langstaff, Esq.	225
Chap. CIX.—Of the Chronicles of the Renowned and Ancient City of Gotham	228
XVIII. TUESDAY, NOVEMBER 24, 1807.—The Little Man in Black. By Launcelot Langstaff, Esq	234
Letter from Mustapha Rub-A-Dub Keli Khan, to Asem Hacchem, Principal Slave-Driver to his Highness, the Bashaw of Tripoli	240
XIX. THURSDAY, DECEMBER 31, 1807.—From my Elbow-Chair	246
Letter from Mustapha Rub-A-Dub Keli Khan to Muley Helim al Raggi, surnamed the Agreeable Ragamuffin, chief Mounte-bank and Buffa-dancer to his Highness	247
By Anthony Evergreen, Gent	254
Tea: A Poem	259
XX. MONDAY, JANUARY 25, 1808.—From my Elbow Chair	262
To the Ladies. By Anthony Evergreen, Gent.	269
Farewell	274

SALMAGUNDI.

VOLUME FIRST.

NO. 1.—SATURDAY, JANUARY 24, 1807.

As every body knows, or ought to know, what a SALMAGUNDI is, we shall spare ourselves the trouble of an explanation—besides, we despise trouble as we do every thing that is low and mean; and hold the man who would incur it unnecessarily, as an object worthy our highest pity and contempt. Neither will we puzzle our heads to give an account of ourselves, for two reasons; first, because it is nobody's business; secondly, because if it were, we do not hold ourselves bound to attend to any body's business but our own; and even *that* we take the liberty of neglecting when it suits our inclination. To these we might add a third, that very few men *can* give a tolerable account of themselves, let them try ever so hard; but this reason, we candidly avow, would not hold good with ourselves.

There are, however, two or three pieces of information which we bestow gratis on the public, chiefly because it suits our own pleasure and convenience that they should be known, and partly because we do not wish that there should be any ill will between us at the commencement of our acquaintance.

Our intention is simply to instruct the young, reform the old, correct the town, and castigate the age; this is an arduous task, and, therefore, we undertake it with confidence. We intend for this purpose to present a striking picture of the town; and as every body is anxious to see his own phiz on canvas, however stupid or ugly it may be, we have no doubt but the whole town will flock to our exhibition. Our picture will necessarily include a vast variety of figures: and should any gentleman or lady be displeased with the inveterate truth of their likenesses, they may ease their spleen by laughing at those of their neighbours—this being what *we* understand by POETICAL JUSTICE.

Like all true and able editors, we consider ourselves infallible, and, therefore, with the customary diffidence of our brethren of the quill, we shall take the liberty of interfering in all matters either of a public or private nature. We are critics, amateurs, dilettanti, and cognoscenti; and as we know "by the pricking of our thumbs," that every opinion which we may advance in either of those characters will be correct, we are determined, though it may be questioned, contradicted, or even controverted, yet it shall never be revoked.

We beg the public particularly to understand that we solicit no patronage. We are determined, on the contrary, that the patronage shall be entirely on our side. We have nothing to do with the pecuniary concerns of the paper; its success will yield us neither pride nor profit—nor will its failure occasion to us either loss or mortification. We advise the public, therefore, to purchase our numbers merely for their own sakes:—if they do not, let them settle the affair with their consciences and posterity.

To conclude, we invite all editors of newspapers and literary journals to praise us heartily in advance, as we assure them that we intend to deserve their praises. To our next-door neighbour "Town," we hold out a hand of amity, declaring to him that, after ours, his paper will stand the best chance for immortality. We proffer an exchange of civilities; he shall furnish us with notices of epic poems and tobacco:—and we in return will enrich him with original speculations on all manner of subjects; together with "the rummaging of my grandfather's mahogany chest of drawers," "the life and amours of mine uncle John," "anecdotes of the Cockloft family," and learned quotations from that unheard-of writer of folios, *Linkum Fidelius.*

PUBLISHER'S NOTICE.

THIS work will be published and sold by D. Longworth. It will be printed on hot prest vellum paper, as that is held in highest estimation for buckling up young ladies' hair—a purpose to which similar works are usually appropriated; it will be a small, neat duodecimo size, so that when enough numbers are written, it may form a volume sufficiently portable to be carried in old ladies' pockets and young ladies' work-bags.

As the above work will not come out at stated periods, notice will be given when another number will be published. The price will depend on the size of the number, and must be paid on delivery. The publisher professes the same sublime contempt for money as his authors. The liberal patronage bestowed by his discerning fellow-citizens on various works of taste which he has published, has left him no *inclination* to ask for further favours at their hands; and be publishes this work in the mere hope of requiting their bounty.*

FROM THE ELBOW-CHAIR OF LAUNCELOT LANGSTAFF, ESQ.

WE were a considerable time in deciding whether we should be at the pains of introducing ourselves to the public. As we care for nobody, and as we are not yet at the bar, we do not feel bound to hold up our hands and answer to our names.

Willing, however, to gain at once that frank, confidential footing, which we are certain of ultimately possessing in this, doubtless, "best of all possible cities;" and, anxious to spare its worthy inhabitants the trouble of making a thousand *wise* conjectures, not one of which would be worth a "tobacco-stopper," we have thought it in some degree a necessary exertion of charitable condescension to furnish them with a slight clue to the truth.

Before we proceed further, however, we advise every body, man, woman, and child, that can read, or get any friend to read for them, to purchase this paper:—not that we write for money;—for, in common with all philosophical wiseacres, from Solomon downwards, we hold it in supreme contempt. The public are welcome to buy this work, or not, just as they choose. If it be purchased freely, so much the better for the public—and the publisher:—we gain not a stiver. If it be not

---

* It was not originally the intention of the authors to insert the above address in the work; but, unwilling that a *morceau* so precious should be lost to posterity, they have been induced to alter their minds. This will account for any repetition of idea that may appear in the introductory essay.

purchased we give fair warning—we shall burn all our essays, critiques, and epigrams, in one promiscuous blaze; and, like the books of the sybils, and the Alexandrian library, they will be lost for ever to posterity. For the sake, therefore, of our publisher, for the sake of the public, and for the sake of the public's children, to the nineteenth generation, we advise them to purchase our paper. We beg the respectable old matrons of this city, not to be alarmed at the appearance we make; we are none of those outlandish geniuses who swarm in New-York, who live by their wits, or rather by the little wit of their neighbours; and who spoil the genuine honest American tastes of their daughters, with French slops and fricasseed sentiment.

We have said we do not write for money;—neither do we write for fame:—we know too well the variable nature of public opinion to build our hopes upon it—we *care* not what the public think of us; and we suspect, before we reach the tenth number, they will not *know* what to think of us. In two words—we write for no other earthly purpose but to please ourselves—and this we shall be sure of doing; for we are all three of us determined beforehand to be pleased with what we write. If, in the course of this work, we edify and instruct and amuse the public, so much the better for the public:—but we frankly acknowledge that so soon as we get tired of reading our own works, we shall discontinue them without the least remorse; whatever the public may think of it.—While we continue to go on, we will go on merrily:—if we moralize, it shall be but seldom; and, on all occasions, we shall be more solicitous to make our readers laugh than cry; for we are laughing philosophers, and clearly of opinion, that wisdom, true wisdom, is a plump, jolly dame, who sits in her arm-chair, laughs right merrily at the farce of life—and takes the world as it goes.

We intend particularly to notice the conduct of the fashionable world: nor in this shall we be governed by that carping spirit with which narrow-minded book-worm cynics squint at the little extravagances of the ton; but with that liberal toleration which actuates every man of fashion. While we keep more than a Cerberus watch over the guardian rules of female delicacy and decorum—we shall not discourage any little sprightliness of demeanour, or innocent vivacity of character. Before we advance one line further we must let it be understood, as our firm opinion, void of all prejudice or partiality, that the ladies of New-York are the fairest, the finest, the most accomplished, the most bewitching, the most ineffable beings, that walk, creep, crawl, swim, fly, float, or vegetate in any or all of the four elements; and that they only want to be cured of certain whims, eccentricities, and unseemly conceits, by our superintending cares, to render them absolutely perfect. They will, therefore, receive a large portion of those attentions directed to the fashionable world;—nor will the gentlemen, who *doze* away their time in the circles of the *haut-ton*, escape our currying. We mean those stupid fellows who sit stock still upon their chairs, without saying a word, and then complain how damned stupid it was at Miss ——'s party.

This department will be under the peculiar direction and control of ANTHONY EVERGREEN, gent., to whom all communications on this subject are to be addressed. This gentleman, from his long experience in the routine of balls, tea-parties, and assemblies, is eminently qualified for the task he has undertaken. He is a kind of patriarch in the fashionable world; and has seen generation after generation pass away into the silent tomb of matrimony while he remains unchangeably the same. He can recount the amours and courtships of the fathers, mothers, uncles and aunts, and even the grandames, of all the belles of the present day; provided their pedigrees extend so far back without being lost in obscurity. As, however, treating of pedigrees is rather an ungrateful task in this city, and as we mean to be perfectly good-natured, he has promised to be cautious in this particular. He recollects perfectly the time when young ladies used to go sleigh-riding at night, without their mammas or grandmammas; in short, without being matronized at all: and can relate a thousand pleasant stories about Kissing-bridge. He likewise remembers the time when ladies paid tea-visits at three in the afternoon, and returned before dark to see that the house was shut up and the servants on duty. He has often played cricket in the orchard in the rear of old Vauxhall, and remembers when the Bull's-head was quite out of town. Though he has slowly and gradually given into modern fashions, and still flourishes in the *beau-monde*, yet he seems a little prejudiced in favor of the dress and manners of the *old school;* and his chief commendation of a new mode is "that it is the same good old fashion we had before the war." It has cost us much trouble to make him confess that a cotillion is superior to a minuet, or an unadorned crop to a pigtail and powder. Custom and fashion have, however, had more effect on him than all our lectures; and he tempers, so happily, the grave and ceremonious gallantry of the old school with the "hail fellow" familiarity of the new, that, we trust, on a little acquaintance, and making allowance for his old-fashioned prejudices, he will become a very considerable favourite with our readers;—if not, the worse for themselves; as they will have to endure his company.

In the territory of criticism, WILLIAM WIZARD, Esq., has undertaken to preside; and though we may all dabble in it a little by turns, yet we have willingly ceded to him all discretionary powers in this respect, though Will has not had the advantage of an education at Oxford or Cambridge, or even at Edinburgh, or Aberdeen, and though he is but little versed in Hebrew, yet we have no doubt he will be found fully competent to the undertaking. He has improved his taste by a long residence abroad, particularly at Canton, Calcutta, and the gay and polished court of Hayti. He has also had an opportunity of seeing the best singing-girls and tragedians of China, is a great connoisseur in mandarine dresses, and porcelain, and particularly values himself on his intimate knowledge of the buffalo, and war dances of the northern Indians. He is likewise promised the assistance of a gentleman, lately from London, who was born and bred in that centre of science and *bongout*, the vicinity of Fleetmarket, where he has been edified, man and boy, these six-and-twenty years, with the harmonious jingle of Bow-bells. His taste, therefore, has attained to such an exquisite pitch of refinement that there are few exhibitions of any kind which do not put him in a fever. He has assured Will, that if Mr. Cooper emphasises "*and*" instead of "*but*"— or Mrs. Oldmixon pins her kerchief a hair's breadth awry—or Mrs. Darley offers to dare to look less than the "daughter of a senator of Venice"—the standard of a senator's daughter being exactly six feet—they shall all hear of it in good time. We have, however, advised Will Wizard to keep his friend in check, lest by opening the eyes of the public to the wretchedness of the actors by whom they have hitherto been entertained, he might cut off one source of amusement from our fellow-citizens. We hereby give notice, that we have taken the whole corps, from the manager in his mantle of gorgeous copper-lace, to honest *John* in his green coat and black breeches, under our wing—and wo be unto him who injures a hair of their heads. As we have no design against the patience of our fellow-citizens, we shall not dose them with copious draughts of theatrical criticism; we well know that they have already been well physicked with them of late; our theatrics shall take up but a small part of our paper; nor shall they be altogether confined to the stage,. but extend from time to time, to those incorrigible offenders against the peace of society, the stage-critics, who not unfrequently create the fault they find, in order to yield an opening for their witticisms—censure an actor for a gesture he never made, or an emphasis he never gave; and, in their attempt to show off *new readings*, make the sweet swan of Avon cackle like a goose. If any one should feel himself offended by our remarks, let him attack us in return—we shall not wince from the combat. If his passes be successful, we will be the first to cry out, a hit! a hit! and we doubt not we shall frequently lay ourselves open to the weapons of our assailants. But let them have a care how they run a tilting with us—they have to deal with stubborn foes, who can bear a world of pummeling; we will be relentless in our vengeance, and will fight "till from our bones the flesh be hackt."

What other subjects we shall include in the range of our observations, we have not determined, or rather we shall not trouble ourselves to detail. The public have already more information concerning us, than we intended to impart. We owe them no favours, neither do we ask any. We again advise them, for their own sakes, to read our papers when they come out. We recommend to all mothers to purchase them for their daughters, who will be taught the true line of propriety, and the most advisable method of managing their beaux. We advise all daughters to purchase them for the sake of their mothers, who shall be initiated into the arcana of the bon ton, and cured of all those rusty old notions which they acquired during the last century: parents shall be taught how to govern their children, girls how to get husbands, and old maids how to do without them.

As we do not measure our wits by the yard or the bushel, and as they do not flow periodically nor constantly, we shall not restrict our paper as to size or the time of its appearance. It will be published whenever we have sufficient matter to constitute a number, and the size of the number shall depend on the stock in hand. This will best suit our negligent habits, and leave us that full liberty and independence which is the joy and pride of our souls. As we have before hinted, that we do not concern ourselves about the pecuniary matters of our paper, we leave its price to be regulated by our publisher, only recommending him for his own interest, and the honour of his authors, not to sell their invaluable productions too cheap.

Is there any one who wishes to know more about us?—let him read SALMAGUNDI, and grow wise apace. Thus much we will say—there are three of us, "Bardolph, Peto, and I," all townsmen good and true;—many a time and oft have we three amused the town without its knowing to whom it was indebted; and many a time have we seen the midnight lamp twinkle faintly on our studious phizes, and heard the morning salutation of "past three o'clock," before we sought our pillows. The result of these midnight studies is now offered to the public; and little as we care for the opinion of this exceedingly stupid world, we shall take care, as far as lies in our careless natures, to fulfil the promises made in this introduction; if we do not, we shall have so many examples to justify us, that we feel little solicitude on that account.

THEATRICS.

CONTAINING THE QUINTESSENCE OF MODERN CRITICISM. BY WILLIAM WIZARD, ESQ.

MACBETH was performed to a very crowded house, and much to our satisfaction. As, however, our neighbor TOWN has been very voluminous already in his criticisms on this play, we shall make but few remarks. Having never seen KEMBLE in this character, we are absolutely at a loss to say whether Mr. COOPER performed it well or not. We think, however, there was an error in his *costume*, as the learned Linkum Fidelius is of opinion, that in the time of Macbeth the Scots did not wear sandals, but wooden shoes. Macbeth also was noted for wearing his jacket open, that he might play the Scotch fiddle more conveniently;—that being an hereditary accomplishment in the Glamis family.

We have seen this character performed in China by the celebrated *Chow-Chow*, the Roscius of that great empire, who in the dagger scene always electrified the audience by blowing his nose like a trumpet. Chow-Chow, in compliance with the opinion of the sage Linkum Fidelius, performed Macbeth in wooden shoes; this gave him an opportunity of producing great effect, for on first seeing the "air-drawn dagger," he always cut a prodigious high caper, and kicked his shoes into the pit at the heads of the critics; whereupon the audience were marvellously delighted, flourished their hands, and stroked their whiskers three times, and the matter was carefully recorded in the next number of a paper called the *flim flam*. (*English*—town.)

We were much pleased with Mrs. VILLIERS in Lady MACBETH; but we think she would have given a greater effect to the night-scene, if, instead of holding the candle in her hand or setting it down on the table, which is sagaciously censured by neighbour Town, she had stuck it in her night-cap. This would have been extremely picturesque, and would have marked more strongly the derangement of her mind.

Mrs. Villiers, however, is not by any means large enough for the character; Lady Macbeth having been, in our opinion, a woman of extraordinary size, and of the race of the giants, notwithstanding what she says of her "little hand"—which being said in her sleep, passes for nothing. We should be happy to see this character in the hands of the lady who played *Glumdalca*, queen of the giants, in Tom Thumb; she is exactly of imperial dimensions; and, provided she is well shaved, of a most interesting physiognomy; as she appears likewise to be a lady of some nerve, I dare engage she will read a letter about witches vanishing in air, and such common occurrences, without being unnaturally surprised, to the annoyance of honest "Town."

We are happy to observe that Mr. Cooper profits by the instructions of friend Town, and does not dip the daggers in blood so deep as formerly by a matter of an inch or two. This was a violent outrage upon our immortal bard. We differ with Mr. Town in his *reading* of the words, "this is a *sorry sight*." We are of opinion the force of the sentence should be thrown on the word *sight*, because Macbeth, having been shortly before most confoundedly humbugged with an aerial dagger, was in doubt whether the daggers actually in his hands were real, or whether they were not mere shadows; or as the old English *may* have termed it, *syghtes;* (this, at any rate, will establish our skill in *new readings*.) Though we differ in this respect from our neighbour Town, yet we heartily agree with him in censuring Mr. Cooper for omitting that passage so remarkable for "beauty of imagery," &c., beginning with "and pity, like a naked, new-born babe," &c. It is one of those passages of Shakspeare which should always be retained, for the purpose of showing how sometimes that great poet could talk like a buzzard; or, to speak more plainly, like the famous mad poet Nat Lee.

As it is the first duty of a friend to advise—and as we profess and do actually feel a friendship for honest "Town"—we warn him, never in his criticisms to meddle with a lady's "petticoats," or to quote Nic Bottom. In the first instance he may "catch a tartar;" and in the second, the ass's head may rise up in judgment against him; and when it is once afloat there is no knowing where some unlucky hand may place it. We would not, for all the money in our pockets, see Town flourishing his critical quill under the auspices of an ass's head, like the great Franklin in his *Monterio Cap*.

NEW-YORK ASSEMBLY.

BY ANTHONY EVERGREEN, GENT.

THE assemblies this year have gained a great accession of beauty. Several brilliant stars have arisen from the east and from the north to brighten the firmament of fashion; among the number I have discovered *another planet*, which rivals even Venus in lustre, and I claim equal honour with Herschel for my discovery. I shall take some future opportunity to describe this planet, and the numerous satellites which revolve around it.

At the last assembly the company began to make some show about eight, but the most fashionable delayed their appearance until about nine—nine being the number of the muses, and therefore the best possible hour for beginning to exhibit the graces. (This is meant for a pretty play upon words, and I assure my readers that I think it very tolerable.)

Poor WILL HONEYCOMB, whose memory I hold in special consideration, even with his half century of experience, would have been puzzled to point out the humours of a lady by her prevailing colours; for the "rival queens" of fashion, Mrs. TOOLE and Madame BOUCHARD, appeared to have exhausted their wonderful inventions in the different disposition, variation, and combination of tints and shades. The philosopher who maintained that black was white, and that of course there was no such colour as white, might have given some colour to his theory on this occasion, by the absence of poor forsaken white muslin. I was, however, much pleased to see that red maintains its ground against all other colours, because red is the colour of Mr. Jefferson's * * * * * *, Tom Paine's nose, and my slippers.

Let the grumbling smellfungi of this world, who cultivate taste among books, cobwebs, and spiders, rail at the extravagance of the age; for my part, I was delighted with the magic of the scene, and as the ladies tripped through the mazes of the dance, sparkling and glowing and dazzling, I, like the honest Chinese, thanked them heartily for the jewels and finery with which they loaded themselves, merely for the entertainment of by-standers, and blessed my stars that I was a bachelor.

The gentlemen were considerably numerous, and being as usual equipt in their appropriate black uniforms, constituted a sable regiment which contributed not a little to the brilliant gayety of the ball-room. I must confess I am indebted for this remark to our friend, the cockney, Mr. 'SBIDLIKENSFLASH, or *'Sbidlikens*, as he is called for shortness. He is a fellow of infinite verbosity—stands in high favour—with himself—and, like Caleb Quotem, is "up to every thing." I remember when a comfortable, plumb-looking citizen led into the room a fair damsel, who looked for all the world like the personification of a rainbow: 'Sbidlikens observed that it reminded him of a fable, which he had read somewhere, of the marriage of an honest, painstaking snail; who had once walked six feet in an hour for a wager, to a butterfly whom he used to gallant by the elbow, with the aid of much puffing and exertion. On being called upon to tell where he had come across this story, 'Sbidlikens absolutely refused to answer.

It would but be repeating an old story to say, that the ladies of New-York dance well;—and well may they, since they learn it scientifically, and begin their lessons before they have quit their swaddling clothes. The immortal DUPORT has usurped despotic sway over all the female heads and heels in this city; —hornbooks, primers, and pianos are neglected to attend to his positions; and poor CHILTON, with his pots and kettles and chemical crockery, finds him a more potent enemy than the whole collective force of the "North River Society." 'Sbidlikens insists that this dancing mania will inevitably continue as long as a dancing-master will charge the fashionable price of five-and-twenty dollars a quarter and all the other accomplishments are so vulgar as to be attainable at "half the money;"—but I put no faith in 'Sbidlikens' candour in this particular. Among his infinitude of endowments he is but a poor proficient in dancing; and though he often flounders through a cotillion, yet he never cut a pigeon-wing in his life.

In my mind there's no position more positive and unexceptionable than that most Frenchmen, dead or alive, are born dancers. I came pounce upon this discovery at the assembly, and I immediately noted it down in my register of indisputable facts:—the public shall know all about it. As I never dance cotillions, holding them to be monstrous distorters of the human frame, and tantamount in their operations to being broken and dislocated on the wheel, I generally take occasion, while they are going on, to make my remarks on the company. In the course of these observations I was struck with the energy and eloquence of sundry limbs, which seemed to be flourishing about without appertaining to any body. After much investigation and difficulty, I at length traced them to their respective owners, whom I found to be all Frenchmen to a man. Art may have meddled somewhat in these affairs, but nature certainly did more. I have since been considerably employed in calculations on this subject; and by the most accurate computation I have determined that a Frenchman passes at least three-fifths of his time between the heavens and the earth, and partakes eminently of the nature of a gossamer or soap-bubble. One of these jack-o'-lantern heroes, in taking a figure which neither Euclid or Pythagoras himself could demonstrate, unfortunately wound himself—I mean his feet, his better part—into a lady's cobweb muslin robe; but perceiving it at the instant, he set himself a spinning the other way, like a top, unravelled his step without omitting one angle or curve, and extricated himself without breaking a thread of the lady's dress! he then sprung up, like a sturgeon, crossed his feet four times, and finished this wonderful evolution by quivering his left leg, as a cat does her paw when she has accidentally dipped it in water. No man "of woman born," who was not a Frenchman or a mountebank, could have done the like.

Among the new faces, I remarked a blooming nymph, who has brought a fresh supply of roses from the country to adorn the wreath of beauty, where lilies too much predominate. As I wish well to every sweet face under heaven, I sincerely hope her roses may survive the frosts and dissipations of winter, and lose nothing by a comparison with the loveliest offerings of the spring. 'Sbidlikens, to whom I made similar remarks, assured me that they were very just, and very prettily exprest; and that the lady in question was a prodigious fine piece of flesh and blood. Now could I find it in my heart to baste these cockneys like their own roast-beef—they can make no distinction between a fine woman and a fine horse.

I would praise the sylph-like grace with which another young lady acquitted herself in the dance, but that she excels in far more valuable accomplishments. Who praises the rose for its beauty, even though it is beautiful.

The company retired at the customary hour to the supper-room, where the tables were laid out with their usual splendour and profusion. My friend, 'Sbidlikens, with the native forethought of a cockney, had carefully stowed his pocket with cheese and crackers, that he might not be tempted again to venture his limbs in the crowd of hungry fair ones who throng the supper-room door; his precaution was unnecessary, for the company entered the room with surprising order and decorum. No gowns were torn—no ladies fainted—no noses bled—nor was there any need of the interference of either managers or peace officers.

NO. II.—WEDNESDAY, FEB'Y 4, 1807.

FROM THE ELBOW-CHAIR OF LAUNCELOT LANGSTAFF, ESQ.

In the conduct of an epic poem, it has been the custom, from time immemorial, for the poet occasionally to introduce his reader to an intimate acquaintance with the heroes of his story, by conducting him into their tents, and giving him an opportunity of observing them in their night-gown and slippers. However I despise the servile genius that would descend to follow a precedent, though furnished by Homer himself, and consider him as on a par with the cart that follows at the heels of the horse, without ever taking the lead, yet at the present moment my whim is opposed to my opinion; and whenever this is the case, my opinion generally surrenders at discretion. I am determined, therefore, to give the town a peep into our divan; and I shall repeat it as often as I please, to show that I intend to be sociable.

The other night Will Wizard and Evergreen called upon me, to pass away a few hours in social chat and hold a kind of council of war. To give a zest to our evening I uncorked a bottle of London particular, which has grown old with myself, and which never fails to excite a smile in the countenances of my old cronies, to whom alone it is devoted. After some little time the conversation turned on the effect produced by our first number; every one had his budget of information, and I assure my readers that we laughed most unceremoniously at their expense; they will excuse us for our merriment—'tis a way we've got. Evergreen, who is equally a favourite and companion of young and old, was particularly satisfactory in his details; and it was highly amusing to hear how different characters were tickled with different passages. The old folks were delighted to find there was a bias in our junto towards the "good old times;" and he particularly noticed a worthy old gentleman of his acquaintance, who had been somewhat a beau in his day, whose eyes brightened at the bare mention of Kissing-bridge. It recalled to his recollection several of his youthful exploits, at that celebrated pass, on which he seemed to dwell with great pleasure and self-complacency;—he hoped, he said, that the bridge might be preserved for the benefit of posterity, and as a monument of the gallantry of their grandfathers; and even hinted at the expediency of erecting a tollgate, to collect the forfeits of the ladies. But the most flattering testimony of approbation, which our work has received, was from an old lady, who never laughed but once in her life, and that was at the conclusion of the last war. She was detected by friend Anthony in the very fact of laughing most obstreporously at the description of the little dancing Frenchman. Now it glads my very heart to find our effusions have such a pleasing effect. I venerate the aged, and joy whenever it is in my power to scatter a few flowers in their path.

The young people were particularly interested in the account of the assembly. There was some difference of opinion respecting the new planet, and the blooming nymph from the country; but as to the compliment paid to the fascinating little sylph who danced so gracefully—every lady modestly took that to herself.

Evergreen mentioned also that the young ladies were extremely anxious to learn the true mode of managing their beaux; and Miss DIANA WEARWELL, who is as chaste as an icicle, has seen a few superfluous winters pass over her head, and boasts of having slain her thousands, wished to know how old maids were to do without husbands;—not that she was very curious about the matter, she "only asked for information." Several ladies expressed their earnest desire that we would not spare those wooden gentlemen who perform the parts of mutes, or stalking horses, in their drawing-rooms; and their mothers were equally anxious that we would show no quarter to those lads of spirit, who now and then cut their bottles to enliven a tea-party with the humours of the dinner-table.

Will Wizard was not a little chagrined at having been mistaken for a gentleman, "who is no more like me," said Will, "than I like Hercules."—"I was well assured," continued Will, "that as our characters were drawn from nature, the originals would be found in every society. And so it has happened—every little circle has its 'Sbidlikens; and the cockney, intended merely as the representative of his species, has dwindled into an insignificant individual, who having recognised his own likeness, has foolishly appropriated to himself a picture for which he never sat. Such, too, has been the case with DING-DONG, who has kindly undertaken to be my representative;—not that I care much about the matter, for it must be acknowledged that the animal is a good animal enough;— and what is more, a fashionable animal—and this is saying more than to call him a conjurer. But, I am much mistaken if he can claim any affinity to the *Wizard* family.—Surely every body knows Ding-dong, the gentle Ding-dong, who pervades all space, who is here and there and every where; no tea-party can be complete without Ding-dong—and his appearance is sure to occasion a smile. Ding-dong has been the occasion of much wit in his day; I have even seen many whipsters attempt to be dull at his expense, who were as much inferior to him as the gad-fly is to the ox that he buzzes about. Does any witling want to distress the company with a miserable pun? nobody's name presents sooner than Ding-dong's; and it has been played upon with equal skill and equal entertainment to the by-standers as Trinity-bells. Ding-dong is profoundly devoted to the ladies, and highly entitled to their regard; for I know no man who makes a better bow, or talks less to the purpose than Ding-dong. Ding-dong has acquired a prodigious fund of knowledge by reading Dilworth when a boy; and the other day, on being asked who was the author of Macbeth, answered, without the least hesitation—Shakspeare! Ding-dong has a quotation for every day of the year, and every hour of the day, and every minute of the hour; but he often commits petty larcenies on the poets—plucks the gray hairs of old Chaucer's head, and claps them on the chin of Pope; and filches Johnson's wig, to cover the bald pate of Homer;—but his blunders pass undetected by one-half of his hearers. Ding-dong, it is true, though he has long wrangled at our bar, cannot boast much of his legal knowledge, nor does his forensic eloquence entitle him to rank with a Cicero or a Demosthenes; but bating his professional deficiencies, he is a man of most delectable discourse, and can hold forth for an hour upon the colour of a riband or the construction of a workbag. Ding-dong is now in his fortieth year, or perhaps a little more—rivals all the little beaux in the town, in his attentions to the ladies—is in a state of rapid improvement; and there is no doubt but that by the time he arrives at years of discretion, he will be a very accomplished, agreeable young fellow."—I advise all clever, good-for-nothing, "learned and authentic gentlemen," to take care how they wear this cap, however well it fits; and to bear in mind, that our characters are not individuals, but species: if, after this warning, any person chooses to represent Mr. Ding-dong, the sin is at his own door; we wash our hands of it.

We all sympathized with Wizard, that he should be mistaken for a person so very different; and I hereby assure my readers, that William Wizard is no other person in the whole world but William Wizard; so I beg I may hear no more conjectures on the subject. Will is, in fact, a wiseacre by inheritance. The Wizard family has long been celebrated for knowing more than their neighbours, particularly concerning their neighbours' affairs. They were anciently called JOSSELIN; but Will's great uncle, by the father's side, having been accidentally burnt for a witch in Connecticut, in consequence of blowing up his own house in a philosophical experiment, the family, in order to perpetuate the recollection of this memorable circumstance, assumed the name and arms of Wizard; and have borne them ever since.

In the course of my customary morning's walk, I stopped in a book-store, which is noted for being the favourite haunt of a number of literati, some of whom rank high in the opinion of the world, and others rank equally high in their own. Here I found a knot of queer fellows listening to one of their company who was reading our paper; I particularly noticed Mr. ICHABOD FUNGUS among the number.

Fungus is one of those fidgeting, meddling quidnuncs, with which this unhappy city is pestered: one of your "Q in a corner fellows," who speaks volumes with a wink;—conveys most portentous information, by laying his finger beside his nose,—and is always smelling a rat in the most trifling occurrence. He listened to our work with the most frigid gravity—every now and then gave a mysterious shrug—a humph—or a screw of the mouth; and on being asked his opinion at the conclusion, said, he did not know what to think of it;—he hoped it did not mean any thing against the government—that no lurking treason was couched in all this talk. These were dangerous times—times of plot and conspiracy; he did not at all like those stars after Mr. Jefferson's name, they had an air of concealment. DICK PADDLE, who was one of the group, undertook our cause. Dick is known to the world, as being a most knowing genius, who can see as far as any body—into a millstone; maintains, in the teeth of all argument, that a spade is a spade; and will labour a good half hour by St. Paul's clock, to establish a self-evident fact. Dick assured old Fungus, that those stars merely stood for Mr. Jefferson's red *what-d'ye-call-'ems;* and that so far from a conspiracy against their peace and prosperity, the authors, whom he knew very well, were only expressing their high respect for them. The old man shook his head, shrugged his shoulders, gave a mysterious Lord Burleigh nod, said he hoped it might be so; but he was by no means satisfied with this attack upon the President's breeches, as "thereby hangs a tale."

MR. WILSON'S CONCERT.

BY ANTHONY EVERGREEN, GENT.

IN my register of indisputable facts I have noted it conspicuously that all modern music is but the mere dregs and draining of the ancient, and that all the spirit and vigour of harmony has entirely evaporated in the lapse of ages. Oh! for the chant of the Naiades, and Dryades, the shell of the Tritons, and the sweet warblings of the Mermaids of ancient days! where now shall we seek the Amphion, who built walls with a turn of his hurdy-gurdy, the Orpheus who made stones to whistle about his ears, and trees hop in a country dance, by the mere quavering of his fiddle-stick! ah! had I the power of the former how soon would I build up the new City-Hall, and save the cash and credit of the Corporation; and how much sooner would I build myself a snug house in Broadway:—nor would it be the first time a house has been obtained there for a song. In my opinion, the Scotch bag-pipe is the only instrument that rivals the ancient lyre; and I am surprised it should be almost the only one entirely excluded from our concerts.

Talking of concerts reminds me of that given a few nights since by Mr. WILSON; at which I had the misfortune of being present. It was attended by a numerous company, and gave great satisfaction, if I may be allowed to judge from the frequent gapings of the audience; though I will not risk my credit as a connoisseur, by saying whether they proceeded from wonder or a violent inclination to doze. I was delighted to find in the mazes of the crowd, my particular friend SNIVERS, who had put on his cognoscenti phiz—he being, according to his own account, a profound adept in the science of music. He can tell a crotchet at first sight; and, like a true Englishman, is delighted with the plum-pudding rotundity of a semibref; and, in short, boasts of having incontinently climbed up Paff's musical tree, which hangs every day upon the poplar, from the fundamental concord, to the fundamental major discord; and so on from branch to branch, until he reached the very top, where he sung "Rule Britannia," clapped his wings, and then—came down again. Like all true trans-atlantic judges, he suffers most horribly at our musical entertainments, and assures me, that what with the confounded scraping, and scratching, and grating of our fiddlers, he thinks the sitting out one of our concerts tantamount to the punishment of that unfortunate saint, who was frittered in two with a hand-saw.

The concert was given in the tea-room, at the City-Hotel; an apartment admirably calculated, by its dingy walls, beautifully marbled with smoke, to show off the dresses and complexions of the ladies; and by the flatness of its ceiling to repress those impertinent reverberations of the music, which, whatever others may foolishly assert, are, as Snivers says, "no better than repetitions of old stories."

Mr. Wilson gave me infinite satisfaction by the gentility of his demeanour, and the roguish looks he now and then cast at the ladies, but we fear his excessive modesty threw him into some little confusion, for he absolutely forgot himself, and in the whole course of his entrances and exits, never once made his bow to the audience. On the whole, however, I think he has a fine voice, sings with great taste, and is a very modest, good-looking little man; but I beg leave to repeat the advice so often given by the illustrious tenants of the theatrical sky-parlour, to the gentlemen who are charged with the "nice conduct" of chairs and tables — "make a bow, Johnny—Johnny, make a bow!"

I cannot, on this occasion, but express my surprise that certain amateurs should be so frequently at concerts, considering what agonies they suffer while a piece of music is playing. I defy any man of common humanity, and who has not the heart of a Choctaw, to contemplate the countenance of one of these unhappy victims of a fiddle-stick without feeling a sentiment of compassion. His whole visage is distorted; he rolls up his eyes, as M'Sycophant says, "like a duck in thunder," and the music seems to operate upon him like a fit of the colic: his very bowels seem to sympathize at every twang of the cat-gut, as if he heard at that moment the wailings of the helpless animal that had been sacrificed to harmony. Nor does the hero of the orchestra seem less affected; as soon as the signal is given, he seizes his fiddle-stick, makes a most horrible grimace, scowls fiercely upon his music-book, as though he would grin every crotchet and quaver out of countenance. I have sometimes particularly noticed a hungry-looking Gaul, who torments a huge bass-viol, and who is, doubtless, the original of the famous "Raw-head-and-bloody-bones," so potent in frightening naughty children.

The person who played the French-horn was very excellent in his way, but Snivers could not relish his performance, having sometime since heard a gentleman amateur in Gotham play a solo on his *proboscis*, in a style infinitely superior;—Snout, the bellows-mender, never turned his wind instrument more musically; nor did the celebrated "knight of the burning lamp," ever yield more exquisite entertainment with his nose; this gentleman had latterly ceased to exhibit this prodigious accomplishment, having, it was whispered, hired out his snout to a ferryman, who had lost his conch-shell;—the consequence was that he did not show his nose in company so frequently as before.

SITTING late the other evening in my elbow-chair, indulging in that kind of indolent meditation, which I consider the perfection of human bliss, I was roused from my reverie by the entrance of an old servant in the COCKLOFT livery, who handed me a letter, containing the following address from my cousin and old college chum, PINDAR COCKLOFT.

Honest ANDREW, as he delivered it, informed me that his master, who resides a little way from town, on reading a small pamphlet in a neat yellow cover, rubbed his hands with symptoms of great satisfaction, called for his favourite Chinese inkstand, with two sprawling Mandarines for its supporters, and wrote the letter which he had the honour to present me.

As I foresee my cousin will one day become a great favourite with the public, and as I know him to be somewhat punctilious as it respects etiquette, I shall take this opportunity to gratify the old gentleman by giving him a proper introduction to the fashionable world. The Cockloft family, to which I have the comfort of being related, has been fruitful in old bachelors and humourists, as will be perceived when I come to treat more of its history. My cousin Pindar is one of its most conspicuous members—he is now in his fifty-eighth year—is a bachelor, partly through choice, and partly through chance, and an oddity of the first water. Half his life has been employed in writing odes, sonnets, epigrams, and elegies, which he seldom shows to any body but myself after they are written; and all the old chests, drawers, and chair-bottoms in the house, teem with his productions.

In his younger days he figured as a dashing blade in the great world; and no young fellow of the town wore a longer pig-tail, or carried more buckram in his skirts. From sixteen to thirty he was continually in love, and during that period, to use his own words, he be-scribbled more paper than would serve the theatre for snow-storms a whole season. The evening of his thirtieth birthday, as he sat by the fireside, as much in love as ever was man in the world and writing the name of his mistress in the ashes, with an old tongs that had lost one of its legs, he was seized with a whim-wham that he was an old fool to be in love at his time of life. It was ever one of the Cockloft characteristics to strike to whim; and had Pindar stood out on this occasion he would have brought the reputation of his mother in question. From that time he gave up all particular attentions to the ladies; and though he still loves their company, he has never been known to exceed the bounds of common courtesy in his intercourse with them. He was the life and ornament of our family circle in town, until the epoch of the French revolution, which sent so many unfortunate dancing-masters from their country to polish and enlighten our hemisphere. This was a sad time for Pindar, who had taken a genuine Cockloft prejudice against every thing French, ever since he was brought to death's door by a *ragout:* he groaned at Ca Ira, and the Marseilles Hymn had much the same effect upon him that sharpening a knife on a dry whetstone has upon some people;—it set his teeth chattering. He might in time have been reconciled to these rubs, had not the introduction of French cockades on the hats of our citizens absolutely thrown him into a fever. The first time he saw an instance of this kind, he came home with great precipitation, packed up his trunk, his old-fashioned writing-desk, and his Chinese ink-stand, and made a kind of growling retreat to Cockloft-Hall, where he has resided ever since.

My cousin Pindar is of a mercurial disposition,—a humourist without ill-nature—he is of the true gun-powder temper;—one flash and all is over. It is true when the wind is easterly, or the gout gives him a gentle twinge, or he hears of any new successes of the French, he will become a little splenetic; and heaven help the man, and more particularly the woman, that crosses his humour at that moment;—she is sure to receive no quarter. These are the most sublime moments of Pindar. I swear to you, dear ladies and gentlemen, I would not lose one of these splenetic bursts for the best wig in my wardrobe; even though it were proved to be the identical wig worn by the sage Linkum Fidelius, when he demonstrated before the whole university of Leyden, that it was possible to make bricks without straw. I have seen the old gentleman blaze forth such a volcanic explosion of wit, ridicule, and satire, that I was almost tempted to believe him inspired. But these sallies only lasted for a moment, and passed like summer clouds over the benevolent sunshine which ever warmed his heart and lighted up his countenance.

Time, though it has dealt roughly with his person, has passed lightly over the graces of his mind, and left him in full possession of all the sensibilities of youth. His eye kindles at the relation of a noble and generous action, his heart melts at the story of distress, and he is still a warm admirer of the fair. Like all old bachelors, however, he looks back with a fond and lingering eye on the period of his boyhood; and would sooner suffer the pangs of matrimony than acknowledge that the world, or any thing in it, is half so clever as it was in those good old times that are "gone by."

I believe I have already mentioned, that with all his good qualities he is a humourist, and a humourist of the highest order. He has some of the most intolerable whim-whams I ever met with in my life, and his oddities are sufficient to eke out a hundred tolerable originals. But I will not enlarge on them—enough has been told to excite a desire to know more; and I am much mistaken, if in the course of half a dozen of our numbers, he don't tickle, plague, please, and perplex the whole town, and completely establish his claim to the laureateship he has solicited, and with which we hereby invest him, recommending him and his effusions to public reverence and respect.

LAUNCELOT LANGSTAFF.

TO LAUNCELOT LANGSTAFF, ESQ.

DEAR LAUNCE,
   As I find you have taken the quill,
To put our gay town, and its fair under drill,
I offer my hopes for success to your cause,
And send you unvarnish'd my mite of applause.
 Ah, Launce, this poor town has been wofully fash'd;
Has long been be-Frenchman'd, be-cockney'd, be-trash'd;
And our ladies be-devil'd, bewilder'd astray,
From the rules of there grandames have wander'd away.
No longer that modest demeanour we meet,
Which whilom the eyes of our fathers did greet;—
No longer be-mobbled, be-ruffled, be-quill'd,
Be-powder'd, be-hooded, be-patch'd, and be-frill'd,—
No longer our fair ones their grograms display,
And stiff in brocade, strut "like castles" away.
 Oh, how fondly my soul forms departed have traced,
When our ladies in stays, and in boddice well laced,
When bishop'd, and cushion'd, and hoop'd to the chin,
Well callash'd without, and well bolster'd within;
All cased in their buckrams, from crown down to tail,
Like O'Brallagan's mistress, were shaped like a pail.
 Well—peace to those fashions—the joy of our eyes—
Tempora mutantur,—new follies will rise;
Yet, "like joys that are past," they still crowd on the mind,
In moments of thought, as the soul looks behind.
 Sweet days of our boyhood, gone by, my dear Launce,
Like the shadows of night, or the forms in a trance;
Yet oft we retrace those bright visions again,
Nos mutamur, 'tis true—but those visions remain—
I recall with delight, how my bosom would creep,
When some delicate foot from its chamber would peep;
And when I a neat stocking'd ankle could spy,
—By the sages of old, I was rapt to the sky!

All then was retiring—was modest—discreet;
The beauties, all shrouded, were left to conceit;
To the visions which fancy would form in her eye,
Of graces that snug in soft ambush would lie;
And the heart, like the poets, in thought would pursue
The elysium of bliss, which was veil'd from its view.
 We are old-fashion'd fellows, our nieces will say:
Old-fashion'd, indeed, coz—and swear it they may—
For I freely confess that it yields me no pride,
To see them all blaze what their mothers would hide:
To see them, all shivering, some cold winter's day,
So lavish their beauties and graces display,
And give to each fopling that offers his hand,
Like Moses from Pisgah—a peep at the land.
 But a truce with complaining—the object in view
Is to offer my help in the work you pursue;
And as your effusions and labours sublime,
May need, now and then, a few touches of rhyme,
I humbly solicit, as cousin and friend,
A quiddity, quirk, or remonstrance to send:
Or should you a laureate want in your plan,
By the muff of my grandmother, I am your man!
You must know I have got a poetical mill,
Which with odd lines, and couplets, and triplits I fill;
And a poem I grind, as from rags white and blue
The paper-mill yields you a sheet fair and new.
I can grind down an ode, or an epic that's long,
Into sonnet, acrostic, conundrum, or song:
As to dull hudibrastic, so boasted of late,
The doggerel discharge of some muddled brain'd pate,
I can grind it by wholesale—and give it its point,
With billingsgate dish'd up in rhymes out of joint.
 I have read all the poets—and got them by heart,
Can slit them, and twist them, and take them apart;
Can cook up an ode out of patches and shreds,
To muddle my readers, and bother their heads.
Old Homer, and Virgil, and Ovid I scan,
Anacreon, and Sappho, who changed to a swan;—
Iambics and sapphics I grind at my will,
And with ditties of love every noddle can fill.
  Oh, 'twould do your heart good, Launce, to see my mill grind
Old stuff into verses, and poems refin'd;—

Dan Spencer, Dan Chaucer, those poets of old,
Though cover'd with dust, are yet true sterling gold;
I can grind off their tarnish, and bring them to view,
New modell'd, new mill'd, and improved in their hue.
 But I promise no more—only give me the place,
And I'll warrant I'll fill it with credit and grace;
By the living! I'll figure and cut you a dash
—As bold as Will Wizard, or 'SBIDLIKENS-FLASH!
PINDAR COCKLOFT.

ADVERTISEMENT.

PERHAPS the most fruitful source of mortification to a merry writer who, for the amusement of himself and the public, employs his leisure in sketching odd characters from imagination, is, that he cannot flourish his pen, but every Jack-pudding imagines it is pointed directly at himself:—he cannot, in his gambols, throw a fool's cap among the crowd, but every queer fellow insists upon puttng it on his own head; or chalk an outlandish figure, but every outlandish genius is eager to write his own name under it. However we may be mortified, that these men should each individually think himself of sufficient consequence to engage our attention, we should not care a rush about it, if they did not get into a passion and complain of having been ill-used.

It is not in our hearts to hurt the feelings of one single mortal, by holding him up to public ridicule; and if it were, we lay it down as one of our indisputable facts, that no man can be made ridiculous but by his own folly. As, however, we are aware that when a man by chance gets a thwack in the crowd, he is apt to suppose the blow was intended exclusively for himself, and so fall into unreasonable anger, we have determined to let these crusty gentry know what kind of satisfaction they are to expect from us. We are resolved not to fight, for three special reasons; first, because fighting is at all events extremely troublesome and inconvenient, particularly at this season of the year; second, because if either of us should happen to be killed, it would be a great loss to the public, and rob them of many a good laugh we have in store for their amusement; and third, because if we should chance to kill our adversary, as is most likely, for we can every one of us split balls upon razors, and snuff candles, it would be a loss to our publisher, by depriving him of a good customer. If any gentleman casuist will give three as good reasons for fighting, we promise him a complete set of Salmagundi for nothing.

But though we do not fight in our own proper persons, let it not be supposed that we will not give ample satisfaction to all those who may choose to demand it—for this would be a mistake of the first magnitude, and lead very valiant gentlemen perhaps into what is called a quandary. It would be a thousand and one pities, that any honest man, after taking to himself the cap and bells which we merely offered to his acceptance, should not have the privilege of being cudgeled into the bargain. We pride ourselves upon giving satisfaction in every department of our paper; and to fill that of fighting have engaged two of those strapping heroes of the theatre, who figure in the retinues of our ginger-bread kings and queens; now hurry an old stuff petticoat on their backs, and strut senators of Rome, or aldermen of London;—and now be-whisker their muffin faces with burnt cork, and swagger right valiant warriors, armed cap-a-pie, in buckram. Should, therefore, any great little man about town, take offence at our good-natured villainy, though we intend to offend nobody under heaven, he will please to apply at any hour after twelve o'clock, as our champions will then be off duty at the theatre and ready for anything. They have promised to fight "with or without balls,"—to give two tweaks of the nose for one—to submit to be kicked, and to cudgel their applicant most heartily in return; this being what we understand by "the satisfaction of a gentleman."

NO. III.—FRIDAY. FEBRUARY 13, 1807.

FROM MY ELBOW-CHAIR.

As I delight in every thing novel and eccentric, and would at any time give an old coat for a new idea, I am particularly attentive to the manners and conversation of strangers, and scarcely ever a traveler enters this city, whose appearance promises any thing original, but by some means or another I form an acquaintance with him. I must confess I often suffer manifold afflictions from the intimacies thus contracted: my curiosity is frequently punished by the stupid details of a blockhead, or the shallow verbosity of a coxcomb. Now I would prefer at any time to travel with an ox-team through a Carolina sand-flat rather than plod through a heavy unmeaning conversation with the former; and as to the latter, I would sooner hold sweet converse with the wheel of a knife grinder than endure his monotonous chattering. In fact, the strangers who flock to this most pleasant of all earthly cities, are generally mere birds of passage whose plumage is often gay enough, I own, but their notes, "heaven save the mark," are as unmusical as those of that classic night bird, which the ancients humorously selected as the emblem of wisdom. Those from the south, it is true, entertain me with their horses, equipages, and puns: and it is excessively pleasant to hear a couple of these *four in hand* gentlemen detail their exploits over a bottle. Those from the east have often induced me to doubt the existence of the wise men of yore, who are said to have flourished in that quarter; and as for those from parts beyond seas—oh! my masters, ye shall hear more from me anon. Heaven help this unhappy town!—hath it not goslings enow of its own hatching and rearing, that it must be overwhelmed by such an inundation of ganders from other climes? I would not have any of my courteous and gentle readers suppose that

I am running *a muck*, full tilt, cut and slash upon all foreigners indiscriminately. I have no national antipathies, though related to the Cockloft family. As to honest John Bull, I shake him heartily by the hand, assuring him that I love his jolly countenance, and moreover am lineally descended from him; in proof of which I allege my invincible predilection for roast beef and pudding. I therefore look upon all his children as my kinsmen; and I beg when I tackle a cockney I may not be understood as trimming an Englishman; they being very distinct animals, as I shall clearly demonstrate in a future number. If any one wishes to know my opinion of the Irish and Scotch, he may find it in the characters of those two nations, drawn by the first advocate of the age. But the French, I must confess, are my favourites; and I have taken more pains to argue my cousin Pindar out of his antipathy to them, than I ever did about any other thing. When, therefore, I choose to hunt a Monsieur for my own particular amusement, I beg it may not be asserted that I intend him as a representative of his countrymen at large. Far from this —I love the nation, as being a nation of right merry fellows, possessing the true secret of being happy; which is nothing more than thinking of nothing, talking about any thing, and laughing at every thing. I mean only to tune up those little thing-o-mys, who represent nobody but themselves; who have no national trait about them but their language, and who hop about our town in swarms like little toads after a shower.

Among the few strangers whose acquaintance has entertained me, I particularly rank the magnanimous MUSTAPHA RUB-A-DUB KELI KHAN, a most illustrious captain of a ketch, who figured some time since, in our fashionable circles, at the head of a ragged regiment of Tripolitan prisoners. His conversation was to me a perpetual feast;—I chuckled with inward pleasure at his whimsical mistakes and unaffected observations on men and manners; and I rolled each odd conceit "like a sweet morsel under my tongue."

Whether Mustapha was captivated by my iron-bound physiognomy, or flattered by the attentions which I paid him, I won't determine; but I so far gained his confidence, that, at his departure, he presented me with a bundle of papers, containing, among other articles, several copies of letters, which he had written to his friends at Tripoli.—The following is a translation of one of them.—The original is in Arabic-Greek; but by the assistance of Will Wizard, who understands all languages, not excepting that manufactured by Psalmanzar, I have been enabled to accomplish a tolerable translation. We should have found little difficulty in rendering it into English, had it not been for Mustapha's confounded pot-hooks and trammels.

LETTER FROM MUSTAPHA RUB-A-DUB KELI KHAN,

CAPTAIN OF A KETCH, TO ASEM HACCHEM, PRINCIPAL SLAVE-DRIVER TO HIS HIGHNESS THE BASHAW OF TRIPOLI.

Thou wilt learn from this letter, most illustrious disciple of Mahomet, that I have for some time resided in New-York; the most polished, vast, and magnificent city of the United States of America. But what to me are its delights! I wander a captive through its splendid streets, I turn a heavy eye on every rising day that beholds me banished from my country. The Christian husbands here lament most bitterly any short absence from home, though they leave but one wife behind to lament their departure;—what then must be the feelings of thy unhappy kinsman, while thus lingering at an immeasurable distance from three-and-twenty of the most lovely and obedient wives in all Tripoli! Oh, Allah! shall thy servant never again return to his native land, nor behold his beloved wives, who beam on his memory beautiful as the rosy morn of the east, and graceful as Mahomet's camel!

Yet beautiful, oh, most puissant slave-driver, as are my wives, they are far exceeded by the women of this country. Even those who run about the streets with bare arms and necks (*et cetera*) whose habiliments are too scanty to protect them either from the inclemency of the season, or the scrutinizing glances of the curious, and who it would seem belong to nobody, are lovely as the houris that people the elysium of true believers. If, then, such as run wild in the highways, and whom no one cares to appropriate, are thus beauteous; what must be the charms of those who are shut up in the seraglios and never permitted to go abroad! surely the region of beauty, the valley of the graces, can contain nothing so inimitably fair!

But, notwithstanding the charms of these infidel women, they are apt to have one fault, which is extremely troublesome and inconvenient. Wouldst thou believe it, Asem, I have been positively assured by a famous dervise, or doctor as he is here called, that at least one-fifth part of them—have souls! incredible as it may seem to thee, I am the more inclined to believe them in possession of this monstrous superfluity, from my own little experience, and from the information which I have derived from others. In walking the streets I have actually seen an exceedingly good-looking woman with soul enough to box her husband's ears to his heart's content, and my very whiskers trembled with indignation at the abject state of these wretched infidels. I am told, moreover, that some of the women have soul enough to usurp the breeches of the men, but these I suppose are married and kept close; for I have not, in my rambles, met with any so extravagantly accoutred; others, I am informed, have soul enough to swear! —yea! by the beard of the great Omar, who prayed three times to each of. the one hundred and twenty-four thousand prophets of our most holy faith, and who never swore but once in his life—they actually swear!

Get thee to the mosque, good Asem! return thanks to our most holy prophet that he has been thus mindful of the comfort of all true Mussulmen, and has given them wives with no more souls than cats and dogs and other necessary animals of the household.

Thou wilt doubtless be anxious to learn our reception in this country, and how we were treated by a people whom we have been accustomed to consider as unenlightened barbarians.

On landing, we were waited upon to our lodgings, I suppose according to the directions of the municipality, by a vast and respectable escort of boys and negroes; who shouted and threw up their hats, doubtless to do honour to the magnanimous Mustapha, captain of a ketch; they were somewhat ragged and dirty in their equipments, but this we attributed to their republican simplicity. One of them, in the zeal of admiration, threw an old shoe, which gave thy friend rather an ungentle salutation on one side of the head, whereat I was not a little offended, until the interpreter informed us that this was the customary manner in which great men were honoured in this country; and that the more distinguished they were, the more they were subjected to the attacks and peltings of the mob. Upon this I bowed my head three times, with my hands to my turban, and made a speech in Arabic-Greek, which gave great satisfaction and occasioned a shower of old shoes, hats, and so forth, that was exceedingly refreshing to us all.

Thou wilt not as yet expect that I should give thee an account of the laws and politics of this country. I will reserve them for some future letter, when I shall be more experienced in their complicated and seemingly contradictory nature.

This empire is governed by a grand and most puissant bashaw, whom they dignify with the title of president. He is chosen by persons who are chosen by an assembly elected by the people—hence the mob is called the sovereign people; and the country, free; the body politic doubtless resembling a vessel, which is best governed by its tail. The present bashaw is a very plain old gentleman—something, they say, of a humourist, as he amuses himself with impaling butterflies and pickling tadpoles; he is rather declining in popularity, having given great offence by wearing red breeches, and tying his horse to a post. The people of the United States have assured me that they themselves are the most enlightened nation under the sun; but thou knowest that the barbarians of the desert, who assemble at the summer solstice to shoot their arrows at that glorious luminary, in order to extinguish his burning rays, make precisely the same boast;—which of them have the superior claim, I shall not attempt to decide.

I have observed, with some degree of surprise, that the men of this country do not seem in haste to accommodate themselves even with the single wife which alone the laws permit them to marry; this backwardness is probably owing to the misfortune of their absolutely having no female mutes among them. Thou knowest how invaluable are these silent companions;—what a price is given for them in the east, and what entertaining wives· they make. What delightful entertainment arises from beholding the silent eloquence of their signs and gestures; but a wife possessed both of a tongue and a soul—monstrous! monstrous! is it astonishing that these unhappy infidels should shrink from a union with a woman so preposterously endowed.

Thou hast doubtless read in the works of Abul Faraj, the Arabian historian, the tradition which mentions that the muses were once upon the point of falling together by the ears about the admission of a tenth among their number, until she assured them by signs that she was dumb; whereupon they received her with great rejoicing. I should, perhaps, inform thee that there are but nine Christian muses, who were formerly pagans, but have since been converted, and that in this country we never hear of a tenth, unless some crazy poet wishes to pay a hyperbolical compliment to his mistress; on which occasion it goes hard, but she figures as a tenth muse, or fourth grace, even though she should be more illiterate than a Hottentot, and more ungraceful than a dancing-bear! Since my arrival in this country I have met with not less than a hundred of these supernumerary muses and graces—and may Allah preserve me from ever meeting with any more!

When I have studied this people more profoundly, I will write thee again; in the mean time, watch over my household, and do not beat my beloved wives unless you catch them with their noses out at the window. Though far distant and a slave, let me live in thy heart as thou livest in mine:—think not, O friend of my soul, that the splendours of this luxurious capital, its gorgeous palaces, its stupendous masques, and the beautiful females who run wild in herds about its streets, can obliterate thee from my remembrance. Thy name shall still be mentioned in the five-and-twenty prayers which I offer up daily; and may our great prophet, after bestowing on thee all the blessings of this life, at length, in good old age, lead thee gently by the hand to enjoy the dignity of bashaw of three tails in the blissful bowers of Eden.

MUSTAPHA.

FASHIONS.

BY ANTHONY EVERGREEN, GENT.

THE FOLLOWING ARTICLE IS FURNISHED ME BY A YOUNG LADY OF UNQUESTIONABLE TASTE, AND WHO IS THE ORACLE OF FASHION AND FRIPPERY, BEING DEEPLY INITIATED INTO ALL THE MYSTERIES OF THE TOILET, SHE HAS PROMISED ME FROM TIME TO TIME A SIMILAR DETAIL.

MRS. TOOLE has for some time reigned unrivalled in the fashionable world, and had the supreme direction of caps, bonnets, feathers, flowers, and tinsel. She has dressed and undressed our ladies just as she pleased; now loading them with velvet and wadding, now turning them adrift upon the world to run shivering through the streets with scarcely a covering to their——backs; and now obliging them to drag a long train at their heels, like the tail of a paper kite. Her despotic sway, however, threatens to be limited. A dangerous rival has sprung up in the person of Madame BOUCHARD, an intrepid little woman, fresh from the head-quarters of fashion and folly, and who has burst, like a second Bonaparte, upon the fashionable world.—Mrs. Toole, notwithstanding, seems determined to dispute her ground bravely for the honour of old England. The ladies have begun to arrange themselves under the banner of one or other of these heroines of the needle, and everything portends open war. Madame Bouchard marches gallantly to the field, flourishing a flaming red robe for a standard, "flouting the skies;" and Mrs. Toole, no ways dismayed, sallies out under cover of a forest of artificial flowers, like Malcolm's host. Both parties possess great merit, and both deserve the victory. Mrs. Toole charges the highest—but Madame Bouchard makes the lowest courtesy. Madame Bouchard is a little short lady—nor is there any hope of her growing larger; but then she is perfectly genteel, and so is Mrs. Toole. Mrs. Toole lives in Broadway, and Madame Bouchard in Courtlandt-street; but Madame atones for the inferiority of her *stand* by making two courtesies to Mrs. Toole's one, and talking French like an angel. Mrs. Toole is the best looking—but Madame Bouchard wears a most bewitching little scrubby wig.—Mrs. Toole is the tallest—but Madame Bouchard has the longest nose.—Mrs. Toole is fond of roast beef—but Madame is loyal in her adherence to onions: in short, so equally are the merits of the two ladies balanced, that there is no judging which will " kick the beam." It, however, seems to be the prevailing opinion that Madame Bouchard will carry the day, because she wears a wig, has a long nose, talks French, loves onions, and does not charge above ten times as much for a thing as it is worth.

UNDER THE DIRECTION OF THESE HIGH PRIESTESSES OF THE BEAU-MONDE, THE FOLLOWING IS THE FASHIONABLE MORNING DRESS FOR WALKING.

If the weather be very cold, a thin muslin gown, or frock, is most advisable; because it agrees with the season, being perfectly cool. The neck, arms, and particularly the elbows bare, in order that they may be agreeably painted and mottled by Mr. JOHN FROST, nose-painter-general, of the colour of Castile soap. Shoes of kid, the thinnest that can possibly be procured —as they tend to promote colds, and make a lady look interesting—(*i. e.*, *grizzly*.) Picnic silk stockings, with lace clocks, flesh-coloured are most fashionable, as they have the appearance of bare legs—*nudity* being all the rage. The stockings carelessly bespattered with mud, to agree with the gown, which should be bordered about three inches deep with the most fashionable coloured mud that can be found: the ladies permitted to hold up their trains, after they have swept two or three streets, in order to show——the clocks of their stockings. The shawl, scarlet, crimson, flame, orange, salmon, or any other combustible or brimstone colour, thrown over one shoulder; like an Indian blanket, with one end dragging on the ground.

N. B. If the ladies have not a red shawl at hand, a red petticoat turned topsy-turvy, over the shoulders, would do just as well. This is called being dressed *a la drabble*.

When the ladies do not go abroad of a morning, the usual chimney-corner dress is a dotted, spotted, striped, or cross-barred gown;—a yellowish, whitish, smokish, dirty-coloured shawl, and the hair curiously ornamented with little bits of newspapers, or pieces of a letter from a dear friend. This is called the "Cinderella-dress."

The recipe for a full dress is as follows: take of spider-net, crape, satin, gymp, cat-gut, gauze, whale-bone, lace, bobbin, ribands, and artificial flowers, as much as will rig out the congregation of a village church; to these, add as many spangles, beads, and gew-gaws, as would be sufficient to turn the heads of all the fashionable fair ones of Nootka-sound. Let Mrs. Toole or Madame Bouchard patch all these articles together, one upon another, dash them plentifully over with stars, bugles, and tinsel, and they will altogether form a dress, which hung upon a lady's back, cannot fail of supplying the place of beauty, youth, and grace, and of reminding the spectator of that celebrated region of finery, called *Rag Fair*.

ONE of the greatest sources of amusement incident to our humourous knight errantry, is to ramble about and hear the various conjectures of the town respecting our worships, whom every body pretends to know as well as Falstaff did Prince Hal at Gads-hill. We have sometimes seen a sapient, sleepy fellow, on being tickled with a straw, make a furious effort and fancy he had fairly caught a gnat in his grasp; so, that many-headed monster, the public, who, with all its heads, is, we fear, sadly off for brains, has, after long hovering, come souse down, like a king-fisher, on the authors of Salmagundi, and caught them as certainly as the aforesaid honest fellow caught the gnat.

Would that we were rich enough to give every one of our numerous readers a cent, as a reward for their ingenuity! not that they have really conjectured within a thousand leagues of the truth, but that we consider it a great stretch of ingenuity even to have guessed wrong; and that we hold ourselves much obliged to them for having taken the trouble to guess at all.

One of the most tickling, dear, mischievous pleasures of this life is to laugh in one's sleeve—to sit snug in the corner, unnoticed and unknown, and hear the wise men of Gotham, who are profound judges of horse-flesh, pronounce, from the style of our work, who are the authors. This listening incog., and receiving a hearty praise over another man's back, is a situation so celestially whimsical, that we have done little else than laugh in our sleeve ever since our first number was published.

The town has at length allayed the titilations of curiosity, by fixing on two young gentlemen of literary talents—that is to say, they are equal to the composition of a newspaper squib, a hodge podge criticism, or some such trifle, and may occasionally raise a smile by their effusions; but pardon us, sweet sirs, if we modestly doubt your capability of supporting the burthen of Salmagundi, or of keeping up a laugh for a whole fortnight, as we have done, and intend to do, until the whole town becomes a community of laughing philosophers like ourselves. We have no intention, however, of undervaluing the abilities of these two young men, whom we verily believe, according to common acceptation, young men *of promise.*

Were we ill-natured, we might publish something that would get our representatives into difficulties; but far be it from us to do anything to the injury of persons to whom we are under such obligations.

While they stand before us, we, like little Teucer, behind the sevenfold shield of Ajax, can launch unseen our sportive arrows, which we trust will never inflict a wound, unless like his they fly "heaven directed," to some conscious-struck bosom.

Another marvellous great source of pleasure to us, is the abuse our work has received from several wooden gentlemen, whose censures we covet more than ever we did any thing in our lives. The moment we declared open war against folly and stupidness, we expected no quarter; and to provoke a confederacy of all the blockheads in town. For it is one of our indisputable facts that so sure as you catch a gander by the tail, the whole flock, geese, goslings, one and all, have a fellow-feeling on the occasion, and begin to cackle and hiss like so many devils bewitched. As we have a profound respect for these ancient and respectable birds, on the score of their once having saved the capitol, we hereby declare that we mean no offence to the aforesaid confederacy. We have heard in our walks such criticisms on Salmagundi, as almost induced a belief that folly had here, as in the east, her moments of inspired idiotism. Every silly royster has, as if by an instinctive sense of anticipated danger, joined in the cry; and condemned us without mercy. All is thus as it should be. It would have mortified us very sensibly, had we been disappointed in this particular, as we should have been apprehensive that our shafts had fallen to the ground, innocent of the "blood or brains" of a single numbskull. Our efforts have been crowned with wonderful success. All the queer fish, the grubs, the flats, the noddies, and the live oak and timber gentlemen, are pointing their empty guns at us; and we are threatened with a most puissant confederacy of the "pigmies and cranes," and other "light militia," backed by the heavy armed artillery of dullness and stupidity. The veriest dreams of our most sanguine moments are thus realized. We have no fear of the censures of the wise, the good, or the fair; for they will ever be sacred from our attacks. We reverence the wise, love the good, and adore the fair; we declare ourselves champions in their cause;—in the cause of morality;—and we throw our gauntlet to all the world besides.

While we profess and feel the same indifference to public applause as at first, we most earnestly invite the attacks and censures of all the wooden warriors of this sensible city; and especially of that distinguished and learned body, heretofore celebrated under the appellation of "the North-river society."

The thrice valiant and renowned Don Quixote never made such work among the wool-clad warriors of Trapoban, or the puppets of the itinerant showman, as we promise to make among these fine fellows; and we pledge ourselves to the public in general, and the Albany skippers in particular, that the North river shall not be set on fire this winter at least, for we shall give the authors of that nefarious scheme, ample employment for some time to come.

PROCLAMATION,

FROM THE MILL OF PINDAR COCKLOFT, ESQ.

To all the young belles who enliven our scene,
From ripe five-and-forty, to blooming fifteen;
Who racket at routs, and who rattle at plays,
Who visit, and fidget, and dance out their days:
Who conquer all hearts, with a shot from the eye,
Who freeze with a frown, and who thaw with a sigh:—
To all those bright youths who embellish the age,
Whether young boys, or old boys, or numskull or sage:
Whether DULL DOGS, who cringe at their mistress' feet,
Who sigh and who whine, and who try to look sweet;
Whether TOUGH DOGS, who squat down stock still in a row
And play wooden gentlemen stuck up for a show;
Or SAD DOGS, who glory in running their rigs,
Now dash in their sleighs, and now whirl in their gigs;
Who riot at Dyde's on imperial champaign,
And then scour our city—the peace to maintain:
To whoe'er it concerns or may happen to meet,
By these presents their worships I lovingly greet.
Now KNOW YE, that I, PINDAR COCKLOFT, esquire,
Am laureate, appointed at special desire;—
A censor, self-dubb'd, to admonish the fair,
And tenderly take the town under my care.
I'm a ci-devant beau, cousin Launcelot has said—
A remnant of habits long vanish'd and dead:
But still, though my heart dwells with rapture sublime,
On the fashions and customs which reign'd in my prime,
I yet can perceive—and still candidly praise,
Some maxims and manners of these "latter days;"
Still own that some wisdom and beauty appears,
Though almost entomb'd in the rubbish of years.
No fierce nor tyrannical cynic am I,
Who frown on each foible I chance to espy;
Who pounce on a novelty, just like a kite,
And tear up a victim through malice or spite:
Who expose to the scoffs of an ill-natured crew,
A trembler for starting a whim that is new.

No, no—I shall cautiously hold up my glass,
To the sweet little blossoms who heedlessly pass;
My remarks not too pointed to wound or offend,
Nor so vague as to miss their benevolent end:
Each innocent fashion shall have its full sway;
New modes shall arise to astonish Broadway:
Red hats and red shawls still illumine the town,
And each belle, like a bon-fire, blaze up and down.

 Fair spirits, who brighten the gloom of our days,
Who cheer this dull scene with your heavenly rays,
No mortal can love you more firmly and true,
From the crown of the head, to the sole of your shoe.
I'm old fashioned, 'tis true,—but still runs in my heart
That affectionate stream, to which youth gave the start,
More calm in its current—yet potent in force;
Less ruffled by gales—but still stedfast in course.
Though the lover, enraptur'd, no longer appears,—
'Tis the guide and the guardian enlighten'd by years.
All ripen'd, and mellow'd, and soften'd by time,
The asperities polish'd which chafed in my prime;
I am fully prepared for that delicate end,
The fair one's instructor, companion and friend.
—And should I perceive you in fashion's gay dance,
Allured by the frippery mongers of France,
Expose your weak frames to a chill wintry sky,
To be nipp'd by its frosts, to be torn from the eye;
My soft admonitions shall fall on your ear—
Shall whisper those parents to whom you are dear—
Shall warn you of hazards you heedlessly run,
And sing of those fair ones whom frost has undone;
Bright suns that would scarce on our horizon dawn,
Ere shrouded from sight, they were early withdrawn;
Gay sylphs, who have floated in circles below,
As pure in their souls, and as transient as snow;
Sweet roses, that bloom'd and decay'd to my eye,
And of forms that have flitted and pass'd to the sky.
But as to those brainless pert bloods of our town,
Those sprigs of the ton who run decency down;
Who lounge and who lout, and who booby about,
No knowledge within, and no manners without;
Who stare at each beauty with insolent eyes;
Who rail at those morals their fathers would prize;

Who are loud at the play—and who impiously dare
To come in their cups to the routs of the fair;
I shall hold up my mirror, to let them survey
The figures they cut as they dash it away:
Should my good-humoured verse no amendment produce,
Like scare-crows, at least, they shall still be of use;
I shall stitch them, in effigy, up in my rhyme,
And hold them aloft through the progress of time,
As figures of fun to make the folks laugh,
Like that b——h of an angel erected by Paff,
"What shtops," as he says, "all de people what come·
What smiles on dem all, and what peats on de trum."

NO. IV.—TUESDAY, FEBRUARY 24, 1807.

FROM MY ELBOW-CHAIR.

PERHAPS there is no class of men to which the curious and literary are more indebted than travellers;—I mean travel-mongers, who write whole volumes about themselves, their horses and their servants, interspersed with anecdotes of inn-keepers,—droll sayings of stage-drivers, and interesting memoirs of—the Lord knows who. They will give you a full account of a city, its manners, customs, and manufactures; though, perhaps, all their knowledge of it was obtained by a peep from their inn-windows, and an interesting conversation with the landlord or the waiter. America has had its share of these buzzards; and in the name of my countrymen I return them profound thanks for the compliments they have lavished upon us, and the variety of particulars concerning our own country, which we should never have discovered without their assistance.

Influenced by such sentiments, I am delighted to find that the Cockloft family, among its other whimsical and monstrous productions, is about to be enriched with a genuine travel-writer. This is no less a personage than Mr. JEREMY COCKLOFT, the only son and darling pride of my cousin, Mr. CHRISTOPHER COCKLOFT. I should have said Jeremy Cockloft, *the younger*, as he so styles himself, by way of distinguishing him from IL SIGNORE JEREMY COCKLOFTICO, a gouty old gentleman, who flourished about the time that Pliny the elder was smoked to death with the fire and brimstone of Vesuvius; and whose travels, if he ever wrote any, are now lost for ever to the world. Jeremy is at present in his one-and-twentieth year, and a young fellow of wonderful quick parts, if you will trust to the word of his father, who, having begotten him, should be the best judge of the matter. He is the oracle of the family, dictates to his sisters on every occasion, though they are some dozen or more years older than himself:—and never did son give mother better advice than Jeremy.

As old Cockloft was determined his son should be both a scholar and a gentleman, he took great pains with his education, which was completed at our university, where he became exceedingly expert in quizzing his teachers and playing billiards. No student made better squibs and crackers to blow up the chemical professor; no one chalked more ludicrous caricatures on the walls of the college; and none were more adroit in shaving pigs and climbing lightning-rods. He moreover learned all the letters of the Greek alphabet; could demonstrate that water never "of its own accord" rose above the level of its source, and that air was certainly the principle of life; for he had been entertained with the humane experiment of a cat worried to death in an air-pump. He once shook down the ash-house, by an artificial earthquake; and nearly blew his sister Barbara, and her cat, out of the window with thundering powder. He likewise boasts exceedingly of being thoroughly acquainted with the composition of Lacedemonian black broth; and once made a pot of it, which had well-nigh poisoned the whole family, and actually threw the cook-maid into convulsions. But above all, he values himself upon his logic, has the old college conundrum of the cat with three tails at his finger's ends, and often hampers his father with his syllogisms, to the great delight of the old gentleman; who considers the major, minor, and conclusions, as almost equal in argument to the pulley, the wedge, and the lever, in mechanics. In fact, my cousin Cockloft was once nearly annihilated with astonishment, on hearing Jeremy trace his derivation of Mango from Jeremiah King;—as Jeremiah King, Jerry King! Jerkin -Girkin! cucumber, Mango! in short, had Jeremy been a student at Oxford or Cambridge, he would, in all probability, have been promoted to the dignity of a *senior wrangler*. By this sketch, I mean no disparagement to the abilities of other students of our college, for I have no doubt that every commencement ushers into society luminaries full as brilliant as *Jeremy Cockloft the younger*.

Having made a very pretty speech on graduating, to a numerous assemblage of old folks and young ladies, who all declared that he was a very fine young man, and made very handsome gestures, Jeremy was seized with a great desire to see, or rather to be seen by the world; and as his father was anxious to give him every possible advantage, it was determined Jeremy should visit foreign parts. In consequence of this resolution, he has spent a matter of three or four months in visiting strange places; and in the course of his travels has tarried some few days at the splendid metropolis' of Albany and Philadelphia.

Jeremy has travelled as every modern man of sense should do; that is, he judges of things by the sample next at hand; if he has ever any doubt on a subject, always decides against the city where he happens to sojourn; and invariably takes *home*, as the standard by which to direct his judgment.

Going into his room the other day, when he happened to be absent, I found a manuscript volume lying on his table; and was overjoyed to find it contained notes and hints for a book of travels which he intends publishing. He seems to have taken a late fashionable *travel-monger* for his model, and I have no doubt his work will be equally instructive and amusing with that of his prototype. The following are some extracts, which may not prove uninteresting to my readers.

MEMORANDUMS FOR A TOUR, TO BE ENTITLED "THE STRANGER IN NEW JERSEY; OR, COCKNEY TRAVELLING."

BY JEREMY COCKLOFT, THE YOUNGER.

CHAPTER I.

THE man in the moon*—preparations for departure—hints to travellers about packing their trunks†—straps, buckles, and bed-cords—case of pistols, *a la cockney*—five trunks—three bandboxes—a cocked hat—and a medicine chest, *a la Francaise* —parting advice of my two sisters—quere, why old maids are so particular in their cautions against naughty women—description of Powles-Hook ferry-boats—might be converted into gunboats, and defend our port equally well with Albany sloops— BROM, the black ferryman—Charon—river Styx—ghosts;— major Hunt—good story—ferryage nine-pence;—city of Harsimus—built on the spot where the folk once danced on their stumps, while the devil fiddled;—quere, why do the Harsimites

---

* *vide* Carr's Stranger in Ireland. † *vide* Weld.

SALMAGUNDI. 47

talk Dutch?—story of the tower of Babel, and confusion of tongues—get into the stage—driver a wag—famous fellow for running stage races—killed three passengers and crippled nine in the course of his practice—philosophical reasons why stage drivers love grog—causeway—ditch on each side for folk to tumble into—famous place for *skilly-pots;* Philadelphians call 'em tarapins—roast them under the ashes as we do potatoes—quere, may not this be the reason that the Philadelphians are all turtle-heads?—Hackensack bridge—good painting of a blue horse jumping over a mountain—wonder who it was painted by;—mem. to ask the *Baron de Gusto* about it on my return;—Rattle-snake hill, so called from abounding with butterflies;—salt marsh, *surmounted* here and there by a solitary haystack;—more tarapins—wonder why the Philadelphians don't establish a fishery here, and get a patent for it;—bridge over the Passaic—rate of toll—description of toll-boards—toll man had but one eye—story how it *is possible* he *may* have lost the other—pence-table, etc.*

CHAPTER II.

NEWARK—noted for its fine breed of fat mosquitoes—sting through the thickest boot †—story about *Gallynipers*—Archer Gifford and his man Caliban—jolly fat fellows;—a knowing traveller always judges of every thing by the inn-keepers and waiters; ‡ set down Newark people all fat as butter—learned dissertation on Archer Gifford's green coat, with philosophical reasons why the Newarkites wear red worsted night-caps, and turn their noses to the south when the wind blows—Newark academy full of windows—sunshine excellent to make little boys grow—Elizabeth-town—fine girls—vile mosquitoes—plenty of oysters—quere, have oysters any feeling?—good story about the fox catching them by his tail—ergo, foxes might be of great use in the pearl-fishery;—landlord member of the legislature—treats every body who has a vote—mem., all the inn-keepers members of legislature in New-Jersey; Bridge-town, vulgarly called *Spank-town,* from a story of a quondam parson and his wife—real name, according to Linkum Fidelius, Bridge-town, from *bridge,* a contrivance to get dry shod over a river or

---

* *vide* Carr. † *vide* Weld.
‡ *vide* Carr. *vide* Moore. *vide* Weld. *vide* Parkinson. *vide* Priest. *vide* Linkum Fidelius, and *vide* Messrs. Tag, Rag, and Bobtail.

brook; and *town*, an appellation given in America to the accidental assemblage of a church, a tavern, and a blacksmith's shop—Linkum as right as my left leg;—Rahway-river—good place for gun-boats—wonder why Mr. Jefferson don't send a *river fleet* there to protect the hay-vessels ?—Woodbridge—landlady mending her husband's breeches—sublime apostrophe to conjugal affection and the fair sex;*—Woodbridge famous for its crab-fishery—sentimental correspondence between a crab and a lobster—digression to Abelard and Eloisa;—mem., when the moon is in *Pisces*, she plays the devil with the crabs.

CHAPTER III.

BRUNSWICK—oldest town in the state—division-line between two counties in the middle of the street;—posed a lawyer with the case of a man standing with one foot in each county—wanted to know in which he was *domicil*—lawyer couldn't tell for the soul of him—mem., all the New-Jersey lawyers *nums.;* —Miss Hay's boarding-school—young ladies not allowed to eat mustard—and why?—fat story of a mustard-pot, with a good saying of Ding-Dong's;—Vernon's tavern—fine place to sleep, if the noise would let you—another Caliban!—Vernon *slew*-eyed —people of Brunswick, of course, all squint;—Drake's tavern —fine old blade—wears square buckles in his shoes—tells bloody long stories about last war—people, of course, all do the same; Hook'em Snivy, the famous fortune-teller, born here—cotemporary with mother Shoulders—particulars of his history—died one day—lines to his memory, *which found their way into my pocket-book;*†—melancholy reflections on the death of great men—beautiful epitaph on myself.

CHAPTER IV.

PRINCETON—college—professors wear boots!—students famous for their love of a jest—set the college on fire, and burnt out the professors; an excellent joke, but not worth repeating —mem., American students very much addicted to burning down colleges—reminds me of a good story, nothing at all to the purpose—two societies in the college—good notion—encourages emulation, and makes little boys fight;—students famous for their eating and erudition—saw two at the tavern,

---

* *vide* The Sentimental Kotzebue.
† *vide* Carr and *Blind Bet !*

who had just got their allowance of spending-money—laid it all out in a supper—got fuddled, and d——d the professors for nincoms. N. B. Southern gentlemen — Church-yard—apostrophe to grim death—saw a cow feeding on a grave—metempsychosis—who knows but the cow may have been eating up the soul of one of my ancestors—made me melancholy and pensive for fifteen minutes;—man planting cabbages*—wondered how he could plant them so straight—method of mole-catching—and all that—quere, whether it would not be a good notion to ring their noses as we do pigs—mem., to propose it to the American Agricultural Society—get a premium, perhaps; —commencement—students give a ball and supper—company from New-York, Philadelphia, and Albany—great contest which spoke the best English—Albanians vociferous in their demand for sturgeon—Philadelphians gave the preference to racoon † and splacnuncs—gave them a long dissertation on the phlegmatic nature of a goose's gizzard—students can't dance—always set off with the wrong foot foremost—Duport's opinion on that subject—Sir Christopher Hatton the first man who ever turned out his toes in dancing—great favourite with Queen Bess on that account—Sir Walter Raleigh—good story about his smoking—his descent into New Spain—El Dorado— Candid—Dr. Pangloss—Miss Cunegunde—earthquake at Lisbon—Baron of Thundertentronck—Jesuits—Monks—Cardinal Woolsey—Pope Joan—Tom Jefferson—Tom Paine, and Tom the —— whew! N.B.—Students got drunk as usual.

Chapter V.

LEFT Princeton—country finely diversified with sheep and hay-stacks ‡—saw a man riding alone in a wagon! why the deuce didn't the blockhead ride in a chair? fellow must be a fool—particular account of the construction of wagons—carts, wheelbarrows and quail-traps—saw a large flock of crows— concluded there must be a dead horse in the neighbourhood— mem. country remarkable for crows—won't let the horses die in peace—anecdote of a jury of crows—stopped to give the horses water—good-looking man came up, and asked me if I had seen his wife? heavens! thought I, how strange it is that this virtuous man should ask *me* about his wife—story of Cain and Abel—stage-driver took a *swig*—mem. set down all the

---

* *vide* Carr.   † *vide* Priest.   ‡ *vide* Carr.

people as drunkards—old house had moss on the top—swallows built in the roof—better place than old men's beards—story about that—derivation of words *kippy, kippy, kippy* and *shoopig* *—negro driver could not write his own name—languishing state of literature in this country;†—philosophical inquiry of 'Sbidlikens, why the Americans are so much inferior to the nobility of Cheapside and Shoreditch, and why they do not eat plum-pudding on Sundays;—superfine reflections about any thing.

CHAPTER VI.

TRENTON—built above the head of navigation to encourage commerce—capital of the State ‡—only wants a castle, a bay, a mountain, a sea, and a volcano, to bear a strong resemblance to the Bay of Naples—supreme court sitting—fat chief justice— used to get asleep on the bench after dinner—gave judgment, I suppose, like Pilate's wife, from his dreams—reminded me of Justice Bridlegoose deciding by a throw of a die, and of the oracle of the holy bottle—attempted to kiss the chambermaid —boxed my ears till they rung like our theatre-bell—girl had lost one tooth—mem. all the American ladies prudes, and have bad teeth;—Anacreon Moore's opinion on the matter.—Statehouse—fine place to see the sturgeons jump up—quere, whether sturgeons jump up by an impulse of the tail, or whether they bounce up from the bottom by the elasticity of their noses— Linkum Fidelius of the latter opinion—I too—sturgeons' nose capital for tennis-balls—learnt that at school—went to a ball— negro wench principal musician !—N.B. People of America have no fiddlers but females!—origin of the phrase, "fiddle of your heart"—reasons why men fiddle better than women;—expedient of the Amazons who were expert at the bow:—waiter at the city-tavern—good story of his—nothing to the purpose— never mind—fill up my book like Carr—make it sell. Saw a democrat get into the stage followed by his dog.§ N.B. This town remarkable for dogs and democrats—superfine sentiment ∥ —good story from Joe Miller—ode to a piggin of butter—pensive meditations on a mouse-hole—make a book as clear as a whistle!

---

* *vide* Carr's learned derivation of *gee* and *whoa*.
† Moore. ‡ Carr. § Moore. ∥ Carr.

NO. V.—SATURDAY, MARCH 7, 1807.

FROM MY ELBOW-CHAIR.

THE following letter of my friend Mustapha appears to have been written some time subsequent to the one already published. Were I to judge from its contents, I should suppose it was suggested by the splendid review of the twenty-fifth of last November; when a pair of colours was presented at the City-Hall, to the regiments of artillery; and when a huge dinner was devoured, by our corporation, in the honourable remembrance of the evacuation of this city. I am happy to find that the laudable spirit of military emulation which prevails in our city has attracted the attention of a stranger of Mustapha's sagacity; by military emulation I mean that spirited rivalry in the size of a hat, the length of a feather, and the gingerbread finery of a sword belt.

LETTER FROM MUSTAPHA RUB-A-DUB KELI KHAN,

TO ABDALLAH EB'N AL RAHAB, SURNAMED THE SNORER, MILITARY SENTINEL AT THE GATE OF HIS HIGHNESS' PALACE.

THOU hast heard, oh Abdallah, of the great magician, MULEY FUZ, who could change a blooming land, blessed with all the elysian charms of hill and dale, of glade and grove, of fruit and flower, into a desert, frightful, solitary, and forlorn;—who with the wave of his wand could transform even the disciples of Mahomet into grinning apes and chattering monkeys. Surely, thought I to myself this morning, the dreadful Muley has been exercising his infernal enchantments on these unhappy infidels. Listen, oh Abdallah, and wonder! Last night I committed myself to tranquil slumber, encompassed with all the monotonous tokens of peace, and this morning I awoke enveloped in the noise, the bustle, the clangor, and the shouts of war. Every thing was changed as if by magic. An immense army had sprung up, like mushrooms, in a night; and all the cobblers, tailors, and tinkers of the city had mounted the nodding plume; had become, in the twinkling of an eye, helmetted heroes and war-worn veterans.

Alarmed at the beating of drums, the braying of trumpets, and the shouting of the multitude, I dressed myself in haste, sallied forth, and followed a prodigious crowd of people to a place called the battery. This is so denominated, I am told, from having once been defended with formidable *wooden* bulwarks which in the course of a hard winter were *thriftily* pulled to pieces by an *economic* corporation, to be distributed for fire-wood among the poor; this was done at the hint of a cunning old engineer, who assured them it was the only way in which their fortifications would ever be able to keep up a warm fire. ECONOMIC, my friend, is the watch-word of this nation; I have been studying for a month past to divine its meaning, but truly am as much perplexed as ever. It is a kind of national starvation; an experiment how many comforts and necessaries the body politic can be deprived of before it perishes. It has already arrived to a lamentable degree of debility, and promises to share the fate of the Arabian philosopher, who proved that he could live without food, but unfortunately died just as he had brought his experiment to perfection.

On arriving at the battery, I found an immense army of SIX HUNDRED MEN, drawn up in a true Mussulman crescent. At first I supposed this was in compliment to myself, but my interpreter informed me that it was done merely for want of room; the corporation not being able to afford them sufficient to display in a straight line. As I expected a display of some grand evolutions, and military manœuvres, I determined to remain a tranquil spectator, in hopes that I might possibly collect some hints which might be of service to his highness.

This great body of men I perceived was under the command of a small *bashaw*, in yellow and gold, with white nodding plumes, and most formidable whiskers; which, contrary to the Tripolitan fashion, were in the neighbourhood of his ears instead of his nose. He had two attendants called aid-de-camps, (or *tails*) being similar to a bashaw with two tails. The bashaw, though commander-in-chief, seemed to have little more to do than myself; he was a spectator within the lines and I without: he was clear of the rabble and I was encompassed by them; this was the only difference between us, except that he had the best opportunity of showing his clothes. I waited an hour or two with exemplary patience, expecting to see some grand military evolutions or a sham battle exhibited; but no such thing took place; the men stood stock still, supporting their arms, groaning under the fatigues of war, and now and then sending out a foraging party to levy contributions of beer and a favourite beverage which they denominate grog. As I perceived the crowd very active in examining the line, from one extreme to the other, and as I could see no other purpose for which these sunshine warriors should be exposed so long to the merciless attacks of wind and weather, I of course concluded that this must be *the review*.

In about two hours the army was put in motion, and marched through some narrow streets, where the economic corporation had carefully provided a soft carpet of mud, to a magnificent castle of painted brick, decorated with grand pillars of pine boards. By the ardor which brightened in each countenance, I soon perceived that this castle was to undergo a vigorous attack. As the ordnance of the castle was perfectly silent, and as they had nothing but a straight street to advance through, they made their approaches with great courage and admirable regularity, until within about a hundred feet of the castle a pump opposed a formidable obstacle in their way, and put the whole army to a nonplus. The circumstance was sudden and unlooked for; the commanding officer ran over all the military tactics with which his head was crammed, but none offered any expedient for the present awful emergency. The pump maintained its post, and so did the commander; there was no knowing which was most at a stand. The commanding officer ordered his men to wheel and take it in flank;—the army accordingly wheeled and came full butt against it in the rear, exactly as they were before.—"Wheel to the left!" cried the officer; they did so, and again as before the inveterate pump intercepted their progress. "Right about face!" cried the officer; the men obeyed, but bungled:—they *faced back to back*. Upon this the bashaw with two tails, with great coolness, undauntedly ordered his men to push right forward, pell-mell, pump or no pump; they gallantly obeyed; after unheard-of acts of bravery the pump was carried, without the loss of a man, and the army firmly entrenched itself under the very walls of the castle. The bashaw had then a council of war with his officers; the most vigorous measures were resolved on. An advance guard of musicians were ordered to attack the castle without mercy. Then the whole band opened a most tremendous battery of drums, fifes, tambourines, and trumpets, and kept up a thundering assault, as if the castle, like the walls of Jericho, spoken of in the Jewish chronicles, would tumble down at the blowing of rams' horns. After some time a parley ensued. The grand bashaw of the city appeared on the battlements of the castle, and as far as I could understand from circumstances, dared the little bashaw of two tails to single combat;—this thou knowest was in the style of ancient chivalry;—the little bashaw dismounted with great intrepidity, and ascended the battlements of the castle, where the great bashaw waited to receive him, attended by numerous dignitaries and worthies of his court, one of whom bore the splendid banners of the castle. The battle was carried on entirely by words, according to the universal custom of this country, of which I shall speak to thee more fully hereafter. The grand bashaw made a furious attack in a speech of considerable length; the little bashaw, by no means appalled, retorted with great spirit. The grand bashaw attempted to rip him up with an argument, or stun him with a solid fact; but the little bashaw parried them both with admirable adroitness, and run him clean through and through with a syllogism. The grand bashaw was overthrown, the banners of the castle yielded up to the little bashaw, and the castle surrendered after a vigorous defence of three hours,—during which the besieger suffered great extremity from muddy streets and a drizzling atmosphere.

On returning to dinner I soon discovered that as usual I had been indulging in a great mistake. The matter was all clearly explained to me by a fellow lodger, who on ordinary occasions moves in the humble character of a tailor, but in the present instance figured in a high military station denominated *corporal*. He informed me that what I had mistaken for a castle was the splendid palace of the municipality, and that the supposed attack was nothing more than the delivery of a flag given by the authorities, to the army, for its magnanimous defence of the town for upwards of twenty years past, that is, ever since the last war. Oh! my friend, surely every thing in this country is on a great scale!——the conversation insensibly turned upon the military establishment of the nation; and I do assure thee that my friend, the tailor, though being, according to a national proverb, but the ninth part of a man, yet acquitted himself on military concerns as ably as the grand bashaw of the empire himself. He observed that their rulers had decided that wars were very useless and expensive, and ill befitting an economic, philosophic nation; they had therefore made up their minds never to have any wars, and consequently there was no need of soldiers or military discipline. As, however, it was thought highly ornâmental to a city to have a number of men drest in fine clothes and *feathers*, strutting about the streets on a holiday—and as the women and children were particularly fond of such *raree shows*, it was ordered that the tailors of the different cities throughout the empire should, forthwith, go to work, and cut out and manufacture soldiers, as fast as their shears and needles would permit.

These soldiers have no pecuniary pay; and their only recompense for the immense services which they render their country, in their voluntary parades, is the plunder of smiles, and winks, and nods which they extort from the ladies. As they have no opportunity, like the vagrant Arabs, of making inroads on their neighbors; and as it is necessary to keep up their military spirit, the town is therefore now and then, but particularly on two days of the year, given up to their ravages. The arrangements are contrived with admirable address, so that every officer, from the bashaw down to the drum-major, the chief of the eunuchs, or musicians, shall have his share of that invaluable booty, the admiration of the fair. As to the soldiers, poor animals, they, like the privates in all great armies, have to bear the brunt of danger and fatigue, while their officers receive all the glory and reward. The narrative of a parade day will exemplify this more clearly.

The chief bashaw, in the plenitude of his authority, orders a grand review of the whole army at two o'clock. The bashaw with two tails, that he may have an opportunity of vapouring about as greatest man on the field, orders the army to assemble at twelve. The kiaya, or colonel, as he is called, that is, commander of one hundred and twenty men, orders his regiment or tribe to collect one mile at least from the place of parade at eleven. Each captain, or fag-rag as we term them, commands his squad to meet at ten at least a half mile from the regimental parade; and to close all, the chief of the eunuchs orders his infernal concert of fifes, trumpets, cymbals, and kettle-drums to assemble at ten! from that moment the city receives no quarter. All is noise, hooting, hubbub, and combustion. Every window, door, crack, and loop-hole, from the garret to the cellar, is crowded with the fascinating fair of all ages and of all complexions. The mistress smiles through the windows of the drawing-room; the chubby chambermaid lolls out of the attic casement, and a host of sooty wenches roll their white eyes and grin and chatter from the cellar door. Every nymph seems anxious to yield voluntarily that tribute which the heroes of their country demand. First struts the chief eunuch, or drum-major, at the head of his sable band, magnificently arrayed in tarnished scarlet. Alexander himself could not have spurned the earth more superbly. A host of ragged boys shout in his train, and inflate the bosom of the warrior with tenfold self-complacency. After he has rattled his kettle-drums through the town, and swelled and swaggered like a turkey-cock before all the dingy Floras, and Dinahs, and Junoes, and Didoes of his acquaintance, he repairs to his place of destination loaded with a rich booty of smiles and approbation. Next comes the FAG-RAG, or captain, at the head of his mighty band, consisting of one lieutenant, one ensign, or mute, four sergeants, four corporals, one drummer, one fifer, and if he has any privates, so much the better for himself. In marching to the regimental parade he is sure to paddle through the street or lane which is honoured with the residence of his mistress or intended, whom he resolutely lays under a heavy contribution. Truly it is delectable to behold these heroes, as they march along, cast side glances at the upper windows; to collect the smiles, the nods, and the winks, which the enraptured fair ones lavish profusely on the magnanimous defenders of their country.

The Fag-rags having conducted their squads to their respective regiments, then comes the turn of the colonel, a bashaw with no tails, for all eyes are now directed to him; and the fag-rags, and the eunuchs, and the kettle-drummers, having had their hour of notoriety, are confound and lost in the military crowd. The colonel sets his whole regiment in motion; and, mounted on a mettlesome charger, frisks and fidgets, and capers, and plunges in front, to the great entertainment of the multitude and the great hazard of himself and his neighbours. Having displayed himself, his trappings, his horse, and his horsemanship, he at length arrives at the place of general rendezvous; blessed with the universal admiration of his country-women. I should perhaps mention a squadron of hardy veterans, most of whom have seen a deal of service during the nineteen or twenty years of their existence, and who, most gorgeously equipped in tight green jackets and breeches, trot and amble, and gallop and scamper like little devils through every street and nook and corner and poke-hole of the city, to the great dread of all old people and sage matrons with young children. This is truly sublime! this is what I call making a mountain out of a mole-hill. Oh, my friend, on what a great scale is every thing in this country. It is in the style of the wandering Arabs of the desert *El-tih*. Is a village to be attacked, or a hamlet to be plundered, the whole desert, for weeks beforehand, is in a buzz;—such marching and countermarching, ere they can concentrate their ragged force! and the consequence is, that before they can bring their troops into action, the whole enterprise is blown.

The army being all happily collected on the battery, though, perhaps, two hours after the time appointed, it is now the turn of the bashaw, with two tails, to distinguish himself. Ambition, my friend, is implanted alike in every heart; it pervades each bosom, from the bashaw to the drum-major. This is a sage truism, and I trust, therefore, it will not be disputed. The bashaw, fired with that thirst for glory, inseparable from the noble mind, is anxious to reap a full share of the laurels of the day and bear off his portion of female plunder. The drums beat, the fifes whistle, the standards wave proudly in the air. The signal is given! thunder roars the cannon! away goes the bashaw, and away go the tails! The review finished, evolutions and military manœuvres are generally dispensed with for three excellent reasons; first, because the army knows very little about them; second, because as the country has determined to remain always at peace, there is no necessity for them to know any thing about them; and third, as it is growing late, the bashaw must despatch, or it will be too dark for him to get his quota of the plunder. He of course orders the whole army to march: and now, my friend, now come the tug of war, now is the city completely sacked. Open fly the battery-gates, forth sallies the bashaw with his two tails, surrounded by a shouting body-guard of boys and negroes! then pour forth his legions, potent as the pismires of the desert! the customary salutations of the country commence—those tokens of joy and admiration which so much annoyed me on first landing: the air is darkened with old hats, shoes, and dead cats; they fly in showers like the arrows of the Parthians. The soldiers, no ways disheartened, like the intrepid followers of Leonidas, march gallantly under their shade. On they push, splash dash, mud or no mud. Down one lane, up another;—the martial music resounds through every street; the fair ones throng to their windows,—the soldiers look every way but straight forward. "Carry arms," cries the bashaw—"tanta ra-ra," brays the trumpet—"rub-a-dub," roars the drum—"hurraw," shout the ragamuffins. The bashaw smiles with exultation—every fag-rag feels himself a hero—"none but the brave deserve the fair!" head of the immortal Amrou, on what a great scale is every thing in this country.

Ay, but you'll say, is not this unfair that the officers should share all the sports while the privates undergo all the fatigue? truly, my friend, I indulged the same idea, and pitied from my heart the poor fellows who had to drabble through the mud and the mire, toiling under ponderous cocked hats, which seemed as unwieldy and cumbrous as the shell which the snail lumbers along on his back. I soon found out, however, that they have their quantum of notoriety. As soon as the army is dismissed, the city swarms with little scouting parties, who fire off their guns at every corner, to he great delight of all the women and children in their vicinity; and wo unto any dog, or pig, or hog, that falls in the way of these magnanimous warriors; they are shown no quarter. Every gentle swain repairs to pass the evening at the feet of his dulcinea, to play "the soldier tired of war's alarms," and to captivate her with the glare of his regimentals; excepting some ambitious heroes who strut to the theatre, flame away in the front boxes, and hector every old apple-woman in the lobbies.

Such, my friend, is the gigantic genius of this nation, and its faculty of swelling up nothings into importance. Our bashaw of Tripoli will review his troops, of some thousands, by an early hour in the morning. Here a review of six hundred men is made the mighty work of a day! with us a bashaw of two tails is never appointed to a command of less than ten thousand men; but here we behold every grade, from the bashaw down to the drum-major, in a force of less than one-tenth of the number. By the beard of Mahomet, but every thing here is indeed on a great scale!

BY ANTHONY EVERGREEN, GENT.

I was not a little surprised the other morning at a request from Will Wizard that I would accompany him that evening to Mrs. ——'s ball. The request was simple enough in itself, it was only singular as coming from Will;—of all my acquaintance Wizard is the least calculated and disposed for the society of ladies—not that he dislikes their company; on the contrary, like every man of pith and marrow, he is a professed admirer of the sex; and had he been born a poet, would undoubtedly have bespattered and be-rhymed some hard-named goddess, until she became as famous as Petrarch's Laura, or Waller's Sacharissa; but Will is such a confounded bungler at a bow, has so many odd bachelor habits, and finds it so troublesome to be gallant, that he generally prefers smoking his segar and telling his story among cronies of his own gender:—and thundering long stories they are, let me tell you;—set Will once a going about China or Crim Tartary, or the Hottentots, and heaven help the poor victim who has to endure his prolixity; he might better be tied to the tail of a jack-o'-lantern. In one word—Will talks like a traveller. Being well acquainted with his character, I was the more alarmed at his inclination to visit a party; since he has often assured me, that he considered it as equivalent to being stuck up for three hours in a steam-engine. I even wondered how he had received an invitation;— this he soon accounted for. It seems Will, on his last arrival from Canton, had made a present of a case of tea to a lady for whom he had once entertained a sneaking kindness when at grammar school; and she in return had invited him to come and drink some of it; a cheap way enough of paying off little obligations. I readily acceded to Will's proposition, expecting much entertainment from his eccentric remarks; and as he has been absent some few years, I anticipated his surprise at the splendour and elegance of a modern rout.

On calling for Will in the evening, I found him full dressed, waiting for me. I contemplated him with absolute dismay. As he still retained a spark of regard for the lady who once reigned in his affections, he had been at unusual pains in decorating his person, and broke upon my sight arrayed in the the true style that prevailed among our beaux some years ago. His hair was turned up and tufted at the top, frizzled out at the ears, a profusion of powder puffed over the whole, and a long plaited club swung gracefully from shoulder to shoulder, describing a pleasing semicircle of powder and pomatum. His claret-coloured coat was decorated with a profusion of gilt buttons, and reached to his calves. His white casimere small-clothes were so tight that he seemed to have grown up in them; and his ponderous legs, which are the thickest part of his body, were beautifully clothed in sky-blue silk stockings, once considered so becoming. But above all, he prided himself upon his waistcoat of China silk, which might almost have served a good housewife for a shortgown; and he boasted that the roses and tulips upon it were the work of *Nang Fou*, daughter of the great *Chin-Chin-Fou*, who had fallen in love with the graces of his person, and sent it to him as a parting present; he assured me she was a remarkable beauty, with sweet obliquity of eyes, and a foot no larger than the thumb of an alderman;—he then dilated most copiously on his silver-sprigged dickey, which he assured me was quite the rage among the dashing young mandarins of Canton.

I hold it an ill-natured office to put any man out of conceit with himself; so, though I would willingly have made a little alteration in my friend Wizard's picturesque costume, yet I politely complimented him on his rakish appearance.

On entering the room I kept a good look-out on Will, expecting to see him exhibit signs of surprise; but he is one of those knowing fellows who are never surprised at any thing, or at least will never acknowledge it. He took his stand in the middle of the floor, playing with his great steel watch-chain; and looking around on the company, the furniture, and the pictures, with the air of a man "who had seen d——d finer things in his time;" and to my utter confusion and dismay, I saw him coolly pull out his villainous old japanned tobacco-box, ornamented with a bottle, a pipe, and a scurvy motto, and help himself to a quid in face of all the company.

I knew it was all in vain to find fault with a fellow of Will's socratic turn, who is never to be put out of humour with himself; so, after he had given his box its prescriptive rap and returned it to his pocket, I drew him into a corner where he might observe the company without being prominent objects ourselves.

"And pray who is that stylish figure," said Will, "who blazes away in red, like a volcano, and who seems wrapped in flames like a fiery dragon?"—That, cried I, is MISS LAURELIA DASHAWAY;—she is the highest flash of the ton—has much whim and more eccentricity, and has reduced many an unhappy gentleman to stupidity by her charms; you see she holds out the red flag in token of "no quarter." "Then keep me safe out of the sphere of her attractions," cried Will. "I would not e'en come in contact with her train, lest it should scorch me like the tail of a comet.——But who, I beg of you, is that amiable youth who is handing along a young lady, and at the same contemplating his sweet person in a mirror, as he passes?" His name, said I, is BILLY DIMPLE;—he is a universal smiler, and would travel from Dan to Beersheba and smile on every body as he passed. Dimple is a slave to the ladies—a hero at tea-parties, and is famous at the *pirouet* and the pigeon-wing; a fiddle-stick is his idol, and a dance his elysium. "A very pretty young gentleman, truly," cried Wizard; "he reminds me of a cotemporary beau at Hayti. -You must know that the magnanimous Dessalines gave a great ball to his court one fine sultry summer's evening; Dessy and me were great cronies;—hand and glove:—one of the most condescending great men I ever knew. Such a display of black and yellow beauties! such a show of Madras handkerchiefs, red beads, cock's-tails and peacock's feathers!—it was, as here, who should wear the highest top-knot, drag the longest tails, or exhibit the greatest variety of combs, colours and gew-gaws. In the middle of the rout, when all was buzz, slip-shod, clack, and perfume, who should enter but TUCKY SQUASH! The yellow beauties blushed blue, and the black ones blushed as red as they could, with pleasure; and there was a universal agitation of fans; every eye brightened and whitened to see Tucky; for he was the pride of the court, the pink of courtesy, the mirror of fashion, the adoration of all the sable fair ones of Hayti. Such breadth of nose, such exuberance of lip! his shins had the true cucumber curve; his face in dancing shone like a kettle; and, provided you kept to windward of him in summer, I do not known a sweeter youth in all Hayti than Tucky Squash. When he laughed, there appeared from ear to ear a chevaux-de-frize of teeth, that rivalled the shark's in whiteness; he could whistle like a north-wester; play on a three-stringed fiddle like Apollo; and as to dancing, no Long-Island negro could shuffle you "double-trouble," or "hoe corn and dig potatoes" more scientifically:—in short, he was a second Lothario. And the dusky nymphs of Hayti, one and all, declared him a perpetual Adonis. Tucky walked about, whistling to himself, without regarding any body; and his *nonchalance* was irresistible."

I found Will had got neck and heels into one of his travellers' stories; and there is no knowing how far he would have run his parallel between Billy Dimple and Tucky Squash, had not the music struck up, from an adjoining apartment, and summoned the company to the dance. The sound seemed to have an inspiring effect on honest Will, and he procured the hand of an old acquaintance for a country dance. It happened to be the fashionable one of "the Devil among the tailors," which is so vociferously demanded at every ball and assembly: and many a torn gown, and many an unfortunate toe did rue the dancing of that night; for Will, thundering down the dance like a coach and six, sometimes right, somewrong; now running over half a score of little Frenchmen, and now making sad inroads into ladies' cobweb muslins and spangled tails. As every part of Will's body partook of the exertion, he shook from his capacious head such volumes of powder, that like pious Eneas on the first interview with Queen Dido, he might be said to have been enveloped in a cloud. Nor was Will's partner an insignificant figure in the scene; she was a young lady of most voluminous proportions, that quivered at every skip; and being braced up in the fashionable style with whalebone, stay-tape, and buckram, looked like an apple-pudding tied in the middle; or, taking her flaming dress into consideration, like a bed and bolsters rolled up in a suit of red curtains. The dance finished—I would gladly have taken Will off, but no;—he was now in one of his happy moods, and there was no doing any thing with him. He insisted on my introducing him to MISS SOPHY SPARKLE, a young lady unrivalled for playful wit and innocent vivacity, and who, like a brilliant, adds lustre to the front of fashion. I accordingly presented him to her, and began a conversation in which, I thought, he might take a share; but no such thing. Will took his stand before her, straddling like a Colossus, with his hands in his pockets, and an air of the most profound attention; nor did he pretend to open his lips for some time; until, upon some lively sally of hers, he electrified the whole company with a most intolerable burst of laughter. What was to be done with such an incorrigible fellow?—to add to my distress, the first word he spoke was to tell Miss Sparkle that something she said reminded him of a circumstance that happened to him in China;—and at it he went, in the true traveller style—described the Chinese mode of eating rice with chop-sticks;—entered into a long eulogium on the succulent qualities of boiled bird's nests; and I made my escape at the very moment when he was on the point of squatting down on the floor, to show how the little Chinese *Joshes* sit cross-legged.

TO THE LADIES.

FROM THE MILL OF PINDAR COCKLOFT, ESQ.

Though jogging down the hill of life,
Without the comfort of a wife;
And though I ne'er a helpmate chose,
To stock my house and mend my hose;
With care my person to adorn,
And spruce me up on Sunday morn;—
Still do I love the gentle sex,
And still with cares my brain perplex
To keep the fair ones of the age
Unsullied as the spotless page;
All pure, all simple, all refined,
The sweetest solace of mankind.
  I hate the loose, insidious jest
To beauty's modest ear addrest,
And hold that frowns should never fail
To check each smooth, but fulsome tale;
But he whose impious pen should dare
Invade the morals of the fair;
To taint that purity divine
Which should each female heart enshrine;
Though soft his vicious strains should swell,
As those which erst from Gabriel fell,
Should yet be held aloft to shame,
And foul dishonour shade his name.
Judge, then, my friends, of my surprise,
The ire that kindled in my eyes,
When I relate, that t'other day
I went a morning-call to pay,

On two young nieces: just come down
To take the polish of the town.
By which I mean no more or less
Than *a la Francaise* to undress;
To whirl the modest waltz' rounds,
Taught by Duport for snug ten pounds.
To thump and thunder through a song,
Play *fortes* soft and *dolce's* strong;
Exhibit loud *piano* feats,
Caught from that crotchet-hero, Meetz:
To drive the rose-bloom from the face,
And fix the lily in its place;
To doff the white, and in its stead
To bounce about in brazen red.

While in the parlour I delay'd,
Till they their persons had array'd,
A dapper volume caught my eye,
That on the window chanced to lie:
A book's a friend—I always choose
To turn its pages and peruse:—
It proved those poems known to fame
For praising every cyprian dame;—
The bantlings of a dapper youth,
Renown'd for gratitude and truth:
A little pest, hight TOMMY MOORE,
Who hopp'd and skipp'd our country o'er;
Who sipp'd our tea and lived on sops,
Revell'd on syllabubs and slops,
And when his brain, of cobweb fine,
Was fuddled with five drops of wine,
Would all his puny loves rehearse,
And many a maid debauch—in verse.
Surprised to meet in open view,
A book of such lascivious hue,
I chid my nieces—but they say,
'Tis all the passion of the day;—
That many a fashionable belle
Will with enraptured accents dwell
On the sweet *morceau* she has found
In this delicious, curst, compound!

Soft do the tinkling numbers roll,
And lure to vice the unthinking soul;

They tempt by softest sounds away,
They lead entranced the heart astray;
And Satan's doctrine sweetly sing,
As with a seraph's heavenly string.
Such sounds, so good, old Homer sung,
Once warbled from the Syren's tongue;—
Sweet melting tones were heard to pour
Along Ausonia's sun-gilt shore;
Seductive strains in æther float,
And every wild deceitful note
That could the yielding heart assail,
Were wafted on the breathing gale;—
And every gentle accent bland
To tempt Ulysses to their strand.
  And can it be this book so base,
Is laid on every window-case?
Oh! fair ones, if you will profane
Those breasts where heaven itself should reign;
And throw those pure recesses wide,
Where peace and virtue should reside
To let the holy pile admit
A guest unhallowed and unfit;
Pray, like the frail ones of the night,
Who hide their wanderings from the light,
So let your errors secret be,
And hide, at least, your fault from me:
Seek some by corner to explore
The smooth, polluted pages o'er.
There drink the insidious poison in,
There slyly nurse your souls for sin:
And while that purity you blight
Which stamps you messengers of light,
And sap those mounds the gods bestow,
To keep you spotless here below;
Still in compassion to our race,
Who joy, not only in the face,
But in that more exalted part,
The sacred temple of the heart;
Oh! hide for ever from our view,
The fatal mischief you pursue:—
Let MEN your praises still exalt,
And none but ANGELS mourn your fault.

NO. VI.—FRIDAY MARCH 20, 1807.

FROM MY ELBOW-CHAIR.

THE Cockloft family, of which I have made such frequent mention, is of great antiquity, if there be any truth in the genealogical tree which hangs up in my cousin's library. They trace their descent from a celebrated Roman knight, cousin to the progenitor of his majesty of Britain, who left his native country on occasion of some disgust; and coming into Wales became a great favourite of prince Madoc, and accompanied that famous argonaut in the voyage which ended in the discovery of this continent. Though a member of the family, I have sometimes ventured to doubt the authenticity of this portion of their annals, to the great vexation of cousin Christopher: who is looked up to as the head of our house; and who, though as orthodox as a bishop, would sooner give up the whole decalogue than lop off a single limb of the family tree. From time immemorial, it has been the rule for the Cocklofts to marry one of their own name; and as they always bred like rabbits, the family has increased and multiplied like that of Adam and Eve. In truth, their number is almost incredible; and you can hardly go into any part of the country without starting a warren of genuine Cocklofts. Every person of the least observation or experience must have observed that where this practice of marrying cousins and second cousins prevails in a family, every member in the course of a few generations becomes queer, humourous, and original; as much distinguished from the common race of mongrels as if he was of a different species. This has happened in our family, and particularly in that branch of it of which Mr. Christopher Cockloft, or, to do him justice, Mr. Christopher Cockloft, Esq., is the head. Christopher is, in fact, the only married man of the name who resides in town; his family is small, having lost most of his children when young, by the excessive care he took to bring them up like vegetables. This was one of his first whim-whams, and a confounded one it was, as his children might have told, had they not fallen victims to this experiment before they could talk. He had got from some quack philosopher or other a notion that there was a complete analogy between children and plants, and that they ought to be both reared alike. Accordingly, he sprinkled them every morning with water, laid them out in the sun, as he did his geraniums; and if the season was remarkably dry, repeated this wise experiment three or four times of a morning. The consequence was, the poor little souls died one after the other, except Jeremy and his two sisters, who, to be sure, are a trio of as odd, runty, mummy-looking originals as ever Hogarth fancied in his most happy moments. Mrs. Cockloft, the larger if not the better half of my cousin, often remonstrated against this vegetable theory; and even brought the parson of the parish in which my cousin's country house is situated to her aid, but in vain: Christopher persisted, and attributed the failure of his plan to its not having been exactly conformed to. As I have mentioned Mrs. Cockloft, I may as well say a little more about her while I am in the humour. She is a lady of wonderful notability, a warm admirer of shining mahogany, clean hearths, and her husband; who she considers the wisest man in the world, bating Will Wizard and the parson of our parish; the last of whom is her oracle on all occasions. She goes constantly to church every Sunday and Saints-day; and insists upon it that no man is entitled to ascend a pulpit unless he has been ordained by a bishop; nay, so far does she carry her orthodoxy, that all the argument in the world will never persuade her that a Presbyterian or Baptist, or even a Calvinist, has any possible chance of going to heaven. Above every thing else, however, she abhors paganism. Can scarcely refrain from laying violent hands on a pantheon when she meets with it; and was very nigh going into hysterics when my cousin insisted one of his boys should be christened after our laureate: because the parson of the parish had told her that Pindar was the name of a pagan writer, famous for his love of boxing matches, wrestling, and horse-racing. To sum up all her qualifications in the shortest possible way, Mrs. Cockloft is, in the true sense of the phrase, a good sort of woman; and I often congratulate my cousin on possessing her. The rest of the family consists of Jeremy Cockloft the younger, who has already been mentioned, and the two Miss Cocklofts, or rather the young ladies, as they have been called by the servants, time out of mind; not that they are really young, the younger being somewhat on the shady side of thirty, but it has ever been the custom to call every member of the family young under fifty. In the southeast corner of the house, I hold quiet possession of an old-fashioned apartment, where myself and my elbow-chair are suffered to amuse ourselves undisturbed, save at meal times. This apartment old Cockloft has facetiously denominated cousin Launce's paradise; and the good old gentleman has two or three favourite jokes about it, which are served up as regularly as the standing family dish of beef-steaks and onions, which every day maintains its station at the foot of the table, in defiance of mutton, poultry, or even venison itself.

Though the family is apparently small, yet, like most old establishments of the kind, it does not want for honorary members. It is the city rendezvous of the Cocklofts; and we are continually enlivened by the company of half a score of uncles, aunts, and cousins, in the fortieth remove, from all parts of the country, who profess a wonderful regard for cousin Christopher, and overwhelm every member of his household, down to the cook in the kitchen, with their attentions. We have for three weeks past been greeted with the company of two worthy old spinsters, who came down from the country to settle a lawsuit. They have done little else but retail stories of their village neighbours, knit stockings, and take snuff all the time they have been here; the whole family are bewildered with churchyard tales of sheeted ghosts, white horses without heads and with large goggle eyes in their buttocks; and not one of the old servants dare budge an inch after dark without a numerous company at his heels. My cousin's visitors, however, always return his hospitality with due gratitude, and now and then remind him of their fraternal regard by a present of a pot of apple-sweetmeats or a barrel of sour cider at Christmas. Jeremy displays himself to great advantage among his country relations, who all think him a prodigy, and often stand astounded, in "gaping wonderment," at his natural philosophy. He lately frightened a simple old uncle almost out of his wits, by giving it as his opinion that the earth would one day be scorched to ashes by the eccentric gambols of the famous comet, so much talked of; and positively asserted that this world revolved round the sun, and that the moon was certainly inhabited.

The family mansion bears equal marks of antiquity with its inhabitants. As the Cocklofts are remarkable for their attachment to every thing that has remained long in the family, they are bigoted towards their old edifice, and I dare say would sooner have it crumble about their ears than abandon it. The consequence is, it has been so patched up and repaired, that it has become as full of whims and oddities as its tenants; requires to be nursed and humoured like a gouty old codger of an alderman, and reminds one of the famous ship in which a certain admiral circumnavigated the globe, which was so patched and timbered, in order to preserve so great a curiosity, that at length not a particle of the original remained. Whenever the wind blows, the old mansion makes a most perilous groaning; and every storm is sure to make a day's work for the carpenter, who attends upon it as regularly as the family physician. This predilection for every thing that has been long in the family shows itself in every particular. The domestics are all grown gray in the service of our house. We have a little, old, crusty, grey-headed negro, who has lived through two or three generations of the Cocklofts; and, of course, has become a personage of no little importance in the household. He calls all the family by their Christian names; tells long stories about how he dandled them on his knee when they were children; and is a complete Cockloft chronicle for the last seventy years. The family carriage was made in the last French war, and the old horses were most indubitably foaled in Noah's ark; resembling marvellously, in gravity of demeanour, those sober animals which may be seen any day of the year in the streets of Philadelphia, walking their snail's pace, a dozen in a row, and harmoniously jingling their bells. Whim-whams are the inheritance of the Cocklofts, and every member of the household is a humourist *sui generis*, from the master down to the footman. The very cats and dogs are humourists; and we have a little, runty scoundrel of a cur, who, whenever the church-bells ring, will run to the street-door, turn up his nose in the wind, and howl most piteously. Jeremy insists that this is owing to a peculiar delicacy in the organization of his ears, and supports his position by many learned arguments which nobody can understand; but I am of opinion that it is a mere Cockloft whim-wham, which the little cur indulges, being descended from a race of dogs which has flourished in the family ever since the time of my grandfather. A propensity to save every thing that bears the stamp of family antiquity, has accumulated an abundance of trumpery and rubbish with which the house is encumbered from the cellar to the garret; and every room and closet, and corner is crammed with three-legged chairs, clocks without hands, swords without scabbards, cocked hats, broken candlesticks, and looking-glasses with frames carved into fantastic shapes of feathered sheep, woolly birds, and other animals that have no name save in books of heraldry. The ponderous mahogany chairs in the parlour are of such unwieldy proportions that it is quite a serious undertaking to gallant one of them across the room; and sometimes make a most equivocal noise when you set down in a hurry; the mantel-piece is decorated with little lacquered earthern shepherdesses; some of which are without toes, and others without noses; and the fire-place is garnished out with Dutch tiles, exhibiting a great variety of scripture pieces, which my good old soul of a cousin takes infinite delight in explaining.—Poor Jeremy hates them as he does poison; for while a yonker, he was obliged by his mother to learn the history of a tile every Sunday morning before she would permit him to join his playmates; this was a terrible affair for Jeremy, who, by the time he had learned the last had forgotten the first, and was obliged to begin again. He assured me the other day, with a round college oath, that if the old house stood out till he inherited it, he would have these tiles taken out and ground into powder, for the perfect hatred he bore them.

My cousin Christopher enjoys unlimited authority in the mansion of his forefathers; he is truly what may be termed a hearty old blade, has a florid, sunshine countenance; and if you will only praise his wine, and laugh at his long stories, himself and his house are heartily at your service.—The first condition is indeed easily complied with, for, to tell the truth, his wine is excellent; but his stories, being not of the best, and often repeated, are apt to create a disposition to yawn; being, in addition to their other qualities, most unreasonably long. His prolixity is the more afflicting to me, since I have all his stories by heart; and when he enters upon one, it reminds me of Newark causeway, where the traveller sees the end at the distance of several miles. To the great misfortune of all his acquaintance, cousin Cockloft is blest with a most provokingly retentive memory; and can give day and date, and name and age and circumstance, with the most unfeeling precision. These, however, are but trivial foibles, forgotten, or remembered, only with a kind of tender, respectful pity, by those who know with what a rich redundant harvest of kindness and generosity his heart is stored. It would delight you to see with what social gladness he welcomes a visitor into his house; and the poorest man that enters his door never leaves it without a cordial invitation to sit down and drink a glass of wine. By the honest farmers round his country-seat, he is looked up to with love and reverence; they never pass him by without his inquiring after the welfare of their families, and receiving a cordial shake of his liberal hand. There are but two classes of people who are thrown out of the reach of his hospitality, and these are Frenchmen and democrats. The old gentleman considers it treason against the majesty of good breeding to speak to any visitor with his hat on; but, the moment a democrat enters his door, he forthwith bids his man Pompey bring his hat, puts it on his head, and salutes him with an appalling "well, sir, what do you want with me?"

He has a profound contempt for Frenchmen, and firmly believes, that they eat nothing but frogs and soup-maigre in their own country. This unluckly prejudice is partly owing to my great aunt, PAMELA, having been many years ago, run away with by a French Count, who turned out to be the son of a generation of barbers;—and partly to a little vivid spark of toryism, which burns in a secret corner of his heart. He was a loyal subject of the crown, has hardly yet recovered the shock of independence; and, though he does not care to own it, always does honour to his majesty's birth-day, by inviting a few cavaliers, like himself, to dinner; and gracing his table with more than ordinary festivity. If by chance the revolution is mentioned before him, my cousin shakes his head; and you may see, if you take good note, a lurking smile of contempt in the corner of his eye, which marks a decided disapprobation of the sound. He once, in the fulness of his heart, observed to me that green peas were a month later than they were under the old government. But the most eccentric manifestation of loyalty he ever gave, was making a voyage to Halifax for no other reason under heaven but to hear his Majesty prayed for in church, as he used to be here formerly. This he never could be brought fairly to acknowledge; but it is a certain fact, I assure you. It is not a little singular that a person, so much given to long story-telling as my cousin, should take a liking to another of the same character; but so it is with the old gentleman:—his prime favourite and companion is Will Wizard, who is almost a member of the family; and will sit before the fire, with his feet on the massy andirons, and smoke his segar, and screw his phiz, and spin away tremendous long stories of his travels, for a whole evening, to the great delight of the old gentleman and lady; and especially of the young ladies, who, like Desdemona, do "seriously incline," and listen to him with innumerable "O dears," "is it possibles," "goody graciouses," and look upon him as a second Sinbad the sailor.

The Miss Cocklofts, whose pardon I crave for not having particularly introduced them before, are a pair of delectable damsels; who, having purloined and locked up the family-Bible, pass for just what age they please to plead guilty to. BARBARA, the eldest, has long since resigned the character of a belle, and adopted that staid, sober, demure, snuff-taking air becoming her years and discretion. She is a good-natured soul, whom I never saw in a passion but once; and that was occasioned by seeing an old favorite beau of hers, kiss the hand of a pretty blooming girl; and, in truth, she only got angry because, as she very properly said, it was spoiling the child. Her sister MARGERY, or MAGGIE, as she is familiarly termed, seemed disposed to maintain her post as a belle, until a few months since; when accidently hearing a gentleman observe that she broke very fast, she suddenly left off going to the assembly, took a cat into high favour, and began to rail at the forward pertness of young misses. From that moment I set her down for an old maid; and so she is, "by the hand of my body." The young ladies are still visited by some half dozen of veteran beaux, who grew and flourished in the *haut ton*, when the Miss Cocklofts were quite children; but have been brushed rather rudely by the hand of time, who, to say the truth, can do almost any thing but make people young. They are, notwithstanding, still warm candidates for female favour; look venerably tender, and repeat over and over the same honeyed speeches and sugared sentiments to the little belles that they poured so profusely into the ears of their mothers. I beg leave here to give notice, that by this sketch, I mean no reflection on old bachelors; on the contrary, I hold that next to a fine lady, the *ne plus ultra*, an old bachelor to be the most charming being upon earth; in as much as by living in "single blessedness," he of course does just as he pleases; and if he has any genius, must acquire a plentiful stock of whims, and oddities, and whalebone habits; without which I esteem a man to be mere beef without mustard; good for nothing at all, but to run on errands for ladies, take boxes at the theatre, and act the part of a screen at tea-parties, or a walking-stick in the streets. I merely speak of these old boys who infest public walks, pounce upon ladies from every corner of the street, and worry and frisk and amble, and caper before, behind, and round about the fashionable belles, like old ponies in a pasture, striving to supply the absence of youthful whim and hilarity, by grimaces and grins, and artificial vivacity. I have sometimes seen one of these "reverend youths" endeavoring to elevate his wintry passions into something like love, by basking in the sunshine of beauty; and it did remind me of an old moth attempting to fly through a pane of glass towards a light, without ever approaching near enough to warm itself, or scorch its wings.

Never, I firmly believe, did there exist a family that went more by tangents than the Cocklofts. Every thing is governed by whim; and if one member starts a new freak, away all the rest follow on like wild geese in a string. As the family, the servants, the horses, cats, and dogs, have all grown old together, they have accommodated themselves to each other's habits completely; and though every body of them is full of odd points, angles, rhomboids, and ins and outs, yet, some how or other, they harmonize together like so many straight lines; and it is truly a grateful and refreshing sight to see them agree so well. Should one, however, get out of tune, it is like a cracked fiddle: the whole concert is ajar; you perceive a cloud over every brow in the house, and even the old chairs seem to creak affetuosso. If my cousin, as he is rather apt to do, betray any symptoms of vexation or uneasiness, no matter about what, he is worried to death with inquiries, which answer no other end but to demonstrate the good-will of the inquirer, and put him in a passion: for every body knows how provoking it is to be cut short in a fit of the blues, by an impertinent question about "what is the matter?" when a man can't tell himself. I remember a few months ago the old gentleman came home in quite a squall; kicked poor Cæsar, the mastiff, out of his way, as he came through the hall; threw his hat on the table with most violent emphasis, and pulling out his box, took three huge pinches of snuff, and threw a fourth into the cat's eyes as he sat purring his astonishment by the fire-side. This was enough to set the body politic going; Mrs. Cockloft began "my dearing" it as fast as tongue could move; the young ladies took each a stand at an elbow of his chair;—Jeremy marshalled in rear;—the servants came tumbling in; the mastiff put up an inquiring nose;—and even grimalkin, after he had cleaned his whiskers and finished sneezing, discovered indubitable signs of sympathy. After the most affectionate inquiries on all sides, it turned out that my cousin, in crossing the street, had got his silk stockings bespattered with mud by a coach, which it seems belonged to a dashing gentleman who had formerly supplied the family with hot rolls and muffins! Mrs. Cockloft thereupon turned up her eyes, and the young ladies their noses; and it would have edified a whole congregation to hear the conversation which took place concerning the insolence of upstarts, and the vulgarity of would-be gentlemen and ladies, who strive to emerge from low life by dashing about in carriages to pay a visit two doors of; giving parties to people who laugh at them, and cutting all their old friends.

THEATRICS.

BY WILLIAM WIZARD, ESQ.

I WENT a few evenings since to the theatre accompanied by my friend Snivers, the cockney, who is a man deeply read in the history of Cinderella, Valentine and Orson, Blue Beard, and all those recondite works so necessary to enable a man to understand the modern drama. Snivers is one of those intolerable fellows who will never be pleased with any thing until he has turned and twisted it divers ways, to see if it corresponds with his notions of congruity; and as he is none of the quickest in his ratiocinations, he will sometimes come out with his approbation, when every body else has forgotten the cause which excited it. Snivers is, moreover, a great critic, for he finds fault with every thing; this being what I understand by modern criticism. He, however, is pleased to acknowledge that our theatre is not so despicable, all things considered; and really thinks Cooper one of our best actors. The play was OTHELLO, and to speak my mind freely, I think I have seen it performed much worse in my time. The actors, I firmly believe, did their best; and whenever this is the case no man has a right to find fault with them, in my opinion.

Little RUTHERFORD, the Roscius of the Philadelphia theatre, looked as big as possible; and what he wanted in size he made up in frowning. I like frowning in tragedy; and if a man but keeps his forehead in proper wrinkle, talks big, and takes long strides on the stage, I always set him down as a great tragedian; and so does my friend Snivers.

Before the first act was over, Snivers began to flourish his critical wooden sword like a harlequin. He first found fault with Cooper for not having made himself as black as a negro; "for," said he, "that Othello was an arrant black, appears from several expressions of the play; as, for instance, 'thick lips,' 'sooty bosom,' and a variety of others. I am inclined to think," continued he, "that Othello was an Egyptian by birth, from the circumstance of the handkerchief given to his mother by a native of that country; and, if so, he certainly was as black as my hat: for Herodotus has told us, that the Egyptians had flat noses and frizzled hair; a clear proof that they were all negroes." He did not confine his strictures to this single error of the actor, but went on to run him down in toto. In this he was seconded by a red hot Philadelphian, who proved, by a string of most eloquent logical puns, that Fennel was unquestionably in every respect a better actor than Cooper. I knew it was vain to contend with them, since I recollected a most obstinate trial of skill these two great *Roscii* had last spring in Philadelphia. Cooper brandished his blood-stained dagger at the theatre—Fennel flourished his snuff-box and shook his wig at the Lyceum, and the unfortunate Philadelphians were a long time at a loss to decide which deserved the palm. The literati were inclined to give it to Cooper, because his name was the most fruitful in puns, but then, on the other side, it was contended that Fennel was the best Greek scholar. Scarcely was the town of Strasburgh in a greater hub-bub about the courteous stranger's nose; and it was well that the doctors of the university did not get into the dispute, else it might have become a battle of folios. At length, after much excellent argument had been expended on both sides, recourse was had to Cocker's arithmetic and a carpenter's rule; the rival candidates were both measured by one of their most steady-handed critics, and by the most exact measurement it was proved that Mr. Fennel was the greater actor by three inches and a quarter. Since this demonstration of his inferiority, Cooper has never been able to hold up his head in Philadelphia.

In order to change a conversation in which my favourite suffered so much, I made some inquiries of the Philadelphian, concerning the two heroes of his theatre, WOOD and CAIN; but I had scarcely mentioned their names, when, whack! he threw a whole handful of puns in my face; 'twas like a bowl of cold water. I turned on my heel, had recourse to my tobacco-box, and said no more about Wood and Cain; nor will I ever more, if I can help it, mention their names in the presence of a Philadelphian. Would that they could leave off punning! for I love every soul of them, with a cordial affection, warm as their own generous hearts, and boundless as their hospitality.

During the performance, I kept an eye on the countenance of my friend, the cockney; because having come all the way from England, and having seen Kemble once, on a visit which he made from the button manufactory to *Lunnun*, I thought his phiz might serve as a kind of thermometer to direct my manifestations of applause or disapprobation. I might as well have looked at the back-side of his head; for I could not, with all my peering, perceive by his features that he was pleased with any thing—except himself. His hat was twitched a little on one side, as much as to say, " demme, I'm your sorts!" He was sucking the end of a little stick; he was a " gemman" from head to foot; but as to his face, there was no more expression in it than in the face of a Chinese lady on a teacup. On Cooper's giving one of his gunpowder explosions of passion, I exclaimed, " fine, very fine!" "Pardon me," said my friend Snivers, "this is damnable!—the gesture, my dear sir, only look at the gesture! how horrible! do you not observe that the actor slaps his forehead, whereas, the passion not having arrived at the proper height, he should only have slapped his—pocket-flap?—this figure of rhetoric is a most important stage trick, and the proper management of it is what peculiarly distinguishes the great actor from the mere plodding mechanical buffoon. Different degrees of passion require different slaps, which we critics have reduced to a perfect manual, improving upon the principle adopted by Frederic of Prussia, by deciding that an actor, like a soldier, is a mere machine; as thus—the actor, for a minor burst of passion merely slaps his pocket-hole; good!—for a major burst, he slaps his breast;—very good!—but for a burst maximus, he whacks away at his forehead, like a brave fellow;—this is excellent!—nothing can be finer than an exit slapping the forehead from one end of the stage to the other." " Except," replied I, " one of those slaps on the breast, which I have sometimes admired in some of our fat heroes and heroines, which make their whole body shake and quiver like a pyramid of jelly."

The Philadelphian had listened to this conversation with profound attention, and appeared delighted with Snivers' mechanical strictures; 'twas natural enough in a man who chose an actor as he would a grenadier. He took the opportunity of a pause, to enter into a long conversation with my friend; and was receiving a prodigious fund of information concerning the true mode of emphasising conjunctions, shifting scenes, snuffing candles, and making thunder and lightning, better than you can get every day from the sky, as practised at the royal theatres; when, as ill luck would have it, they happened to run their heads full butt against a new reading. Now this was "a stumper," as our friend Paddle would say; for the Philadelphians are as inveterate new-reading hunters as the cockneys; and, for aught I know, as well skilled in finding them out. The Philadelphian thereupon met the cockney on his own ground; and at it they went, like two inveterate curs at a bone. Snivers quoted Theobald, Hanmer, and a host of learned commentators, who have pinned themselves on the sleeve of Shakspeare's immortality, and made the old bard, like General Washington, in General Washington's life, a most diminutive figure in his own book;—his opponent chose Johnson for his bottle-holder, and thundered him forward like an elephant to bear down the ranks of the enemy. I was not long in discovering that these two precious judges had got hold of that unlucky passage of Shakspeare which, like a straw, has tickled, and puzzled, and confounded many a somniferous buzzard of past and present time. It was the celebrated wish of Desdemona, that heaven had made her such a man as Othello.—Snivers insisted, that "the gentle Desdemona" merely wished for such a man for a husband, which in all conscience was a modest wish enough, and very natural in a young lady who might possibly have had a predilection for flat noses; like a certain philosophical great man of our day. The Philadelphian contended with all the vehemence of a member of congress, moving the house to have "whereas," or "also," or "nevertheless," struck out of a bill, that the young lady wished heaven had made her a man instead of a woman, in order that she might have an opportunity of seeing the "anthropophagi, and the men whose heads do grow beneath their shoulders;" which was a very natural wish, considering the curiosity of the sex. On being referred to, I incontinently decided in favour of the honourable member who spoke last; inasmuch as I think it was a very foolish, and therefore very natural, wish for a young lady to make before a man she wished to marry. It was, moreover, an indication of the violent inclination she felt to wear the breeches, which was afterwards, in all probability, gratified, if we may judge from the title of "our captain's captain," given her by Cassio, a phrase which, in my opinion, indicates that Othello was, at that time, most ignominiously hen-pecked. I believe my argument staggered Snivers himself, for he looked confoundedly queer, and said not another word on the subject.

A little while after, at it he went again on another tack; and began to find fault with Cooper's manner of dying:—"it was not natural," he said, for it had lately been demonstrated, by a learned doctor of physic, that when a man is mortally stabbed, he ought to take a flying leap of at least five feet, and drop down "dead as a salmon in a fishmonger's basket."—Whenever a man, in the predicament above mentioned, departed from this fundamental rule, by falling flat down, like a log, and rolling about for two or three minutes, making speeches all the time, the said learned doctor maintained that it was owing to the waywardness of the human mind, which delighted in flying in the face of nature, and dying in defiance of all her established rules.—I replied, "for my part, I held that every man had a right of dying in whatever position he pleased; and that the mode of doing it depended altogether on the peculiar character of the person going to die. A Persian could not die in peace unless he had his face turned to the east; —a Mahometan would always choose to have his towards Mecca; a Frenchman might prefer this mode of throwing a somerset; but Mynheer Van Brumblebottom, the Roscius of Rotterdam, always chose to thunder down on his seat of honour whenever he received a mortal wound.—Being a man of ponderous dimensions, this had a most electrifying effect, for the whole theatre "shook like Olympus at the nod of Jove." The Philadelphian was immediately inspired with a pun, and swore that Mynheer must be great in a dying scene, since he knew how to make the most of his latter end.

It is the inveterate cry of stage critics, that an actor does not perform the character naturally, if, by chance, he happens not to die exactly as they would have him. I think the exhibition of a play at Pekin would suit them exactly; and I wish, with all my heart, they would go there and see one: nature is there imitated with the most scrupulous exactness in every trifling particular. Here an unhappy lady or gentleman, who happens unluckily to be poisoned or stabbed, is left on the stage to writhe and groan, and make faces at the audience, until the poet pleases they should die; while the honest folks of the *dramatis personæ*, bless their hearts! all crowd round and yield most potent assistance, by crying and lamenting most vociferously! the audience, tender souls, pull out their white pocket handkerchiefs, wipe their eyes, blow their noses, and swear it is natural as life, while the poor actor is left to die without common Christian comfort. In China, on the contrary, the first thing they do is to run for the doctor and *tchoouc*, or notary. The audience are entertained throughout the fifth act with a learned consultation of physicians, and if the patient must die, he does it *secundum artem*, and always is allowed time to make his will. The celebrated Chow-Chow was the completest hand I ever saw at killing himself; he always carried under his robe a bladder of bull's blood, which, when he gave the mortal stab, spirted out, to the infinite delight of the audience. Not that the ladies of China are more fond of the sight of blood than those of our own country; on the contrary, they are remarkably sensitive in this particular; and we are told by the great Linkum Fidelius, that the beautiful Ninny Consequa, one of the ladies of the emperor's seraglio, once fainted away on seeing a favourite slave's nose bleed; since which time refinement has been carried to such a pitch, that a buskined hero is not allowed to run himself through the body in the face of the audience.—The immortal Chow-Chow, in conformity to this absurd prejudice, whenever he plays the part of Othello, which is reckoned his master-piece, always keeps a bold front, stabs himself slily behind, and is dead before any body suspects that he has given the mortal blow.

P.S. Just as this was going to press, I was informed by Evergreen that Othello had not been performed here the Lord knows when; no matter, I am not the first that has criticised a play without seeing it, and this critique will answer for the last performance, if that was a dozen years ago.

NO. VII.—SATURDAY, APRIL 4, 1807.

LETTER FROM MUSTAPHA RUB-A-DUB KELI KAHN,
TO ASEM HACCHEM, PRINCIPAL SLAVE-DRIVER TO HIS HIGHNESS THE BASHAW OF TRIPOLI.

I PROMISED in a former letter, good Asem, that I would furnish thee with a few hints respecting the nature of the government by which I am held in durance.—Though my inquiries for that purpose have been industrious, yet I am not perfectly satisfied with their results; for thou mayest easily imagine that the vision of a captive is overshadowed by the mists of illusion and prejudice, and the horizon of his speculations must be limited indeed. I find that the people of this country are strangely at a loss to determine the nature and proper character of their government. Even their dervises are extremely in the dark as to this particular, and are continually indulging in the most preposterous disquisitions on the subject: some have insisted that it savours of an aristocracy; others maintain that it is a pure democracy; and a third set of theorists declare absolutely that it is nothing more nor less than a mobocracy. The latter, I must confess, though still wide in error, have come nearest to the truth. You of course must understand the meaning of these different words, as they are derived from the ancient Greek language, and bespeak loudly the verbal poverty of these poor infidels, who cannot utter a learned phrase without laying the dead languages under contribution. A man, my dear Asem, who talks good sense in his native tongue, is held in tolerable estimation in this country; but a fool who clothes his feeble ideas in a foreign or antique garb, is bowed down to as a literary prodigy. While I conversed with these people in plain English, I was but little attended to; but the moment I prosed away in Greek, every one looked up to me with veneration as an oracle.

Although the dervises differ widely in the particulars above mentioned, yet they all agree in terming their government one of the most pacific in the known world. I cannot help pitying their ignorance, and smiling, at times, to see into what ridiculous errors those nations will wander who are unenlightened by the precepts of Mahomet, our divine prophet, and uninstructed by the five hundred and forty-nine books of wisdom of the immortal Ibrahim Hassan al Fusti. To call this nation pacific! most preposterous! it reminds me of the title assumed by the sheik of that murderous tribe of wild Arabs, that desolate the valleys of Belsaden, who styles himself STAR OF COURTESY—BEAM OF THE MERCY-SEAT!

The simple truth of the matter is, that these people are totally ignorant of their own true character; for, according to the best of my observation, they are the most warlike, and, I must say, the most savage nation that I have as yet discovered among all the barbarians. They are not only at war, in their own way, with almost every nation on earth, but they are at the same time engaged in the most complicated knot of civil wars that ever infested any poor unhappy country on which ALLAH has denounced his malediction!

To let thee at once into a secret, which is unknown to these people themselves, their government is a pure unadulterated LOGOCRACY, or government of words. The whole nation does every thing *viva voce*, or by word of mouth; and in this manner is one of the most military nations in existence. Every man who has what is here called the gift of the gab, that is, a plentiful stock of verbosity, becomes a soldier outright; and is forever in a militant state. The country is entirely defended *vi et lingua;* that is to say, by force of tongues. The account which I lately wrote to our friend, the snorer, respecting the immense army of six hundred men, makes nothing against this observation; that formidable body being kept up, as I have already observed, only to amuse their fair countrywomen by their splendid appearance and nodding plumes; and are by way of distinction, denominated the "defenders of the fair."

In a logocracy thou well knowest there is little or no occasion for fire-arms, or any such destructive weapons. Every offensive or defensive measure is enforced by wordy battle, and paper war; he who has the longest tongue or readiest quill, is sure to gain the victory,—will carry horror, abuse, and inkshed into the very trenches of the enemy; and, without mercy or remorse, put men, women, and children to the point of the pen!

There is still preserved in this country some remains of that gothic spirit of knight-errantry, which so much annoyed the faithful in the middle ages of the hegira. As, notwithstanding their martial disposition, they are a people much given to commerce and agriculture, and must, necessarily, at certain seasons be engaged in these employments, they have accommodated themselves by appointing knights, or constant warriors, incessant brawlers, similar to those who, in former ages, swore eternal enmity to the followers of our divine prophet.—These knights, denominated editors or SLANG-WHANGERS, are appointed in every town, village, and district, to carry on both foreign and internal warfare, and may be said to keep up a constant firing "in words." Oh, my friend, could you but witness the enormities sometimes committed by these tremendous slang-whangers, your very turban would rise with horror and astonishment. I have seen them extend their ravages even into the kitchens of their opponents, and annihilate the very cook with a blast; and I do assure thee, I beheld one of these warriors attack a most venerable bashaw, and at one stroke of his pen lay him open from the waistband of his breeches to his chin!

There has been a civil war carrying on with great violence for some time past, in consequence of a conspiracy among the higher classes, to dethrone his highness the present bashaw, and place another in his stead. I was mistaken when I formerly asserted to thee that this dissatisfaction arose from his wearing red breeches. It is true the nation have long held that colour in great detestation, in consequence of a dispute they had some twenty years since with the barbarians of the British islands. The colour, however, is again rising into favour, as the ladies have transferred it to their heads from the bashaw's——body. The true reason, I am told, is, that the bashaw absolutely refuses to believe in the deluge, and in the story of Balaam's ass;—maintaining that this animal was never yet permitted to talk except in a genuine logocracy; where, it is true, his voice may often be heard, and is listened to with reverence, as "the voice of the sovereign people." Nay, so far did he carry his obstinacy, that he absolutely invited a professed antediluvian from the Gallic empire, who illuminated the whole country with his principles——and his nose. This was enough to set the nation in a blaze;—every slang-whanger resorted to his tongue or his pen; and for seven years have they carried on a most inhuman war, in which volumes of words have been expended, oceans of ink have been shed; nor has any mercy been shown to age, sex, or condition. Every day have these slang-whangers made furious attacks on each other, and upon their respective adherents: discharging their heavy artillery, consisting of large sheets loaded with scoundrel! villain! liar! rascal! numbskull! nincompoop! dunderhead! wiseacre! blockhead! jackass! and I do swear, by my beard, though I know thou wilt scarcely credit me, that in some of these skirmishes the grand bashaw himself has been wofully pelted! yea, most ignominiously pelted!—and yet have these talking desperadoes escaped without the bastinado!

Every now and then a slang-whanger, who has a longer head, or rather a longer tongue than the rest, will elevate his piece and discharge a shot quite across the ocean, levelled at the head of the emperor of France, the king of England, or, wouldst thou believe it, oh! Asem, even at his sublime highness the bashaw of Tripoli! these long pieces are loaded with single ball, or language, as tyrant! usurper! robber! tiger! monster! and thou mayest well suppose they occasion great distress and dismay in the camps of the enemy, and are marvellously annoying to the crowned heads at which they are directed. The slang-whanger, though perhaps the mere champion of a village, having fired off his shot, struts about with great self-congratulation, chuckling at the prodigious bustle he must have occasioned, and seems to ask of every stranger, "well, sir, what do they think of me in Europe?"* This is sufficient to show you the manner in which these bloody, or rather windy fellows fight; it is the only mode allowable in a logocracy or government of

---

NOTE, BY WILLIAM WIZARD, ESQ.

* The sage Mustapha, when he wrote the above paragraph, had probably in his eye the following anecdote; related either by Linkum Fidelius, or Josephus Millerius, vulgarly called Joe Miller, of facetious memory.

The captain of a slave-vessel, on his first landing on the coast of Guinea, observed, under a palm-tree, a negro chief, sitting most majestically on a stump; while two women, with wooden spoons, were administering his favourite pottage of boiled rice; which, as his imperial majesty was a little greedy, would part of it escape the place of destination and run down his chin. The watchful attendants were particularly careful to intercept these scapegrace particles, and return them to their proper port of entry. As the captain approached, in order to admire this curious exhibition of royalty, the great chief clapped his hands to his sides, and saluted his visitor with the following pompous question, "well, sir! what do they say of me in England?"

words. I would also observe that their civil wars have a thousand ramifications.

While the fury of the battle rages in the metropolis, every little town and village has a distinct broil, growing like excrescences out of the grand national altercation, or rather agitating within it, like those complicated pieces of mechanism where there is a "wheel within a wheel."

But in nothing is the verbose nature of this government more evident than in its grand national divan, or congress, where the laws are framed; this is a blustering, windy assembly, where everything is carried by noise, tumult and debate; for thou must know, that the members of this assembly do not meet together to find wisdom in the multitude of counsellors, but to wrangle, call each other hard names, and hear themselves talk. When the congress opens, the bashaw first sends them a long message, *i.e.*, a huge mass of words—*vox et preterea nihil*, all meaning nothing; because it only tells them what they perfectly know already. Then the whole assembly are thrown into a ferment, and have a long talk about the quantity of words that are to be returned in answer to this message; and here arises many disputes about the correction of "if so be's," and "how so ever's." A month, perhaps, is spent in thus determining the precise number of words the answer shall contain; and then another, most probably, in concluding whether it shall be carried to the bashaw on foot, on horseback, or in coaches. Having settled this weighty matter, they next fall to work upon the message itself, and hold as much chattering over it as so many magpies over an addled egg. This done they divide the message into small portions, and deliver them into the hands of little juntoes of talkers, called committees: these juntoes have each a world of talking about their respective paragraphs, and return the results to the grand divan, which forthwith falls to and retalks the matter over more earnestly than ever. Now, after all, it is an even chance that the subject of this prodigious arguing, quarrelling, and talking, is an affair of no importance, and ends entirely in smoke. May it not then be said, the whole nation have been talking to no purpose? The people, in fact, seem to be somewhat conscious of this propensity to talk, by which they are characterized, and have a favourite proverb on the subject, viz.: "all talk and no cider;" this is particularly applied when their congress, or assembly of all the sage chatterers of the nation, have chattered through a whole session, in a time of great peril and momentous event, and have done nothing but exhibit the length of their tongues and the emptiness of their heads. This has been the case more than once, my friend; and to let thee into a secret, I have been told in confidence, that there have been absolutely several old women smuggled into congress from different parts of the empire; who, having once got on the breeches, as thou mayest well imagine, have taken the lead in debate, and overwhelmed the whole assembly with their garrulity; for my part, as times go, I do not see why old women should not be as eligible to public councils as old men who possess their dispositions;—they certainly are eminently possessed of the qualifications requisite to govern in a logocracy.

Nothing, as I have repeatedly insisted, can be done in this country without talking; but they take so long to talk over a measure, that by the time they have determined upon adopting it, the period has elapsed which was proper for carry- it into effect. Unhappy nation!—thus torn ·to pieces by intestine talks! never, I fear, will it be restored to tranquillity and silence. Words are but breath; breath is but air; and air put into motion is nothing but wind. This vast empire, therefore, may be compared to nothing more or less than a mighty windmill, and the orators, and the chatterers, and the slang-whangers, are the breezes that put it in motion; unluckily, however, they are apt to blow different ways, and their blasts counteracting each other—the mill is perplexed, the wheels stand still, the grist is unground, and the miller and his family starved.

Every thing partakes of the windy nature of the government. In case of any domestic grievance, or an insult from a foreign foe, the people are all in a buzz;—town-meetings are immediately held where the quidnuncs of the city repair, each like an atlas, with the cares of the whole nation upon his shoulders, each resolutely bent upon saving his country, and each swelling and strutting like a turkey-cock; puffed up with words, and wind, and nonsense. After bustling, and buzzing, and bawling for some time; and after each man has shown himself to be indubitably the greatest personage in the meeting, they pass a string of resolutions, *i.e.* words, which were previously prepared for the purpose; these resolutions, are whimsically denominated the sense of the meeting, and are sent off for the instruction of the reigning bashaw, who receives them graciously, puts them into his red breeches pocket, forgets to read them—and so the matter ends.

As to his highness, the present bashaw, who is at the very top of the logocracy, never was a dignitary better qualified for his station. He is a man of superlative ventosity, and comparable to nothing but a huge bladder of wind. He talks of vanquishing all opposition by the force of reason and philosophy; throws his gauntlet at all the nations of the earth, and defies them to meet him—on the field of argument!—is the national dignity insulted, a case in which his highness of Tripoli would immediately call forth his forces;——the bashaw of America—utters a speech. Does a foreign invader molest the commerce in the very mouth of the harbours; an insult which would induce his highness of Tripoli to order out his fleets;— his highness of America—utters a speech. Are the free citizens of America dragged from on board the vessels of their country, and forcibly detained in the war ships of another power——his highness—utters a speech. Is a peaceable citizen killed by the marauders of a foreign power, on the very shores of his country——his highness utters a speech.—Does an alarming insurrection break out in a distant part of the empire——his highness utters a speech!—nay, more, for here he shows his "energies;"—he most intrepidly despatches a courier on horseback and orders him to ride one hundred and twenty miles a day, with a most formidable army of proclamations, *i.e.* a collection of words, packed up in his saddle bags. He is instructed to show no favour nor affection; but to charge the thickest ranks of the enemy; and to specify and batter by words the conspiracy and the conspirators out of existence. Heavens, my friends, what a deal of blustering is here! it reminds me of a dunghill cock in a farm-yard, who, have accidentally in his scratchings found a worm, inmediately begins a most vociferous cackling;—calls around him his hen-hearted companions, who run chattering from all quarters to gobble up the poor little worm that happened to turn under his eye. Oh, Asem! Asem! on what a prodigious great scale is every thing in this country!

Thus, then, I conclude my observations. The infidel nations have each a separate characteristic trait, by which they may be distinguished from each other;—the Spaniards, for instance, may be said to sleep upon every affair of importance;—the Italians to fiddle upon every thing;—the French to dance upon every thing;—the Germans to smoke upon every thing;—the British islanders to eat upon every thing;—and the windy subjects of the American logocracy to talk upon every thing.

For ever thine,
MUSTAPHA.

FROM THE MILL OF PINDAR COCKLOFT, ESQ.

How oft in musing mood my heart recalls,
From grey-beard father Time's oblivious halls,
The modes and maxims of my early day,
Long in those dark recesses stow'd away:
Drags once more to the cheerful realms of light
Those buckram fashions, long since lost in night,
And makes, like Endor's witch, once more to rise
My grogram grandames to my raptured eyes!
  Shades of my fathers! in your pasteboard skirts,
Your broidered waistcoats and your plaited shirts,
Your formal bag-wigs—wide-extended cuffs,
Your five-inch chitterlings and nine-inch ruffs!
Gods! how ye strut, at times, in all your state,
Amid the visions of my thoughtful pate!
I see ye move the solemn minuet o'er,
The modest foot scarce rising from the floor;
No thundering rigadoon with boisterous prance,
No pigeon-wing disturb your *contre-danse*.
But silent as the gentle Lethe's tide,
Adown the festive maze ye peaceful glide!
  Still in my mental eye each dame appears—
Each modest beauty of departed years;
Close by mamma I see her stately march
Or sit, in all the majesty of starch;—
When for the dance a stranger seeks her hand,
I see her doubting, hesitating, stand;
Yield to his claim with most fastidious grace,
And sigh for her intended in his place!
  Ah! golden days! when every gentle fair
On sacred Sabbath conn'd with pious care
Her holy Bible, or her prayer-book o'er,
Or studied honest Bunyan's drowsy lore;
Travell'd with him the PILGRIM'S PROGRESS through,
And storm'd the famous town of MAN-SOUL too:

Beat Eye and Ear-gate up with thundering jar,
And fought triumphant through the HOLY WAR;
Or if, perchance, to lighter works inclined,
They sought with novels to relax the mind,
'Twas GRANDISON's politely formal page
Or CLELIA or PAMELA were the rage.
  No plays were then—theatrics were unknown—
A learned pig—a dancing monkey shown—
The feats of Punch—a cunning juggler's slight,
Were sure to fill each bosom with delight.
An honest, simple, humdrum race we were,
Undazzled yet by fashion's wildering glare
Our manners unreserved, devoid of guile,
We knew not then the modern monster style:
Style, that with pride each empty bosom swells,
Puffs boys to manhood, little girls to belles.
  Scarce from the nursery freed, our gentle fair
Are yielded to the dancing-master's care;
And e'er the head one mite of sense can gain,
Are introduced 'mid folly's frippery train.
A stranger's grasp no longer gives alarms,
Our fair surrender to their very arms.
And in the insidious waltz * will swim and twine
And whirl and languish tenderly divine!

NOTES, BY WILLIAM WIZARD, ESQ.

* [*Waltz*]. As many of the retired matrons of this city, unskilled in "gestic lore," are doubtless ignorant of the movements and figures of this modest exhibition, I will endeavour to give some account of it, in order that they may learn what odd capers their daughters sometimes cut when from under their guardian wings.

  On a signal being given by the music, the gentleman seizes the lady round her waist; the lady, scorning to be outdone in courtesy, very politely takes the gentleman round the neck, with one arm resting against his shoulder to prevent encroachments. Away then they go, about, and about, and about——"about what, Sir?"——about the room, Madam, to be sure. The whole economy of this dance consists in turning round and round the room in a certain measured step: and it is truly astonishing that this continued revolution does not set all their heads swimming like a top; but I have been positively assured that it only occasions a gentle sensation which is marvellously agreeable. In the course of this circumnavigation, the dancers, in order to give the charm of variety, are continually changing their relative situations;——now the gentleman, meaning no harm in the world, I assure you Madam, carelessly flings his arm about the lady's neck, with an air of celestial impudence; and anon, the lady, meaning as little harm as the gentleman, takes him round the waist with most ingenious modest languishment, to the great delight of numerous spectators and amateurs, who generally form a ring, as the mob do about a pair of amazons pulling caps, or a couple of fighting mastiffs.

  After continuing this divine interchange of hands, arms, et cetera, for half an

Oh, how I hate this loving, hugging, dance;
This imp of Germany—brought up in France:
Nor can I see a niece its windings trace,
But all the honest blood glows in my face.
" Sad, sad refinement this," I often say,
" 'Tis modesty indeed refined away!
" Let France its whim, its sparkling wit supply,
" The easy grace that captivates the eye;
" But curse their waltz—their loose lascivious arts,
" That smooth our manners, to corrupt our hearts!"
Where now those books, from which in days of yore
Our mothers gain'd their literary store?
Alas! stiff-skirted Grandison gives place
To novels of a new and rakish race;
And honest Bunyan's pious dreaming lore,
To the lascivious rhapsodies of MOORE.
And, last of all, behold the mimic stage,
Its morals lend to polish off the age,

---

hour or so, the lady begins to tire, and with " eyes upraised," in most bewitching languor petitions her partner for a little more support. This is always given without hesitation. The lady leans gently on his shoulder, their arms entwine in a thousand seducing, mischievous curves——don't be alarmed, Madam——closer and closer they approach each other, and in conclusion, the parties being overcome with ecstatic fatigue, the lady seems almost sinking into the gentleman's arms, and then——" Well, Sir, and what then?"——lord, Madam, how should I know!

* My friend Pindar, and, in fact, our whole junto, has been accused of an unreasonable hostility to the French nation: and I am informed by a Parisian correspondent, that our first number played the very devil in the court of St. Cloud. His imperial majesty got into a most outrageous passion, and being withal a waspish little gentleman, had nearly kicked his bosom friend, Talleyrand, out of the cabinet, in the paroxysms of his wrath. He insisted upon it that the nation was assailed in its most vital part; being, like Achilles, extremely sensitive to any attacks upon the heel. When my correspondent sent off his despatches, it was still in doubt what measures would be adopted; but it was strongly suspected that vehement representations would be made to our government. Willing, therefore, to save our executive from any embarrassment on the subject, and above all from the disagreeable alternative of sending an apology by the HORNET, we do assure Mr. Jefferson, that there is nothing further from our thoughts than the subversion of the Gallic empire, or any attack on the interests, tranquillity, or reputation of the nation at large, which we seriously declare possesses the highest rank in our estimation. Nothing less than the national welfare could have induced us to trouble ourselves with this explanation; and in the name of the junto, I once more declare, that when we toast a Frenchman, we merely mean one of these *inconnus*, who swarmed to this country, from the kitchens and barbers' shops of Nantz, Bordeaux, and Marseilles; played game of leap-frog at all our balls and assemblies;—set this unhappy town hopping mad;—and passed themselves off on our tender-hearted damsels for unfortunate noblemen—ruined in the revolution! such only can wince at the lash, and accuse us of severity; and we should be mortified in the extreme if they did not feel our well-intended castigation.

With flimsy farce, a comedy miscall'd,
Garnish'd with vulgar cant, and proverbs bald.
With puns most puny, and a plenteous store
Of smutty jokes, to catch a gallery roar.
Or see, more fatal, graced with every art
To charm and captivate the female heart,
The false, "the gallant, gay Lothario," smiles,*
And loudly boasts his base seductive wiles;—
In glowing colours paints Calista's wrongs,
And with voluptuous scenes the tale prolongs,
When COOPER lends his fascinating powers,
Decks vice itself in bright alluring flowers,
Pleased with his manly grace, his youthful fire,
Our fair are lured the villain to admire;
While humbler virtue, like a stalking horse,
Struts clumsily and croaks in honest MORSE.

Ah, hapless days! when trials thus combined,
In pleasing garb assail the female mind;
When every smooth insidious snare is spread
To sap the morals and delude the head!
Not Shadrach, Meshach and Abed-nego,
To prove their faith and virtue here below,
Could more an angel's helping hand require
To guide their steps uninjured through the fire,
Where had but heaven its guardian aid denied,
The holy trio in the proof had died.
If, then, their manly vigour sought supplies
From the bright stranger in celestial guise,
Alas! can we from feebler nature's claim,
To brave seduction's ordeal, free from blame;
To pass through fire unhurt like golden ore,
Though ANGEL MISSIONS bless the earth no more!

---

* [*Fair Penitent*]. The story of this play, if told in its native language, would exhibit a scene of guilt and shame, which no modest ear could listen to without shrinking with disgust; but, arrayed as it is in all the splendour of harmonious, rich, and polished verse, it steals into the heart like some gay, luxurious, smooth-faced villain, and betrays it insensibly to immorality and vice; our very sympathy is enlisted on the side of guilt; and the piety of Altamont, and the gentleness of Lavinia, are lost in the splendid debaucheries of the "gallant, gay Lothario," and the blustering, hollow repentance of the fair Calisto, whose sorrow reminds us of that of Pope's Heloise—"I mourn the lover, not lament the fault." Nothing is more easy than to banish such plays from the stage. Were our ladies, instead of crowding to see them again and again repeated, to discourage their exhibition by absence, the stage would soon be indeed the school of morality, and the number of "Fair Penitents," in all probability, diminished.

NO. VIII.—SATURDAY, APRIL 18 1807.

BY ANTHONY EVERGREEN, GENT.

"In all thy humours, whether grave or mellow,
Thou'rt such a touchy, testy, pleasant fellow;
Hast so much wit, and mirth, and spleen about thee,
There is no living with thee—nor without thee."

"NEVER, in the memory of the oldest inhabitant, has there been known a more backward spring." This is the universal remark among the almanac quidnuncs and weather-wisacres of the day; and I have heard it at least fifty-five times from old Mrs. Cockloft, who, poor woman, is one of those walking almanacs that foretell every snow, rain, or frost, by the shooting of corns, a pain in the bones, or an "ugly stitch in the side." I do not recollect, in the whole course of my life, to have seen the month of March indulge in such untoward capers, caprices, and coquetries, as it has done this year: I might have forgiven these vagaries, had they not completely knocked up my friend Langstaff, whose feelings are ever at the mercy of a weathercock, whose spirits sink and rise with the mercury of a barometer, and to whom an east wind is as obnoxious as a Sicilian *sirocco*. He was tempted some time since, by the fineness of the weather, to dress himself with more than ordinary care and take his morning stroll; but before he had half finished his peregrination, he was utterly discomfited, and driven home by a tremendous squall of wind, hail, rain, and snow; or, as he testily termed it, "a most villainous congregation of vapors."

This was too much for the patience of friend Launcelot; he declared he would honour the weather no longer in its whim-whams; and, according to his immemorial custom on these occasions, retreated in high dudgeon to his elbow-chair to lie in of the spleen and rail at nature for being so fantastical:—"confound the jade," he frequently exclaims, "what a pity nature had not been of the masculine instead of the feminine gender; the almanac makers might then have calculated with some degree of certainty."

When Langstaff invests himself with the spleen, and gives audience to the blue devils from his elbow-chair, I would not advise any of his friends to come within gunshot of his citadel with the benevolent purpose of administering consolation or amusement: for he is then as crusty and crabbed as that famous coiner of false money, Diogenes himself. Indeed, his room is at such times inaccessible; and old Pompey is the only soul that can gain admission, or ask a question with impunity; the truth is, that on these occasions, there is not a straw's difference between them, for Pompey is as grum and grim and cynical as his master.

Launcelot has now been above three weeks in this desolate situation, and has therefore had but little to do in our last number. As he could not be prevailed on to give any account of himself in our introduction, I will take the opportunity of his confinement, while his back is turned, to give a slight sketch of his character;—fertile in whim-whams and bachelorisms, but rich in many of the sterling qualities of our nature. Annexed to this article, our readers will perceive a striking likeness of my friend, which was taken by that cunning rogue Will Wizard, who peeped through the key-hole and sketched it off as honest Launcelot sat by the fire, wrapped up in his flannel *robe de chambre*, and indulging in a mortal fit of the *hyp*. Now take my word for it, gentle reader, this is the most auspicious moment in which to touch off the phiz of a genuine humorist.

Of the antiquity of the Langstaff family I can say but little; except that I have no doubt it is equal to that of most families who have the privilege of making their own pedigree, without the impertinent interposition of a college of heralds. My friend Launcelot is not a man to blazon any th'ng; but I have heard him talk with great complacency of his ancestor, Sir ROWLAND, who was a dashing buck in the days of Hardiknute, and broke the head of a gigantic Dane, at a game of quarter-staff, in presence of the whole court. In memory of this gallant exploit, Sir Rowland was permitted to take the name of Langstoffe, and to assume, as a crest to his arms, a hand grasping a cudgel. It is, however, a foible so ridiculously common in this country for people to claim consanguinity with all the great personages of their own name in Europe, that I should put but little faith in this family boast of friend Langstaff, did I not know him to be a man of most unquestionable veracity.

The whole world knows already that my friend is a bachelor; for he is, or pretends to be, exceedingly proud of his personal independence, and takes care to make it known in all companies where strangers are present. He is forever vaunting the precious state of "single blessedness;" and was not long ago considerably startled at a proposition of one of his great favourites, Miss Sophy Sparkle, "that old bachelors should be taxed as luxuries." Launcelot immediately hied him home, and wrote a tremendous long representation in their behalf, which I am resolved to publish if it is ever attempted to carry the measure into operation. Whether he is sincere in these professions, or whether his present situation is owing to choice or disappointment, he only can tell; but if he ever does tell, I will suffer myself to be shot by the first lady's eye that can twang an arrow. In his youth he was for ever in love; but it was his misfortune to be continually crossed and rivalled by his bosom friend and contemporary beau, Pindar Cockloft, Esq., for as Langstaff never made a confidant on these occasions, his friend never knew which way his affections pointed; and so, between them both, the lady generally slipped through their fingers.

It has ever been the misfortune of Launcelot that he could not for the soul of him restrain a good thing; and this fatality has drawn upon him the ill will of many whom he would not have offended for the world. With the kindest heart under heaven, and the most benevolent disposition toward every being around him, he has been continually betrayed by the mischievous vivacity of his fancy, and the good-humoured waggery of his feelings, into satirical sallies which have been treasured up by the invidious, and retailed out with the bitter sneer of malevolence, instead of the playful hilarity of countenance which originally sweetened and tempered and disarmed them of their sting.—These misrepresentations have gained him many reproaches and lost him many a friend.

This unlucky characteristic played the mischief with him in one of his love affairs. He was, as I have before observed, often opposed in his gallantries by that formidable rival, Pindar Cockloft, Esq., and a most formidable rival he was; for he had Apollo, the nine muses, together with all the joint tenants of Olympus to back him; and every body knows what important confederates they are to a lover. Poor Launcelot stood no chance;—the lady was cooped up in the poet's corner of every weekly paper; and at length Pindar attacked her with a sonnet that took up a whole column, in which he enumerated at least a dozen cardinal virtues, together with innumerable others of inferior consideration. Launcelot saw his case was desperate, and that unless he sat down forthwith, be-churibimed and be-angeled her to the skies, and put every virtue under the sun in requisition, he might as well go hang himself and so make an end of the business. At it, therefore, he went, and was going on very swimmingly, for, in the space of a dozen lines he had enlisted under her command at least three score and ten substantial housekeeping virtues, when, unluckily for Launcelot's reputation as a poet and the lady's as a saint, one of those confounded good thoughts struck his laughter-loving brain;—it was irresistible; away he went full sweep before the wind, cutting and slashing and tickled to death with his own fun; the consequence was, that by the time he had finished, never was poor lady so most ludicrously lampooned since lampooning came into fashion. But this was not half;—so hugely was Launcelot pleased with this frolic of his wits, that nothing would do but he must show it to the lady, who, as well she might, was mortally offended, and forbid him her presence. My friend was in despair; but through the interference of his generous rival, was permitted to make his apology, which, however, most unluckily happened to be rather worse than the original offence; for though he had studied an eloquent compliment, yet, as ill-luck would have it, a most preposterous whim-wham knocked at his pericranium, and inspired him to say some consummate good things, which all put together amounted to a downright hoax, and provoked the lady's wrath to such a degree that sentence of eternal banishment was awarded against him.

Launcelot was inconsolable, and determined, in the true style of novel heroics, to make the tour of Europe, and endeavour to lose the recollection of this misfortune amongst the gayeties of France and the classic charms of Italy; he accordingly took passage in a vessel and pursued his voyage prosperously as far as Sandy Hook, where he was seized with a violent fit of sea-sickness; at which he was so affronted that he put his portmanteau into the first pilot-boat and returned to town completely cured of his love and his rage for travelling.

I pass over the subsequent amours of my friend Langstaff, being but little acquainted with them; for, as I have already mentioned, he never was known to make a confidant of any body. He always affirmed a man must be a fool to fall in love, but an idiot to boast of it;—ever denominated it the villainous passion;—lamented that it could not be cudgelled out of the human heart;—and yet could no more live without being in love with somebody or other than he could without whim-whams.

My friend Launcelot is a man of excessive irritability of nerve, and I am acquainted with no one so susceptible of the petty "miseries of human life;" yet its keener evils and misfortunes he bears without shrinking, and however they may prey in secret on his happiness, he never complains. This was strikingly evinced in an affair where his heart was deeply and irrevocably concerned, and in which his success was ruined by one for whom he had long cherished a warm friendship. The circumstance cut poor Langstaff to the very soul; he was not seen in company for months afterwards, and for a long time he seemed to retire within himself, and battle with the poignancy of his feelings; but not a murmur or a reproach was heard to fall from his lips, though, at the mention of his friend's name, a shade of melancholy might be observed stealing across his face, and his voice assumed a touching tone, that seemed to say, he remembered his treachery "more in sorrow than in anger."—This affair has given a slight tinge of sadness to his disposition, which, however, does not prevent his entering into the amusements of the world; the only effect it occasions, is, that you may occasionally observe him, at the end of a lively conversation, sink for a few minutes into an apparent forgetfulness of surrounding objects, during which time he seems to be indulging in some melancholy retrospection.

Langstaff inherited from his father a love of literature, a disposition for castle-building, a mortal enmity to noise, a sovereign antipathy to cold weather and brooms, and a plentiful stock of whim-whams. From the delicacy of his nerves he is peculiarly sensible to discordant sounds; the rattling of a wheelbarrow is "horrible;" the noise of children "drives him distracted;" and he once left excellent lodgings merely because the lady of the house wore high-heeled shoes, in which she clattered up and down stairs, till, to use his own emphatic expression, "they made life loathsome" to him. He suffers annual martyrdom from the razor-edged zephyrs of our "balmy spring," and solemnly declares that the boasted month of May has become a perfect "vagabond." As some people have a great antipathy to cats, and can tell when one is locked up in a closet, so Launcelot declares his feelings always announce to him the neighbourhood of a broom; a household implement which he abominates above all others. Nor is there any living animal in the world that he holds in more utter abhorrence than what is usually termed a notable house-wife; a pestilent being, who, he protests, is the bane of good-fellowship, and has a heavy charge to answer for the many offences committed against the ease, comfort, and social enjoyments of sovereign man. He told me not long ago, "that he had rather see one of the weird sisters flourish through his key-hole on a broomstick, than one of the servant maids enter the door with a besom."

My friend Launcelot is ardent and sincere in his attachments, which are confined to a chosen few, in whose society he loves to give free scope to his whimsical imagination; he, however, mingles freely with the world, though more as a spectator than an actor; and without an anxiety or hardly a care to please, is generally received with welcome and listened to with complacency. When he extends his hand it is in a free, open, liberal style; and when you shake it, you feel his honest heart throb in its pulsations. Though rather fond of gay exhibitions, he does not appear so frequently at balls and assemblies since the introduction of the drum, trumpet, and tamborine: all of which he abhors on account of the rude attacks they make on his organs of hearing:—in short, such is his antipathy to noise, that though exceedingly patriotic, yet he retreats every fourth of July to Cockloft Hall, in order to get out of the way of the hub-bub and confusion which make so considerable a part of the pleasure of that splendid anniversary.

I intend this article as a mere sketch of Langstaff's multifarious character; his innumerable whim-whams will be exhibited by himself, in the course of this work, in all their strange varieties; and the machinery of his mind, more intricate than the most subtle piece of clock-work, be fully explained. And trust me, gentlefolk, his are the whim-whams of a courteous gentleman full of most excellent qualities; honourable in his disposition, independent in his sentiments, and of unbounded good nature, as may be seen through all his works.

ON STYLE.

BY WILLIAM WIZARD, ESQ.

STYLE, *a manner of writing; title; pin of a dial; the pistil of plants.*—JOHNSON.
STYLE, *is* . . . . *style.*—LINKUM FIDELIUS.

Now I would not give a straw for either of the above definitions, though I think the latter is by far the most satisfactory: and I do wish sincerely every modern numskull, who takes hold of a subject he knows nothing about, would adopt honest Linkum's mode of explanation. Blair's Lectures on this article have not thrown a whit more light on the subject of my inquiries; they puzzled me just as much as did the learned and laborious expositions and illustrations of the worthy professor of our college, in the middle of which I generally had the ill luck to fall asleep.

This same word style, though but a diminutive word, assumes to itself more contradictions, and significations, and eccentricities, than any monosyllable in the language is legitimately entitled to. It is an arrant little humorist of a word, and full of whim-whams, which occasions me to like it hugely; but it puzzled me most wickedly on my first return from a long residence abroad, having crept into fashionable use during my absence; and had it not been for friend Evergreen, and that thrifty sprig of knowledge, Jeremy Cockloft the younger, I should have remained to this day ignorant of its meaning.

Though it would seem that the people of all countries are equally vehement in the pursuit of this phantom, style, yet in almost all of them there is a strange diversity in opinion as to what constitutes its essence; and every different class, like the pagan nations, adore it under a different form. In England, for instance, an honest cit packs up himself, his family, and his style, in a buggy or tim-whisky, and rattles away on Sunday with his fair partner blooming beside him, like an eastern bride, and two chubby children, squatting like Chinese images at his feet. A Baronet requires a chariot and pair;—a Lord must needs have a barouche and four;—but a Duke—oh! a Duke cannot possibly lumber his style along under a coach and six, and half a score of footmen into the bargain. In China a puissant Mandarin loads at least three elephants with style; and an overgrown sheep at the Cape of Good-Hope, trails along his tail and his style on a wheelbarrow. In Egypt, or at Constantinople, style consists in the quantity of fur and fine clothes a lady can put on without danger of suffocation; here it is otherwise, and consists in the quantity she can put off without the risk of freezing. A Chinese lady is thought prodigal of her charms if she expose the tip of her nose, or the ends of her fingers, to the ardent gaze of bystanders: and I recollect that all Canton was in a buzz in consequence of the great belle, Miss Nangfous, peeping out of the window with her face uncovered! Here the style is to show not only the face, but the neck, shoulders, &c.; and a lady never presumes to hide them except when she is not at home, and not sufficiently undressed to see company.

This style has ruined the peace and harmony of many a worthy household; for no sooner do they set up for style, but instantly all the honest old comfortable *sans ceremonie* furniture is discarded; and you stalk, cautiously about, amongst the uncomfortable splendour of Grecian chairs, Egyptian tables, Turkey carpets, and Etruscan vases.—This vast improvement in furniture demands an increase in the domestic establishment; and a family that once required two or three servants for convenience, now employs half a dozen for style.

BELL-BRAZEN, late favourite of my unfortunate friend Dessalines, was one of these patterns of style; and whatever freak she was seized with, however preposterous, was implicitly followed by all who would be considered as admitted in the stylish arcana. She was once seized with a whim-wham that tickled the whole court. She could not lay down to take an afternoon's loll, but she must have one servant to scratch her head, two to tickle her feet, and a fourth to fan her delectable person while she slumbered. The thing took;—it became the rage, and not a sable belle in all Hayti but what insisted upon being fanned, and scratched, and tickled in the true imperial style. Sneer not at this picture, my most excellent townswomen, for who among you but are daily following fashions equally absurd!

Style, according to Evergreen's account, consists in certain fashions, or certain eccentricities, or certain manners of certain people, in certain situations, and possessed of a certain share of fashion or importance. A red cloak, for instance, on the shoulders of an old market-woman is regarded with contempt; it is vulgar, it is odious:—fling, however, its usurping rival, a red shawl, over the fine figure of a fashionable belle, and let her flame away with it in Broadway, or in a ball-room, and it is immediately declared to be the style.

The modes of attaining this certain situation, which entitle its holder to style, are various and opposite; the most ostensible is the attainment of wealth; the possession of which changes, at once, the pert airs of vulgar ignorance into fashionable ease and elegant vivacity. It is highly amusing to observe the gradation of a family aspiring to style, and the devious windings they pursue in order to attain it. While beating up against wind and tide they are the most complaisant beings in the world;—they keep "booing and booing," as M'Sycophant says, until you would suppose them incapable of standing upright; they kiss their hands to every body who has the least claim to style; their familiarity is intolerable, and they absolutely overwhelm you with their friendship and loving-kindness. But having once gained the envied pre-eminence, never were beings in the world more changed. They assume the most intolerable caprices; at one time, address you with importunate sociability; at another, pass you by with silent indifference; sometimes sit up in their chairs in all the majesty of dignified silence; and at another time bounce about with all the obstreperous ill-bred noise of a little hoyden just broke loose from a boarding-school.

Another feature which distinguishes these new-made fashionables, is the inveteracy with which they look down upon the honest people who are struggling to climb up to the same envied height. They never fail to salute them with the most sarcastic reflections; and like so many worthy hodmen, clambering a ladder, each one looks down upon his next neighbour below and makes no scruple of shaking the dust off his shoes into his eyes. Thus by dint of perseverance, merely, they come to be considered as established denizens of the great world; as in some barbarous nations an oyster-shell is of sterling value, and a copper-washed counter will pass current for genuine gold.

In no instance have I seen this grasping after style more whimsically exhibited, than in the family of my old acquaintance, TIMOTHY GIBLET.—I recollect old Giblet when I was a boy, and he was the most surly curmudgeon I ever knew. He was a perfect scare-crow to the small-fry of the day, and inherited the hatred of all these unlucky little shavers; for never could we assemble about his door of an evening to play, and make a little hub-bub, but out he sallied from his nest like a spider, flourishing his formidable horse-whip, and dispersed the whole crew in the twinkling of a lamp. I perfectly remember a bill he sent in to my father for a pane of glass I had accidentally broken, which came well-nigh getting me a sound flogging; and I remember, as perfectly, that the next night I revenged myself by breaking half a dozen. Giblet was as arrant a grub-worm as ever crawled; and the only rules of right and wrong he cared a button for, were the rules of multiplication and addition; which he practiced much more successfully than he did any of the rules of religion or morality. He used to declare they were the true golden rules; and he took special care to put Cocker's arithmetic in the hands of his children, before they had read ten pages in the Bible or the prayer-book. The practice of these favourite maxims was at length crowned with the harvest of success; and after a life of incessant self-denial, and starvation, and after enduring all the pounds, shillings, and pence miseries of a miser, he had the satisfaction of seeing himself worth a plum and of dying just as he had determined to enjoy the remainder of his days in contemplating his great wealth and accumulating mortgages.

His children inherited his money; but they buried the disposition, and every other memorial of their father, in his grave. Fired with a noble thirst for style, they instantly emerged from the retired lane in which themselves and their accomplishments had hitherto been buried; and they blazed, and they whizzed, and they cracked about town, like a nest of squibs and devils in a firework. I can liken their sudden eclat to nothing but that of the locust, which is hatched in the dust, where it increases and swells up to maturity, and after feeling for a moment the vivifying rays of the sun, bursts forth a mighty insect, and flutters, and rattles, and buzzes from every tree. The little warblers who have long cheered the woodlands with their dulcet notes, are stunned by the discordant racket of these upstart intruders, and contemplate, in contemptuous silence, their tinsel and their noise.

Having once started, the Giblets were determined that nothing should stop them in their career, until they had run their full course and arrived at the very tip-top of style. Every tailor, every shoe-maker, every coach-maker, every milliner, every mantua-maker, every paper-hanger, every piano teacher, and every dancing master in the city, were enlisted in their service; and the willing wights most courteously answered their call; and fell to work to build up the fame of the Giblets, as they had done that of many an aspiring family before them. In a little time the young ladies could dance the waltz, thunder Lodoiska, murder French, kill time, and commit violence on the face of nature in a landscape in water colours, equal to the best lady in the land; and the young gentlemen were seen lounging at corners of streets, and driving tandem; heard talking loud at the theatre, and laughing in church; with as much ease, and grace, and modesty, as if they had been gentlemen all the days of their lives.

And the Giblets arrayed themselves in scarlet, and in fine linen, and seated themselves in high places; but nobody noticed them except to honor them with a little contempt. The Giblets made a prodigious splash in their own opinion; but nobody extolled them except the tailors, and the milliners, who had been employed in manufacturing their paraphernalia. The Giblets thereupon being, like Caleb Quotem, determined to have "a place at the review," fell to work more fiercely than ever;—they gave dinners, and they gave balls, they hired cooks, they hired fiddlers, they hired confectioners; and they would have kept a newspaper in pay, had they not been all bought up at that time for the election. They invited the dancing-men and the dancing-women, and the gormandizers, and the epicures of the city, to come and make merry at their expense; and the dancing-men, and the dancing-women, and the epicures, and the gormandizers, did come; and they did make merry at their expense; and they eat, and they drank, and they capered, and they danced, and they—laughed at their entertainers.

Then commenced the hurry and the bustle and the mighty nothingness of fashionable life;—such rattling in coaches! such flaunting in the streets! such slamming of box doors at the theatre! such a tempest of bustle and unmeaning noise wherever they appeared! the Giblets were seen here and there and everywhere;—they visited every body they knew, and every body they did not know; and there was no getting along for the Giblets.—Their plan at length succeeded. By dint of dinners, of feeding and frolicking the town, the Giblet family worked themselves into notice, and enjoyed the ineffable pleasure of being for ever pestered by visitors, who cared nothing about them; of being squeezed, and smothered, and parboiled at nightly balls, and evening tea-parties;—they were allowed the privilege of forgetting the very few old friends they once possessed;—they turned their noses up in the wind at every thing that was not genteel; and there superb manners and sublime affectation at length left it no longer a matter of doubt that the Giblets were perfectly in style.

"——Being, as it were, a small contentmente in a never contenting subjecte; a bitter pleasaunte taste of sweete seasoned sower; and, all in all, a more than ordinarie rejoycing, in an extraordinarie sorrow of delyghts."

LINK. FIDELIUS.

WE have been considerably edified of late by several letters of advice from a number of sage correspondents, who really seem to know more about our work than we do ourselves. One warns us against saying any thing more about SNIVERS, who is a very particular friend of the writer, and who has a singular disinclination to be laughed at.—This correspondent in particular inveighs against personalities, and accuses us of ill nature in bringing forward old Fungus and Billy Dimple, as figures of fun to amuse the public. Another gentleman, who states that he is a near relation of the Cocklofts, proses away most soporifically on the impropriety of ridiculing a respectable old family; and declares that if we make them and their whim-whams the subject of any more essays, he shall be under the necessity of applying to our theatrical champions for satisfaction. A third, who by the crabbedness of the hand-writing, and a few careless inaccuracies in the spelling, appears to be a lady, assures us that the Miss Cocklofts, and Miss Diana Wearwell, and Miss Dashaway, and Mrs. ——, Will Wizard's quondam flame, are so much obliged to us for our notice, that they intend in future to take no notice of us at all, but leave us out of all their tea-parties; for which we make them one of our best bows, and say, "thank you, ladies."

We wish to heaven these good people would attend to their own affairs, if they have any to attend to, and let us alone. It is one of the most provoking things in the world that we cannot tickle the public a little, merely for our own private amusement, but we must be crossed and jostled by these meddling incendiaries, and, in fact, have the whole town about our ears. We are much in the same situation with an unlucky blade of a cockney; who, having mounted his bit of blood to enjoy a little innocent recreation, and display his horsemanship along Broadway, is worried by all those little yelping curs that infest our city; and who never fail to sally out and growl, and bark, and snarl, to the great annoyance of the Birmingham equestrian.

Wisely was it said by the sage Linkum Fidelius, "howbeit, moreover, nevertheless, this thrice wicked towne is charged up to the muzzle with all manner of ill-natures and uncharitablenesses, and is, moreover, exceedinglie naughte." This passage of the erudite Linkum was applied to the city of Gotham, of which he was once Lord Mayor, as appears by his picture hung up in the hall of that ancient city;—but his observation fits this best of all possible cities "to a hair." It is a melancholy truth that this same New-York, although the most charming, pleasant, polished, and praise-worthy city under the sun, and, in a word, the *bonne bouche* of the universe, is most shockingly ill-natured and sarcastic, and wickedly given to all manner of backslidings;—for which we are very sorry indeed. In truth, for it must come out like murder one time or another, the inhabitants are not only ill-natured, but manifestly unjust: no sooner do they get one of our random sketches in their hands, but instantly they apply it most unjustifiably to some "dear friend," and then accuse us vociferously of the personality which originated in their own officious friendship! Truly it is an ill-natured town, and most earnestly do we hope it may not meet with the fate of Sodom and Gomorrah of old.

As, however, it may be thought incumbent upon us to make some apology for these mistakes of the town; and as our good-nature is truly exemplary, we would certainly answer this expectation were it not that we have an invincible antipathy to making apologies. We have a most profound contempt for any man who cannot give three good reasons for an unreasonable thing; and will therefore condescend, as usual, to give the public three special reasons for never apologizing:—first, an apology implies that we are accountable to some body or another for our conduct;—now as we do not care a fiddle-stick, as authors, for either public opinion or private ill-will, it would be implying a falsehood to apologize:—second, an apology would indicate that we had been doing what we ought not to have done. Now, as we never did nor ever intend to do any thing wrong it would be ridiculous to make an apology:—third, we labour under the same incapacity in the art of apologizing that lost Langstaff his mistress; we never yet undertook to make apology without committing a new offence, and making matters ten times worse than they were before; and we are, therefore, determined to avoid such predicaments in future.

But though we have resolved never to apologize, yet we have no particular objection to explain; and if this is all that's wanted, we will go about it directly:——*allons*, gentleman!—— before, however, we enter upon this serious affair, we take this opportunity to express our surprise and indignation at the incredulity of some people.—Have we not, over and over, assured the town that we are three of the best-natured fellows living? And is it not astonishing, that having already given seven convincing proofs of the truth of this assurance, they should still have any doubts on the subject? but as it is one of the impossible things to make a knave believe in honesty, so perhaps it may be another to make this most sarcastic, satirical, and tea-drinking city believe in the existence of good-nature. But to our explanation.——Gentle reader! for we are convinced that none but gentle or genteel readers can relish our excellent productions, if thou art in expectation of being perfectly satisfied with what we are about to say, thou mayest as well "whistle lillebullero" and skip quite over what follows; for never wight was more disappointed than thou wilt be most assuredly.—But to the explanation: We care just as much about the public and its wise conjectures, as we do about the man in the moon and his whim-whams, or the criticisms of the lady who sits majestically in her elbow-chair in the lobster; and who, belying her sex, as we are credibly informed, never says any thing worth listening to. We have launched our bark, and we will steer to our destined port with undeviating perseverance, fearless of being shipwrecked by the way. Good-nature is our steersman, reason our ballast, whim the breeze that wafts us along, and MORALITY our leading star.

NO. IX.—SATURDAY, APRIL 25, 1807.

FROM MY ELBOW-CHAIR.

It in some measure jumps with my humour to be "melancholy and gentleman-like" this stormy night, and I see no reason why I should not indulge myself for once.—Away, then, with joke, with fun, and laughter, for a while; let my soul look back in mournful retrospect, and sadden with the memory of my good aunt CHARITY—who died of a Frenchman!

Stare not, oh, most dubious reader, at the mention of a complaint so uncommon; grievously hath is afflicted the ancient family of the Cocklofts, who carry their absurd antipathy to the French so far, that they will not suffer a clove of garlic in the house: and my good old friend Christopher was once on the point of abandoning his paternal country mansion of Cockloft-hall, merely because a colony of frogs had settled in a neighbouring swamp. I verily believe he would have carried his whim-wham into effect, had not a fortunate drought obliged the enemy to strike their tents, and, like a troop of wandering Arabs, to march off towards a moister part of the country.

My aunt Charity departed this life in the fifty-ninth year of her age, though she never grew older after twenty-five. In her teens she was, according to her own account, a celebrated beauty,—though I never could meet with any body that remembered when she was handsome; on the contrary, Evergreen's father, who used to gallant her in his youth, says she was as knotty a little piece of humanity as he ever saw; and that, if she had been possessed of the least sensibility, she would, like poor old *Acco*, have most certainly run mad at her own figure and face the first time she contemplated herself in a looking-glass. In the good old times that saw my aunt in the hey-day of youth, a fine lady was a most formidable animal, and required to be approached with the same awe and devotion that a Tartar feels in the presence of his Grand Lama. If a gentleman offered to take her hand, except to help her into a carriage, or lead her into a drawing-room, such frowns! such a rustling of brocade and taffeta! her very paste shoe-buckles sparkled with indignation, and for a moment assumed the brilliancy of diamonds: in those days the person of a belle was sacred; it was unprofaned by the sacrilegious grasp of a stranger:——simple souls!—they had not the waltz among them yet!

My good aunt prided herself on keeping up this buckram delicacy; and if she happened to be playing at the old-fashioned game of forfeits, and was fined a kiss, it was always more trouble to get it than it was worth; for she made a most gallant defence, and never surrendered until she saw her adversary inclined to give over his attack. Evergreen's father says he remembers once to have been on a sleighing party with her, and when they came to Kissing-bridge, it fell to his lot to levy contributions on Miss Charity Cockloft; who, after squalling at a hideous rate, at length jumped out of the sleigh plump into a snow-bank; where she stuck fast like an icicle, until he came to her rescue. This latonian feat cost her a rheumatism, from which she never thoroughly recovered.

It is rather singular that my aunt, though a great beauty, and an heiress withal, never got married. The reason she alleged was, that she never met with a lover who resembled Sir Charles Grandison, the hero of her nightly dreams and waking fancy; but I am privately of opinion that it was owing to her never having had an offer. This much is certain, that for many years previous to her decease, she declined all attentions from the gentlemen, and contented herself with watching over the welfare of her fellow-creatures. She was, indeed, observed to take a considerable lean towards Methodism, was frequent in her attendance at love feasts, read Whitefield and Wesley, and even went so far as once to travel the distance of five and twenty miles to be present at a campmeeting. This gave great offence to my cousin Christopher and his good lady, who, as I have already mentioned, are rigidly orthodox; and had not my aunt Charity been of a most pacific disposition, her religious whim-wham would have occasioned many a family altercation. She was, indeed, as good a soul as the Cockloft family ever boasted; a lady of unbounded loving-kindness, which extended to man, woman, and child; many of whom she almost killed with good-nature. Was any acquaintance sick? in vain did the wind whistle and the storm beat; my aunt would waddle through mud and mire, over the whole town, but what she would visit them. She would sit by them for hours together with the most persevering patience; and tell a thousand melancholy stories of human misery, to keep up their spirits. The whole catalogue of *yerb* teas was at her fingers' ends, from formidable wormwood down to gentle balm; and she would descant by the hour on the healing qualities of hoar-hound, catnip, and penny-royal.—Wo be to the patient that came under the benevolent hand of my aunt Charity; he was sure, willy nilly, to be drenched with a deluge of decoctions; and full many a time has my cousin Christopher borne a twinge of pain in silence through fear of being condemned to suffer the martyrdom of her materia-medica. My good aunt had, moreover, considerable skill in astronomy, for she could tell when the sun rose and set every day in the year; and no woman in the whole world was able to pronounce, with more certainty, at what precise minute the moon changed. She held the story of the moon's being made of green cheese, as an abominable slander on her favourite planet; and she had made several valuable discoveries in solar eclipses, by means of a bit of burnt glass, which entitled her at least to an honorary admission in the American-philosophical-society. Hutchings improved was her favourite book; and I shrewdly suspect that it was from this valuable work she drew most of her sovereign remedies for colds, coughs, corns, and consumptions.

But the truth must be told; with all her good qualities my aunt Charity was afflicted with one fault, extremely rare among her gentle sex;—it was curiosity. How she came by it, I am at a loss to imagine, but it played the very vengeance with her and destroyed the comfort of her life. Having an invincible desire to know every body's character, business, and mode of living, she was for ever prying into the affairs of her neighbours; and got a great deal of ill will from people towards whom she had the kindest disposition possible.—If any family on the opposite side of the street gave a dinner; my aunt would mount her spectacles, and sit at the window until the company were all housed; merely that she might know who they were. If she heard a story about any of her acquaintance, she would, forthwith, set off full sail and never rest until, to use her usual expression, she had got "to the bottom of it;" which meant nothing more than telling it to every body she knew.

I remember one night my aunt Charity happened to hear a a most precious story about one of her good friends, but unfortunately too late to give it immediate circulation. It made her absolutely miserable; and she hardly slept a wink all night, for fear her bosom friend, Mrs. SIPKINS, should get the start of her in the morning and blow the whole affair. You must know there was always a contest between these two ladies, who should first give currency to the good-natured things said about every body; and this unfortunate rivalship at length proved fatal to their long and ardent friendship. My aunt got up full two hours that morning before her usual time; put on her pompadour tafeta gown, and sallied forth to lament the misfortune of her dear friend. Would you believe it!— wherever she went Mrs. Sipkins had anticipated her; and, instead of being listened to with uplifted hands and open-mouthed wonder, my unhappy aunt was obliged to sit down quietly and listen to the whole affair, with numerous additions, alterations, and amendments!—now this was too bad; it would almost have provoked Patience Grizzle or a saint;—it was too much for my aunt, who kept her bed for three days afterwards, with a cold, as she pretended; but I have no doubt it was owing to this affair of Mrs. Sipkins, to whom she never would be reconciled.

But I pass over the rest of my aunt Charity's life, chequered with the various calamities and misfortunes and mortifications incident to those worthy old gentlewomen who have the domestic cares of the whole community upon their minds; and I hasten to relate the melancholy incident that hurried her out of existence in the full bloom of antiquated virginity.

In their frolicksome malice the fates had ordered that a French boarding-house, or *Pension Francaise*, as it was called, should be established directly opposite my aunt's residence. Cruel event! unhappy aunt Charity!—it threw her into that alarming disorder denominated the fidgets; she did nothing but watch at the window day after day, but without becoming one whit the wiser at the end of a fortnight than she was at the beginning; she thought that neighbour Pension had a monstrous large family, and somehow or other they were all men! she could not imagine what business neighbour Pension followed to support so numerous a household; and wondered why there was always such a scraping of fiddles in the parlour, and such a smell of onions from neighbour Pension's kitchen; in short, neighbour Pension was continually uppermost in her thoughts, and incessantly on the outer edge of her tongue. This was, I believe, the very first time she had ever failed "to get at the bottom of a thing;" and the disappointment cost her many a sleepless night I warrant you. I have little doubt, however, that my aunt would have ferretted neighbour Pension out, could she have spoken or understood French; but in those times people in general could make themselves understood in plain English; and it was always a standing rule in the Cockloft family, which exists to this day, that not one of the females should learn French.

My aunt Charity had lived, at her window, for some time in vain; when one day, as she was keeping her usual look-out, and suffering all the pangs of unsatisfied curiosity, she beheld a little, meagre, weazel-faced Frenchman, of the most forlorn, diminutive, and pitiful proportions, arrive at neighbour Pension's door. He was dressed in white, with a little pinched-up cocked hat; he seemed to shake in the wind, and every blast that went over him whistled through his bones and threatened instant annihilation. This embodied spirit-of-famine was followed by three carts, lumbered with crazy trunks, chests, band-boxes, bidets, medicine-chests, parrots, and monkeys; and at his heels ran a yelping pack of little black-nosed pug dogs. This was the one thing wanting to fill up the measure of my aunt Charity's afflictions; she could not conceive, for the soul of her, who this mysterious little apparition could be that made so great a display; what he could possibly do with so much baggage, and particularly with his parrots and monkeys; or how so small a carcass could have occasion for so many trunks of clothes. Honest soul! she had never had a peep into a Frenchman's wardrobe; that *depôt* of old coats, hats, and breeches, of the growth of every fashion he has followed in his life.

From the time of this fatal arrival, my poor aunt was in a quandary;—all her inquiries were fruitless; no one could expound the history of this mysterious stranger: she never held up her head afterwards,—drooped daily, took to her bed in a fortnight, and in "one little month" I saw her quietly deposited in the family vault:—being the seventh Cockloft that has died of a whim-wham!

Take warning, my fair country-women! and you, oh, ye excellent ladies, whether married or single, who pry into other people's affairs and neglect those of your own household;—who are so busily employed in observing the faults of others that you have no time to correct your own;—remember the fate of my dear aunt Charity, and eschew the evil spirit of curiosity.

FROM MY ELBOW-CHAIR.

I FIND, by perusal of our last number, that WILL WIZARD and EVERGREEN, taking advantage of my confinement, have been playing some of their gambols. I suspected these rogues of some mal-practices, in consequence of their queer looks and knowing winks whenever I came down to dinner; and of their not showing their faces at old Cockloft's for several days after the appearance of their precious effusions. Whenever these two waggish fellows lay their heads together, there is always sure to be hatched some notable piece of mischief; which, if it tickles nobody else, is sure to make its authors merry. The public will take notice that, for the purpose of teaching these my associates better manners, and punishing them for their high misdemeanors, I have, by virtue of my authority, suspended them from all interference in Salmagundi, until they show a proper degree of repentance; or I get tired of supporting the burthen of the work myself. I am sorry for Will, who is already sufficiently mortified in not daring to come to the old house and tell his long stories and smoke his segar; but Evergreen, being an old beau, may solace himself in his disgrace by trimming up all his old finery and making love to the little girls.

At present my right-hand man is cousin Pindar, whom I have taken into high favour. He came home the other night all in a blaze like a sky-rocket—whisked up to his room in a paroxysm of poetic inspiration, nor did we see any thing of him until late the next morning, when he bounced upon us at breakfast,

"Fire in each eye—and paper in each hand."

This is just the way with Pindar, he is like a volcano; will remain for a long time silent without emitting a single spark, and then, all at once, burst out in a tremendous explosion of rhyme and rhapsody.

As the letters of my friend Mustapha seem to excite considerable curiosity, I have subjoined another. I do not vouch for the justice of his remarks, or the correctness of his conclusions; they are full of the blunders and errors in which strangers continually indulge, who pretend to give an account of this country before they well know the geography of the street in which they live. The copies of my friend's papers being confused and without date, I cannot pretend to give them in systematic order;—in fact, they seem now and then to treat of matters which have occurred since his departure; whether these are sly interpolations of that meddlesome wight Will Wizard, or whether honest Mustapha was gifted with the spirit of prophecy or second sight, I neither know—nor, in fact, do I care. The following seems to have been written when the Tripolitan prisoners were so much annoyed by the ragged state of their wardrobe. Mustapha feelingly depicts the embarrassments of his situation, traveller-like; makes an easy transition from his breeches to the seat of government, and incontinently abuses the whole administration; like a sapient traveller I once knew, who damned the French nation in toto—because they eat sugar with green peas.

LETTER FROM MUSTAPHA RUB-A-DUB KELI KHAN.

CAPTAIN OF A KETCH, TO ASEM HACCHEM, PRINCIPAL SLAVE-DRIVER TO HIS HIGHNESS THE BASHAW OF TRIPOLI.

SWEET, oh, Asem! is the memory of distant friends! like the mellow ray of a departing sun it falls tenderly yet sadly on the heart. Every hour of absence from my native land rolls heavily by, like the sandy wave of the desert; and the fair shores of my country rise blooming to my imagination, clothed in the soft, illusive charms of distance. I sigh, yet no one listens to the sigh of the captive; I shed the bitter tear of recollection, but no one sympathizes in the tear of the turbaned stranger! Think not, however, thou brother of my soul, that I complain of the horrors of my situation;—think not that my captivity is attended with the labours, the chains, the scourges, the insults, that render slavery, with us, more dreadful than the pangs of hesitating, lingering death. Light, indeed, are the restraints on the personal freedom of thy kinsman; but who can enter into the afflictions of the mind?—who can describe the agonies of the heart? they are mutable as the clouds of the air—they are countless as the waves that divide me from my native country.

I have, of late, my dear Asem, laboured under an inconvenience singularly unfortunate, and am reduced to a dilemma most ridiculously embarrassing. Why should I hide it from the companion of my thoughts, the partner of my sorrows and my joys? Alas! Asem, thy friend Mustapha, the invincible captain of a ketch, is sadly in want of a pair of breeches! Thou wilt doubtless smile, oh, most grave Mussulman, to hear me indulge in such ardent lamentations about a circumstance so trivial, and a want apparently so easy to be satisfied; but little canst thou know of the mortifications attending my necessities, and the astonishing difficulty of supplying them. Honoured by the smiles and attentions of the beautiful ladies of this city, who have fallen in love with my whiskers and my turban; courted by the bashaws and the great men, who delight to have me at their feasts; the honour of my company eagerly solicited by every fiddler who gives a concert; think of my chagrin at being obliged to decline the host of invitations that daily overwhelm me, merely for want of a pair of breeches! Oh, Allah! Allah! that thy disciples could come into the world all be-feathered like a bantam, or with a pair of leather breeches like the wild deer of the forest! Surely, my friend, it is the destiny of man to be for ever subjected to petty evils; which, however trifling in appearance, prey in silence on his little pittance of enjoyment, and poison those moments of sunshine which might otherwise be consecrated to happiness.

The want of a garment, thou wilt say, is easily supplied; and thou mayest suppose need only be mentioned, to be remedied at once by any tailor of the land: little canst thou conceive the impediments which stand in the way of my comfort; and still less art thou acquainted with the prodigious great scale on which every thing is transacted in this country. The nation moves most majestically slow and clumsy in the most trivial affairs, like the unwieldy elephant which makes a formidable difficulty of picking up a straw! When I hinted my necessities to the officer who has charge of myself and my companions, I expected to have them forthwith relieved; but he made an amazing long face, told me that we were prisoners of state, that we must, therefore, be clothed at the expense of government; that as no provision had been made by congress for an emergency of the kind, it was impossible to furnish me with a pair of breeches, until all the sages of the nation had been convened to talk over the matter and debate upon the expediency of granting my request. Sword of the immortal Khalid, thought I, but this is great!—this is truly sublime! All the sages of an immense logocracy assembled together to talk about my breeches! Vain mortal that I am!—I cannot but own I was somewhat reconciled to the delay, which must necessarily attend this method of clothing me, by the consideration that if they made the affair a national act, my "name must, of course, be embodied in history," and myself and my breeches flourish to immortality in the annals of this mighty empire!

"But, pray," said I, "how does it happen that a matter so insignificant should be erected into an object of such importance as to employ the representative wisdom of the nation; and what is the cause of their talking so much about a trifle?" —"Oh," replied the officer, who acts as our slave-driver, "it all proceeds from economy. If the government did not spend ten times as much money in debating whether it was proper to supply you with breeches, as the breeches themselves would cost, the people who govern the bashaw and his divan would straightway begin to complain of their liberties being infringed; the national finances squandered! not a hostile slang-whanger throughout the logocracy, but would burst forth like a barrel of combustion, and ten chances to one but the bashaw and the sages of his divan would all be turned out of office together. My good Mussulman," continued he, "the administration have the good of the people too much at heart to trifle with their pockets; and they would sooner assemble and talk away ten thousand dollars, than expend fifty silently out of the treasury; such is the wonderful spirit of economy that pervades every branch of this government." "But," said I, "how is it possible they can spend money in talking; surely words cannot be the current coin of this country?" "Truly," cried he, smiling, "your question is pertinent enough, for words indeed often supply the place of cash among us, and many an honest debt is paid in promises: but the fact is, the grand bashaw and the members of congress, or grand-talkers-of-the-nation, either receive a yearly salary or are paid by the day." "By the nine hundred tongues of the great beast in Mahomet's vision, but the murder is out;—it is no wonder these honest men talk so much about nothing, when they are paid for talking, like day-labourers." "You are mistaken," said my driver, "it is nothing but economy!"

I remained silent for some minutes, for this inexplicable word economy always discomfits me; and when I flatter myself I have grasped it, it slips through my fingers like a jack-o'-lantern. I have not, nor perhaps ever shall acquire, sufficient of the philosophic policy of this government to draw a proper distinction between an individual and a nation. If a man was to throw away a pound in order to save a beggarly penny, and boast, at the same time, of his economy, I should think him on a par with the fool in the fable of Alfanji, who, in skinning a flint worth a farthing, spoiled a knife worth fifty times the sum, and thought he had acted wisely. The shrewd fellow would doubtless have valued himself much more highly on his economy, could he have known that his example would one day be followed by the bashaw of America, and the sages of his divan.

This economic disposition, my friend, occasions much fighting of the spirit, and innumerable contests of the tongue in this talking assembly.—Wouldst thou believe it? they were actually employed for a whole week in a most strenuous and eloquent debate about patching up a hole in the wall of the room appropriated to their meetings! A vast profusion of nervous argument and pompous declamation was expended on the occasion. Some of the orators, I am told, being rather waggishly inclined, were most stupidly jocular on the occasion; but their waggery gave great offence; and was highly reprobated by the more weighty part of the assembly, who hold all wit and humour in abomination, and thought the business in hand much too solemn and serious to be treated lightly. It is supposed by some that this affair would have occupied a whole winter, as it was a subject upon which several gentlemen spoke who had never been known to open their lips in that place except to say yes and no. These silent members are by way of distinction denominated orator mums, and are highly valued in this country on account of their great talent for silence;—a qualification extremely rare in a logocracy.

Fortunately for the public tranquillity, in the hottest part of the debate, when two rampant Virginians, brim-full of logic and philosophy, were measuring tongues, and syllogistically cudgelling each other out of their unreasonable notions, the president of the divan, a knowing old gentleman, one night slyly sent a mason with a hod of mortar, who, in the course of a few minutes, closed up the hole and put a final end to the argument. Thus did this wise old gentleman, by hitting on a most simple expedient, in all probability save his country as much money as would build a gun-boat, or pay a hireling slang-whanger for a whole volume of words. As it happened, only a few thousand dollars were expended in paying these men, who are denominated, I suppose in derision, legislators.

Another instance of their economy I relate with pleasure, for I really begin to feel a regard for these poor barbarians. They talked away the best part of a whole winter before they could determine not to expend a few dollars in purchasing a sword to bestow on an illustrious warrior: yes, Asem, on that very hero who frightened all our poor old women and young children at Derne, and fully proved himself a greater man than the mother that bore him. Thus, my friend, is the whole collective wisdom of this mighty logocracy employed in somniferous debates about the most trivial affairs; like I have sometimes seen a herculean mountebank exerting all his energies in balancing a straw upon his nose. Their sages behold the minutest object with the microscopic eyes of a pismire; mole-hills swell into mountains, and a grain of mustard-seed will set the whole ant-hill in a hub-bub. Whether this indicates a capacious vision, or a diminutive mind, I leave thee to decide; for my part, I consider it as another proof of the great scale on which every thing is transacted in this country.

I have before told thee that nothing can be done without consulting the sages of the nation, who compose the assembly called the congress. This prolific body may not improperly be termed the "mother of inventions;" and a most fruitful mother it is, let me tell thee, though its children are generally abortions. It has lately laboured with what was deemed the conception of a mighty navy.—All the old women and the good wives that assist the bashaw in his emergencies hurried to head-quarters to be busy, like midwives, at the delivery.— All was anxiety, fidgeting, and consultation; when, after a deal of groaning and struggling, instead of formidable first rates and gallant frigates, out crept a litter of sorry little gunboats! These are most pitiful little vessels, partaking vastly of the character of the grand bashaw, who has the credit of begetting them; being flat, shallow vessels that can only sail before the wind;—must always keep in with the land;—are continually foundering or running ashore; and, in short, are only fit for smooth water. Though intended for the defence of the maritime cities, yet the cities are obliged to defend them; and they require as much nursing as so many ricketty little bantlings. They are, however, the darling pets of the grand bashaw, being the children of his dotage, and, perhaps from their diminutive size and palpable weakness, are called the "infant navy of America." The act that brought them into existence was almost deified by the majority of the people as a grand stroke of economy.—By the beard of Mahomet, but this word is truly inexplicable!

To this economic body, therefore, was I advised to address my petition, and humbly to pray that the august assembly of sages would, in the plenitude of their wisdom and the magnitude of their powers, munificently bestow on an unfortunate captive, a pair of cotton breeches! "Head of the immortal Amrou," cried I, "but this would be presumptuous to a degree; what! after these worthies have thought proper to leave their country naked and defenceless, and exposed to all the political storms that rattle without, can I expect that they will lend a helping hand to comfort the extremities of a solitary captive?" My exclamation was only answered by a smile, and I was consoled by the assurance that, so far from being neglected, it was every way probable my breeches might occupy a whole session of the divan, and set several of the longest heads together by the ears. Flattering as was the idea of a whole nation being agitated about my breeches, yet I own I was somewhat dismayed at the idea of remaining *in querpo*, until all the national gray-beards should have made a speech on the occasion, and given their consent to the measure. The embarrassment and distress of mind which I experienced was visible in my countenance, and my guard, who is a man of infinite good-nature, immediately suggested, as a more expeditious plan of supplying my wants—a benefit at the theatre. Though profoundly ignorant of his meaning, I agreed to his proposition, the result of which I shall disclose to thee in another letter.

Fare thee well, dear Asem; in thy pious prayers to our great prophet, never forget to solicit thy friend's return; and when thou numberest up the many blessings bestowed on thee by all-bountiful Allah, pour forth thy gratitude that he has cast thy nativity in a land where there is no assembly of legislative chatterers:—no great bashaw, who bestrides a gun-boat for a hobby-horse:—where the word economy is un-

known;—and where an unfortunate captive is not obliged to call upon the whole nation, to cut him out a pair of breeches.
                                    Ever thine,
                                         MUSTAPHA.

FROM THE MILL OF PINDAR COCKLOFT, ESQ.

    THOUGH enter'd on that sober age,
When men withdraw from fashion's stage,
And leave the follies of the day,
To shape their course a graver way;
Still those gay scenes I loiter round,
In which my youth sweet transport found:
And though I feel their joys decay,
And languish every hour away,—
Yet like an exile doom'd to part,
From the dear country of his heart,
From the fair spot in which he sprung,
Where his first notes of love were sung,
Will often turn to wave the hand,
And sigh his blessings on the land;
Just so my lingering watch I keep,
Thus oft I take my farewell peep.
    And, like that pilgrim who retreats,
Thus lagging from his parent seats,
When the sad thought pervades his mind,
That the fair land he leaves behind
Is ravaged by a foreign foe,
Its cities waste, its temples low,
And ruined all those haunts of joy
That gave him rapture when a boy;
Turns from it with averted eye,
And while he heaves the anguish'd sigh,
Scarce feels regret that the loved shore
Shall beam upon his sight no more;—
Just so it grieves my soul to view,
While breathing forth a fond adieu,
The innovations pride has made,
The fustian, frippery, and parade,
That now usurp with mawkish grace
Pure tranquil pleasure's wonted place!

'Twas joy we look'd for in my prime,
That idol of the olden time;
When all our pastimes had the art
To please, and not mislead, the heart.
Style curs'd us not,—that modern flash,
That love of racket and of trash;
Which scares at once all feeling joys,
And drowns delight in empty noise;
Which barters friendship, mirth, and truth,
The artless air, the bloom of youth,
And all those gentle sweets that swarm
Round nature in her simplest form,
For cold display, for hollow state,
The trappings of the would-be great.

  Oh! once again those days recall,
When heart met heart in fashion's hall;
When every honest guest would flock
To add his pleasure to the stock,
More fond his transports to express,
Than show the tinsel of his dress!
These were the times that clasp'd the soul
In gentle friendship's soft control,
Our fair ones, unprofan'd by art,
Content to gain one honest heart,
No train of sighing swains desired,
Sought to be loved and not admired.
But now 'tis form, not love, unites;
'Tis show, not pleasure, that invites.
Each seeks the ball to play the queen,
To flirt, to conquer, to be seen;
Each grasps at universal sway,
And reigns the idol of the day;
Exults amid a thousand sighs,
And triumphs when a lover dies.
Each belle a rival belle surveys,
Like deadly foe with hostile gaze;
Nor can her "dearest friend" caress,
Till she has slyly scann'd her dress;
Ten conquests in one year will make,
And six eternal friendships break!

  How oft I breathe the inward sigh,
And feel the dew-drop in my eye,

When I behold some beauteous frame,
Divine in every thing but name.
Just venturing, in the tender age,
On fashion's late new-fangled stage!
Where soon the guiltless heart shall cease
To beat in artlessness and peace;
Where all the flowers of gay delight
With which youth decks its prospects bright,
Shall wither 'mid the cares, the strife,
The cold realities of life!
 Thus lately, in my careless mood,
As I the world of fashion view'd
While celebrating great and small
That grand solemnity, a ball,
My roving vision chanced to light
On two sweet forms, divinely bright;
Two sister nymphs, alike in face,
In mien, in loveliness, and grace;
Twin rose-buds, bursting into bloom,
In all their brilliance and perfume:
Like those fair forms that often beam
Upon the Eastern poet's dream!
For Eden had each lovely maid
In native innocence arrayed,—
And heaven itself had almost shed
Its sacred halo round each head!
 They seem'd, just entering hand in hand,
To cautious tread this fairy land;
To take a timid, hasty view,
Enchanted with a scene so new.
The modest blush, untaught by art,
Bespoke their purity of heart;
And every timorous act unfurl'd
Two souls unspotted by the world.
 Oh, how these strangers joy'd my sight,
And thrill'd my bosom with delight!
They brought the visions of my youth
Back to my soul in all their truth;
Recall'd fair spirits into day,
That time's rough hand had swept away!
Thus the bright natives from above,
Who come on messages of love,

Will bless, at rare and distant whiles,
Our sinful dwelling by their smiles!
 Oh! my romance of youth is past,
Dear airy dreams too bright to last!
Yet when such forms as these appear,
I feel your soft remembrance here;
For, ah! the simple poet's heart,
On which fond love once play'd its part,
Still feels the soft pulsations beat,
As loth to quit their former seat.
Just like the harp's melodious wire,
Swept by a bard with heavenly fire,
Though ceased the loudly swelling strain
Yet sweet vibrations long remain.
 Full soon I found the lovely pair
Had sprung beneath a mother's care,
Hard by a neighbouring streamlet's side,
At once its ornament and pride.
The beauteous parent's tender heart
Had well fulfill'd its pious part;
And, like the holy man of old,
As we're by sacred writings told,
Who, when he from his pupil sped,
Pour'd two-fold blessings on his head.
So this fond mother had imprest
Her early virtues in each breast,
And as she found her stock enlarge,
Had stampt new graces on her charge.
 The fair resign'd the calm retreat,
Where first their souls in concert beat,
And flew on expectation's wing,
To sip the joys of life's gay spring;
To sport in fashion's splendid maze,
Where friendship fades and love decays.
So two sweet wild flowers, near the side
Of some fair river's silver tide,
Pure as the gentle stream that laves
The green banks with its lucid waves,
Bloom beauteous in their native ground,
Diffusing heavenly fragrance round;
But should a venturous hand transfer
These blossoms to the gay parterre,

Where, spite of artificial aid,
The fairest plants of nature fade,
Though they may shine supreme awhile
'Mid pale ones of the stranger soil,
The tender beauties soon decay,·
And their sweet fragrance dies away.
  Blest spirits! who, enthroned in air,
Watch o'er the virtues of the fair,
And with angelic ken survey
Their windings through life's chequer'd way;
Who hover round them as they glide
Down fashion's smooth, deceitful tide,
And guard them o'er that stormy deep
Where dissipation's tempests sweep:
Oh, make this inexperienced pair
The objects of your tenderest care.
Preserve them from the languid eye,
The faded cheek, the long-drawn sigh;
And let it be your constant aim
To keep the fair ones still the same:
Two sister hearts, unsullied, bright
As the first beam of lucid light
That sparkled from the youthful sun,
When first his jocund race begun.
So when these hearts shall burst their shrine,
To wing their flight to realms divine,
They may to radiant mansions rise
Pure as when first they left the skies.

NO. X.—SATURDAY, MAY 16, 1807.

FROM MY ELBOW-CHAIR.

THE long interval which has elapsed since the publication of our last number, like many other remarkable events, has given rise to much conjecture and excited considerable solicitude. It is but a day or two since I heard a knowing young gentleman observe, that he suspected Salmagundi would be a nine days' wonder, and had even prophesied that the ninth would be our last effort. But the age of prophecy, as well as that of chivalry, is past; and no reasonable man should now venture to foretell aught but what he is determined to bring about himself:—he may then, if he please, monopolize prediction, and be honoured as a prophet even in his own country.

Though I hold whether we write, or not write, to be none of the public's business, yet as I have just heard of the loss of three thousand votes at least to the Clintonians, I feel in a remarkably dulcet humour thereupon, and will give some account of the reasons which induced us to resume our useful labours:—or rather our amusement; for, if writing cost either of us a moment's labour, there is not a man but what would hang up his pen, to the great detriment of the world at large, and of our publisher in particular; who has actually bought himself a pair of trunk breeches, with the profits of our writings!!

He informs me that several persons having called last Saturday for No. X., took the disappointment so much to heart, that he really apprehended some terrible catastrophe; and one good-looking man, in particular, declared his intention of quitting the country if the work was not continued. Add to this, the town has grown quite melancholy in the last fortnight; and several young ladies have declared, in my hearing, that if another number did not make its appearance soon, they would be obliged to amuse themselves with teasing their beaux and making them miserable. Now I assure my readers there was no flattery in this, for they no more suspected me of being Launcelot Langstaff, than they suspected me of being the emperor of China, or the man in the moon.

I have also received several letters complaining of our indolent procrastination; and one of my correspondents assures me, that a number of young gentlemen, who had not read a book through since they left school, but who have taken a wonderful liking to our paper, will certainly relapse into their old habits unless we go on.

For the sake, therefore, of all these good people, and most especially for the satisfaction of the ladies, every one of whom we would love, if we possibly could, I have again wielded my pen with a most hearty determination to set the whole world to rights; to make cherubims and seraphs of all the fair ones of this enchanting town, and raise the spirits of the poor federalists, who, in truth, seem to be in a sad taking, ever since the American-Ticket met with the accident of being so unhappily thrown out.

TO LAUNCELOT LANGSTAFF, ESQ.

SIR:—I felt myself hurt and offended by Mr. Evergreen's terrible philippic against modern music, in No. II. of your work, and was under serious apprehension that his strictures might bring the art, which I have the honour to profess, into contempt. The opinion of yourself and fraternity appears indeed to have a wonderful effect upon the town.—I am told the ladies are all employed in reading Bunyan and Pamela, and the waltz has been entirely forsaken ever since the winter balls have closed. Under these apprehensions I should have addressed you before, had I not been sedulously employed, while the theatre continued open, in supporting the astonishing variety of the orchestra, and in composing a new chime or Bob-Major for Trinity Church, to be rung during the summer, beginning with ding-dong di-do, instead of di-do ding-dong. The citizens, especially those who live in the neighbourhood of that harmonious quarter, will, no doubt, be infinitely delighted with this novelty.

But to the object of this communication. So far, sir, from agreeing with Mr. Evergreen in thinking that all modern music is but the mere dregs and drainings of the ancient, I trust, before this letter is concluded, I shall convince you and him that some of the late professors of this enchanting art have completely distanced the paltry efforts of the ancients; and that I, in particular, have at length brought it almost to absolute perfection.

The Greeks, simple souls! were astonished at the powers of Orpheus, who made the woods and rocks dance to his lyre; —of Amphion, who converted crotchets into bricks, and quavers into mortar;—and of Arion, who won upon the compassion of the fishes. In the fervency of admiration, their poets fabled that Apollo had lent them his lyre, and inspired them with his own spirit of harmony. What then would they have said had they witnessed the wonderful effects of my skill? had they heard me in the compass of a single piece, describe in glowing notes one of the most sublime operations of nature; and not only make inanimate objects dance, but even speak; and not only speak, but speak in strains of exquisite harmony?

Let me not, however, be understood to say that I am the sole author of this extraordinary improvement in the art, for I confess I took the hint of many of my discoveries from some of those meritorious productions that have lately come abroad and made so much noise under the title of overtures. From some of these, as, for instance, Lodoiska, and the battle of Marengo, a gentleman, or a captain in the city militia, or an amazonian young lady, may indeed acquire a tolerable idea of military tactics, and become very well experienced in the firing of musketry, the roaring of cannon, the rattling of drums, the whistling of fifes; braying of trumpets, groans of the dying, and trampling of cavalry, without ever going to the wars; but it is more especially in the art of imitating inimitable things, and giving the language of every passion and sentiment of the human mind, so as entirely to do away the necessity of speech, that I particularly excel the most celebrated musicians of ancient and modern times.

I think, sir, I may venture to say there is not a sound in the whole compass of nature which I cannot imitate, and even improve upon;—nay, what I consider the perfection of my art, I have discovered a method of expressing, in the most striking manner, that undefinable, indescribable silence which accompanies the falling of snow.

In order to prove to you that I do not arrogate to myself what I am unable to perform, I will detail to you the different movements of a grand piece which I pride myself upon exceedingly, called the "Breaking up of the ice in the North River."

The piece opens with a gentle *andante affetuosso*, which ushers you into the assembly-room in the state-house in Albany, where the speaker addresses his farewell speech, informing the members that the ice is about breaking up, and thanking them for their great services and good behaviour in a manner so pathetic as to bring tears into their eyes.—Flourish of Jacks-a-donkies.—Ice cracks; Albany in a hub-bub:—air, "Three children sliding on the ice, all on a summer's day."—Citizens quarrelling in Dutch;——chorus of a tin trumpet, a cracked fiddle, and a hand-saw!——*allegro moderato*.—Hard frost:—this, if given with proper spirit, has a charming effect, and sets every body's teeth chattering.—Symptoms of snow—consultation of old women who complain of pains in the bones and *rheumatics;*——air, "There was an old woman tossed up in a blanket," &c.——*allegro staccato;* wagon breaks into the ice; —people all run to see what is the matter;——air, *siciliano*— "Can you row the boat ashore, Billy boy, Billy boy;"—*andante;*—frost fish froze up in the ice;——air,—"Ho, why dost thou shiver and shake, Gaffer Gray, and why does thy nose look so blue?"——Flourish of two-penny trumpets and rattlers; —consultation of the North-river society;—determine to set the North-river on fire, as soon as it will burn;—air, "O, what a fine kettle of fish."

Part II.—GREAT THAW.—This consists of the most melting strains, flowing so smoothly as to occasion a great overflowing of scientific rapture; air—"One misty moisty morning." The house of assembly breaks up—air—"The owls came out and flew about."——Assembly-men embark on their way to New-York——air——"The ducks and the geese they all swam over, fal, de ral," &c.——Vessel sets sail—chorus of mariners— "Steer her up, and let her gang." After this a rapid movement conducts you to New York;—the North-river society hold a meeting at the corner of Wall-street, and determine to delay burning till all the assembly-men are safe home, for fear of consuming some of their own members who belong to that respectable body. Return again to the capital.—Ice floats down the river; lamentation of skaters; air, *affetuosso*—"I sigh and lament me in vain," &c.—Albanians cutting up sturgeon;—air,

"O the roast beef of Albany."—Ice runs against Polopoy's island, with a terrible crash.—This is represented by a fierce fellow travelling with his fiddle-stick over a huge bass viol, at the rate of one hundred and fifty bars a minute, and tearing the music to rags;—this being what is called execution.—The great body of ice passes West-point, and is saluted by three or four dismounted cannon, from Fort Putnam.—"Jefferson's march" by a full band;—air, "Yankee doodle," with seventy-six variations, never before attempted, except by the celebrated eagle, which flutters his wings over the copper-bottomed angel at Messrs. Paff's in Broadway. Ice passes New-York: conch-shell sounds at a distance—ferrymen calls o-v-e-r;—people run down Courtlandt-street—ferry-boat sets sail——air—accompanied by the conch-shell—"We'll all go over the ferry."—Rondeau—giving a particular account of BROM the Powles-hook admiral, who is supposed to be closely connected with the North-river society.—The society make a grand attempt to fire the stream, but are utterly defeated by a remarkable high tide, which brings the plot to light; drowns upwards of a thousand rats, and occasions twenty robins to break their necks.*—Society not being discouraged, apply to "Common Sense," for his lantern;——Air—"Nose, nose, jolly red nose." Flock of wild geese fly over the city;—old wives chatter in the fog—cocks crow at Communipaw—drums beat on Governor's island.—The whole to conclude with the blowing up of Sand's powder-house.

Thus, sir, you perceive what wonderful powers of expression have been hitherto locked up in this enchanting art:—a whole history is here told without the aid of speech, or writing; and provided the hearer is in the least acquainted with music, he cannot mistake a single note. As to the blowing up of the powder-house, I look upon it as a *chef d'ouvre*, which I am confident will delight all modern amateurs, who very properly estimate music in proportion to the noise it makes, and delight in thundering cannon and earthquakes.

I must confess, however, it is a difficult part to manage, and I have already broken six pianos in giving it the proper force and effect. But I do not despair, and am quite certain that by the time I have broken eight or ten more, I shall have brought it to such perfection, as to be able to teach any young lady of tolerable ear, to thunder it away to the infinite delight of papa

---

* Vide—Solomon Lang.

and mamma, and the great annoyance of those Vandals, who are so barbarous as to prefer the simple melody of a Scots air, to the sublime effusions of modern musical doctors.

In my warm anticipations of future improvement, I have sometimes almost convinced myself that music will, in time, be brought to such a climax of perfection, as to supersede the necessity of speech and writing; and every kind of social intercourse be conducted by the flute and fiddle.—The immense benefits that will result from this improvement must be plain to every man of the least consideration. In the present unhappy situation of mortals, a man has but one way of making himself perfectly understood; if he loses his speech, he must inevitably be dumb all the rest of his life; but having once learned this new musical language, the loss of speech will be a mere trifle not worth a moment's uneasiness. Not only this, Mr. L., but it will add much to the harmony of domestic intercourse; for it is certainly much more agreeable to hear a lady give lectures on the piano than, *viva voce*, in the usual discord, ant measure. This manner of discoursing may also, I think, be introduced with great effect into our national assemblies, where every man, instead of wagging his tongue, should be obliged to flourish a fiddle-stick, by which means, if he said nothing to the purpose, he would, at all events, "discourse most eloquent music," which is more than can be said of most of them at present. They might also sound their own trumpets without being obliged to a hireling scribbler, for an immortality of nine days, or subjected to the censure of egotism.

But the most important result of this discovery is that it may be applied to the establishment of that great desideratum, in the learned world, a universal language. Wherever this science of music is cultivated, nothing more will be necessary than a knowledge of its alphabet; which being almost the same everywhere, will amount to a universal medium of communication. A man may thus, with his violin under his arm, a piece of rosin, and a few bundles of catgut, fiddle his way through the world, and never be at a loss to make himself understood.

I am, etc.
DEMY SEMIQUAVER.

[END OF VOL. ONE.]

SALMAGUNDI.

VOLUME TWO.

NOTE BY THE PUBLISHER.

Without the knowledge or permission of the authors, and which, if he dared, he would have placed near where their remarks are made on the great difference of manners which exists between the sexes now, from what it did in the days of our grandames. The danger of that cheek-by-jowl familiarity of the present day, must be obvious to many; and I think the following a strong example of one of its evils.

EXTRACTED FROM "THE MIRROR OF THE GRACES."

"I REMEMBER the Count M——, one of the most accomplished and handsomest young men in Vienna; when I was there he was passionately in love with a girl of almost peerless beauty. She was the daughter of a man of great rank, and great influence at court; and on these considerations, as well as in regard to her charms, she was followed by a multitude of suitors. She was lively and amiable, and treated them all with an affability which still kept them in her train, although it was generally known she had avowed a partiality for Count M——; and that preparations were making for their nuptials. The Count was of a refined mind, and a delicate sensibility; he loved her for herself alone: for the virtues which he believed dwelt in her beautiful form; and, like a lover of such perfections, he never approached her without timidity; and when he touched her, a fire shot through his veins, that warned him not to invade the vermillion sanctuary of her lips. Such were his feelings when, one evening, at his intended father-in-law's, a party of young people were met to celebrate a certain festival; several of the young lady's rejected suitors were present. Forfeits were one of the pastimes, and all went on with the greatest merriment, till the Count was commanded, by some witty *mam'selle*, to redeem his glove by saluting the cheek of his intended bride. The Count blushed, trembled, advanced, retreated; again advanced to his mistress;—and,—at last,—with a tremor that shook his whole soul, and every fibre of his frame, with a modest and diffident grace, he took the soft ringlet which played upon her cheek, pressed it to his lips, and retired to demand his redeemed pledge in the most evident confusion. His mistress gaily smiled, and the game went on.

"One of her rejected suitors who was of a merry, unthinking disposition, was adjudged by the same indiscreet crier of the forfeits as "his last treat before he hanged himself" to snatch a kiss from the object of his recent vows. A lively contest ensued between the gentleman and lady, which lasted for more than a minute; but the lady yielded, though in the midst of a convulsive laugh.

"The Count had the mortification—the agony—to see the lips, which his passionate and delicate love would not permit him to touch, kissed with roughness, and repetition, by another man:—even by one whom he really despised. Mournfully and silently, without a word, he rose from his chair—left the room and the house. By that *good-natured kiss* the fair boast of Vienna lost her lover—lost her husband. THE COUNT NEVER SAW HER MORE."

NO. XI.—TUESDAY, JUNE 2, 1807.

LETTER FROM MUSTAPHA RUB-A-DUB KELI KHAN,

CAPTAIN OF A KETCH, TO ASEM HACCHEM, PRINCIPAL SLAVE-DRIVER TO HIS HIGHNESS THE BASHAW OF TRIPOLI.

THE deep shadows of midnight gather around me;—the footsteps of the passengers have ceased in the streets, and nothing disturbs the holy silence of the hour save the sound of distant drums, mingled with the shouts, the bawlings, and the discordant revelry of his majesty, the sovereign mob. Let the hour be sacred to friendship, and consecrated to thee, oh, thou brother of my inmost soul!

Oh, Asem! I almost shrink at the recollection of the scenes of confusion, of licentious disorganization, which I have witnessed during the last three days. I have beheld this whole city, nay, this whole state, given up to the tongue, and the pen; to the puffers, the bawlers, the babblers, and the slang-whangers. I have beheld the community convulsed with a civil war, or civil talk; individuals verbally massacred, families annihilated by whole sheets full, and slang-whangers coolly bathing their pens in ink and rioting in the slaughter of their thousands. I have seen, in short, that awful despot, the people, in the moment of unlimited power, wielding newspapers in one hand, and with the other scattering mud and filth about, like some desperate lunatic relieved from the restraints of his straight waistcoat. I have seen beggars on horseback, ragamuffins riding in coaches, and swine seated in places of honour; I have seen liberty; I have seen equality; I have seen fraternity!—I have seen that great political puppet-show—— AN ELECTION.

A few days ago the friend, whom I have mentioned in some of my former letters, called upon me to accompany him to witness this grand ceremony; and we forthwith sallied out to the polls, as he called them. Though for several weeks before this splendid exhibition, nothing else had been talked of, yet I do assure thee I was entirely ignorant of its nature; and when, on coming up to a church, my companion informed me we were at the poll, I supposed that an election was some great religious ceremony like the fast of Ramazan, or the great festival of Haraphat, so celebrated in the east.

My friend, however, undeceived me at once, and entered into a long dissertation on the nature and object of an election, the substance of which was nearly to this effect: "You know," said he, "that this country is engaged in a violent internal warfare, and suffers a variety of evils from civil dissensions. An election is a grand trial of strength, the decisive battle, when the belligerents draw out their forces in martial array; when every leader, burning with warlike ardour, and encouraged by the shouts and acclamations of tatterdemalions, buffoons, dependents, parasites, toad-eaters, scrubs, vagrants, mumpers, ragamuffins, bravoes, and beggars, in his rear; and puffed up by his bellows-blowing slang-whangers, waves gallantly the banners of faction, and presses forward TO OFFICE AND IMMORTALITY!

"For a month or two previous to the critical period which is to decide this important affair, the whole community is in a ferment. Every man, of whatever rank or degree, such is the wonderful patriotism of the people, disinterestedly neglects his business, to devote himself to his country;—and not an insignificant fellow, but feels himself inspired, on this occasion, with as much warmth in favour of the cause he has espoused, as if all the comfort of his life, or even his life itself, was dependent on the issue. Grand councils of war are, in the first place, called by the different powers, which are dubbed general meetings, where all the head workmen of the party collect, and arrange the order of battle;—appoint the different commanders, and their subordinate instruments, and furnish the funds indispensable for supplying the expenses of the war. Inferior councils are next called in the different classes or wards; consisting of young cadets, who are candidates for offices; idlers who come there for mere curiosity; and orators who appear for the purpose of detailing all the crimes, the faults, or the weaknesses of their opponents, and *speaking the sense of the meeting*, as it is called; for as the meeting generally consists of men whose quota of sense, taken individually would make but a poor figure, these orators are appointed to collect it all in a lump; when I assure you it makes a very formidable appearance, and furnishes sufficient matter to spin an oration of two or three hours.

"The orators who declaim at these meetings are, with a few exceptions, men of most profound and perplexed eloquence; who are the oracles of barbers' shops, market-places, and porter-houses; and who you may see every day at the corners of the streets, taking honest men prisoners by the button, and talking their ribs quite bare without mercy and without end. These orators, in addressing an audience, generally mount a chair, a table, or an empty beer barrel, which last is supposed to afford considerable inspiration, and thunder away their combustible sentiments at the heads of the audience, who are generally so busily employed in smoking, drinking, and hearing themselves talk, that they seldom hear a word of the matter. This, however, is of little moment; for as they come there to agree at all events to a certain set of resolutions, or articles of war, it is not at all necessary to hear the speech; more especially as few would understand it if they did. Do not suppose, however, that the minor persons of the meeting are entirely idle.—Besides smoking and drinking, which are generally practised, there are few who do not come with as great a desire to talk as the orator himself; each has his little circle of listeners, in the midst of whom he sets his hat on one side of his head, and deals out matter-of-fact information; and draws self-evident conclusions, with the pertinacity of a pedant, and to the great edification of his gaping auditors. Nay, the very urchins from the nursery, who are scarcely emancipated from the dominion of birch, on these occasions strut pigmy great men;—bellow for the instruction of gray-bearded ignorance, and, like the frog in the fable, endeavour to puff themselves up to the size of the great object of their emulation —the principal orator."

"But is it not preposterous to a degree," cried I, "for those puny whipsters to attempt to lecture age and experience? They should be sent to school to learn better." "Not at all," replied my friend; "for as an election is nothing more than a war of words, the man that can wag his tongue with the greatest elasticity, whether he speaks to the purpose or not, is entitled to lecture at ward meetings and polls, and instruct all who are inclined to listen to him: you may have remarked a ward meeting of politic dogs, where although the great dog is, ostensibly, the leader, and makes the most noise, yet every little scoundrel of a cur has something to say; and in proportion to his insignificance, fidgets, and worries, and puffs about mightily, in order to obtain the notice and approbation of his betters. Thus it is with these little, beardless, bread-and-butter politicians who, on this occasion, escape from the jurisdiction of their mammas to attend to the affairs of the nation. You will see them engaged in dreadful wordy contest with old cartmen, cobblers, and tailors, and plume themselves not a little if they should chance to gain a victory.—Aspiring spirits! how interesting are the first dawnings of political greatness! an election, my friend, is a nursery or hot-bed of genius in a logocracy; and I look with enthusiasm on a troop of these Lilliputian partisans, as so many chatterers, and orators, and puffers, and slang-whangers in embryo, who will one day take an important part in the quarrels, and wordy wars of their country.

"As the time for fighting the decisive battle approaches, appearances become more and more alarming; committees are appointed, who hold little encampments from whence they send out small detachments of tattlers, to reconnoitre, harass, and skirmish with the enemy, and if possible, ascertain their numbers; every body seems big with the mighty event that is impending; the orators they gradually swell up beyond their usual size; the little orators they grow greater and greater; the secretaries of the ward committees strut about looking like wooden oracles; the puffers put on the airs of mighty consequence; the slang-whangers deal out direful innuendoes, and threats of doughty import; and all is buzz, murmur, suspense, and sublimity!

"At length the day arrives. The storm that has been so long gathering, and threatening in distant thunders, bursts forth in terrible explosion: all business is at an end; the whole city is in a tumult; the people are running helter-skelter, they know not whither, and they know not why; the hackney coaches rattle through the streets with thundering vehemence, loaded with recruiting serjeants who have been prowling in cellars and caves, to unearth some miserable minion of poverty and ignorance, who will barter his vote for a glass of beer, or a ride in a coach with such *fine gentlemen!*—the buzzards of the party scamper from poll to poll, on foot or on horseback; and they worry from committee to committee, and buzz, and fume, and talk big, and—*do nothing:* like the vagabond drone, who wastes his time in the laborious idleness of *see-saw-song*, and busy nothingness."

I know not how long my friend would have continued his detail, had he not been interrupted by a squabble which took place] between two *old continentals*, as they were called. It seems they had entered into an argument on the respective merits of their cause, and not being able to make each other clearly understood, resorted to what is called knock-down arguments, which form the superlative degree of *argumentum ad hominem;* but are, in my opinion, extremely inconsistent with the true spirit of a genuine logocracy. After they had beaten each other soundly, and set the whole mob together by the ears, they came to a full explanation; when it was discovered that they were both of the same way of thinking;—whereupon they shook each other heartily by the hand, and laughed with great glee at their humorous misunderstanding.

I could not help being struck with the exceeding great number of ragged, dirty-looking persons that swaggered about the place and seemed to think themselves the bashaws of the land. I inquired of my friend, if these people were employed to drive away the hogs, dogs, and other intruders that might thrust themselves in and interrupt the ceremony? "By no means," replied he; "these are the representatives of the sovereign people, who come here to make governors, senators, and members of assembly, and are the source of all power and authority in this nation." "Preposterous!" said I, "how is it possible that such men can be capable of distinguishing between an honest man and a knave; or even if they were, will it not always happen that they are led by the nose by some intriguing demagogue, and made the mere tools of ambitious political jugglers? Surely it would be better to trust to providence, or even to chance, for governors, than resort to the discriminating powers of an ignorant mob.—I plainly perceive the consequence. A man who possesses superior talents, and that honest pride which ever accompanies this possession, will always be sacrificed to some creeping insect who will prostitute himself to familiarity with the lowest of mankind; and, like the idolatrous Egyptian, worship the wallowing tenants of filth and mire."

" All this is true enough," replied my friend, "but after all, you cannot say but that this is a free country, and that the people can get drunk cheaper here, particularly at elections, than in the despotic countries of the east." I could not, with any degree of propriety or truth, deny this last assertion; for just at that moment a patriotic brewer arrived with a load of beer, which, for a moment, occasioned a cessation of argument.——The great crowd of buzzards, puffers, and "old continentals" of all parties, who throng to the polls, to persuade, to cheat, or to force the freeholders into the right way, and to maintain the freedom of suffrage, seemed for a moment to forget their antipathies and joined, heartily, in a copious libation of this patriotic and argumentative beverage.

These beer-barrels indeed seem to be most able logicians, well stored with that kind of sound argument best suited to the comprehension, and most relished by the mob, or sovereign people; who are never so tractable as when operated upon by this convincing liquor, which, in fact, seems to be imbued with the very spirit of a logocracy. No sooner does it begin its operation, than the tongue waxes exceeding valorous, and becomes impatient for some mighty conflict. The puffer puts himself at the head of his body-guard of buzzards, and his legion of ragamuffins, and wo then to every unhappy adversary who is uninspired by the deity of the beer-barrel—he is sure to be talked and argued into complete insignificance.

While I was making these observations, I was surprised to observe a bashaw, high in office, shaking a fellow by the hand, that looked rather more ragged than a scare-crow, and inquiring with apparent solicitude concerning the health of his family; after which he slipped a little folded paper into his hand, and turned away. I could not help applauding his humility in shaking the fellow's hand, and his benevolence in relieving his distresses, for I imagined the paper contained something for the poor man's necessities; and truly he seemed verging towards the last stage of starvation. My friend, however, soon undeceived me by saying that this was an elector, and that the bashaw had merely given him the list of candidates for whom he was to vote. "Ho! ho!" said I, "then he is a particular friend of the bashaw?" "By no means," replied my friend, "the bashaw will pass him without notice the day after the election, except, perhaps, just to drive over him with his coach."

My friend then proceeded to inform me that for some time before, and during the continuance of an election, there was a most delectable courtship, or intrigue, carried on between the great bashaws and the mother mob. That mother mob generally preferred the attentions of the rabble, or of fellows of her own stamp; but would sometimes condescend to be treated to a feasting, or any thing of that kind, at the bashaw's expense; nay, sometimes when she was in good humour, she would condescend to toy with them in her rough way:—but wo be to the bashaw who attempted to be familiar with her, for she was the most pestilent, cross, crabbed, scolding, thieving, scratching, toping, wrong-headed, rebellious, and abominable termagant that ever was let loose in the world, to the confusion of honest gentlemen bashaws.

Just then a fellow came round and distributed among the crowd a number of hand-bills, written by the ghost of Washington, the fame of whose illustrious actions, and still more illustrious virtues, has reached even the remotest regions of the east, and who is venerated by this people as the Father of his country. On reading this paltry paper, I could not restrain my indignation. "Insulted hero," cried I, "is it thus thy name is profaned, thy memory disgraced, thy spirit drawn down from heaven to administer to the brutal violence of party rage!—It is thus the necromancers of the east, by their infernal incantations, sometimes call up the shades of the just, to give their sanction to frauds, to lies, and to every species of enormity." My friend smiled at my warmth, and observed, that raising ghosts, and not only raising them, but making them speak, was one of the miracles of elections. "And believe me," continued he, "there is good reason for the ashes of departed heroes being disturbed on these occasions, for such is the sandy foundation of our government, that there never happens an election of an alderman, or a collector, or even a constable, but we are in imminent danger of losing our liberties, and becoming a province of France, or tributary to the British islands." "By the hump of Mahomet's camel," said I, "but this is only another striking example of the prodigious great scale on which every thing is transacted in this country!"

By this time, I had become tired of the scene; my head ached with the uproar of voices, mingling in all the discordant tones of triumphant exclamation, nonsensical argument, intemperate reproach, and drunken absurdity.—The confusion was such as no language can adequately describe, and it seemed as if all the restraints of decency, and all the bands of law, had been broken, and given place to the wide ravages of licentious brutality. These, thought I, are the orgies of liberty! these are the manifestations of the spirit of independence! these are the symbols of man's sovereignty! Head of Mahomet! with what a fatal and inexorable despotism do empty names and ideal phantoms exercise their dominion over the human mind! The experience of ages has demonstrated, that in all nations, barbarous or enlightened, the mass of the people, the mob, must be slaves, or they will be tyrants; but their tyranny will not be long:—some ambitious leader, having at first condescended to be their slave, will at length become their master; and in proportion to the vileness of his former servitude, will be the severity of his subsequent tyranny.—Yet, with innumerable examples staring them in the face, the people still bawl out liberty; by which they mean nothing but freedom from every species of legal restraint, and a warrant for all kinds of licentiousness: and the bashaws and leaders, in courting the mob, convince them of their power; and by administering to their passions, for the purposes of ambition, at length learn, by fatal experience, that he who worships the beast that carries him on his back, will sooner or later be thrown into the dust and trampled under foot by the animal who has learnt the secret of its power by this very adoration.

Ever thine,

MUSTAPHA.

FROM MY ELBOW-CHAIR.

MINE UNCLE JOHN.

To those whose habits of abstraction may have led them into some of the secrets of their own minds, and whose freedom from daily toil has left them at leisure to analyze their feelings, it will be nothing new to say that the present is peculiarly the season of remembrance. The flowers, the zephyrs, and the warblers of spring, returning after their tedious absence, bring naturally to our recollection past times and buried feelings; and the whispers of the full-foliaged grove, fall on the ear of contemplation, like the sweet tones of far distant friends whom the rude jostlers of the world have severed from us and cast far beyond our reach. It is at such times, that casting backward many a lingering look we recall, with a kind of sweet-souled melancholy, the days of our youth, and the jocund companions who started with us the race of life, but parted midway in the journey to pursue some winding path that allured them with a prospect more seducing—and never returned to us again. It is then, too, if we have been afflicted with any heavy sorrow, if we have even lost—and who has not!—an old friend, or chosen companion, that his shade will hover around us; the memory of his virtues press on the heart; and a thousand endearing recollections, forgotten amidst the cold pleasures and midnight dissipations of winter, arise to our remembrance.

These speculations bring to my mind MY UNCLE JOHN, the history of whose loves, and disappointments, I have promised to the world. Though I must own myself much addicted to forgetting my promises, yet, as I have been so happily reminded of this, I believe I must pay it at once, "and there is an end.". Lest my readers—good-natured souls that they are!—should, in the ardour of peeping into millstones, take my uncle for an old acquaintance, I here inform them, that the old gentleman died a great many years ago, and it is impossible they should ever have known him:—I pity them—for they would have known a good-natured, benevolent man, whose example might have been of service.

The last time I saw my uncle John was fifteen years ago, when I paid him a visit at his old mansion. I found him reading a newspaper—for it was election time, and he was always a warm federalist, and had made several converts to the true political faith in his time;—particularly one old tenant, who always, just before the election, became a violent anti;—in order that he might be convinced of his errors by my uncle, who never failed to reward his conviction by some substantial benefit.

After we had settled the affairs of the nation, and I had paid my respects to the old family chronicles in the kitchen,—an indispensable ceremony,—the old gentleman exclaimed, with heart-felt glee, "Well, I suppose you are for a trout-fishing;—I have got every thing prepared;—but first you must take a walk with me to see my improvements." I was obliged to consent; though I knew my uncle would lead me a most villainous dance, and in all probability treat me to a quagmire, or a tumble into a ditch. If my readers choose to accompany me in this expedition, they are welcome; if not, let them stay at home like lazy fellows—and sleep—or be hanged.

Though I had been absent several years, yet there was very little alteration in the scenery, and every object retained the same features it bore when I was a school-boy: for it was in this spot that I grew up in the fear of ghosts, and in the breaking of many of the ten commandments. The brook, or river as they would call it in Europe, still murmured with its wonted sweetness through the meadow; and its banks were still tufted with dwarf willows, that bent down to the surface. The same echo inhabited the valley, and the same tender air of repose pervaded the whole scene. Even my good uncle was but little altered, except that his hair was grown a little grayer, and his forehead had lost some of its former smoothness. He had, however, lost nothing of his former activity, and laughed heartily at the difficulty I found in keeping up with him as he stumped through bushes, and briers, and hedges; talking all the time about his improvements, and telling what he would do with such a spot of ground and such a tree. At length, after showing me his stone fences, his famous two-year-old bull, his new invented cart, which was to go before the horse, and his Eclipse colt, he was pleased to return home to dinner.

After dinner and returning thanks,—which with him was not a ceremony merely, but an offering from the heart,—my uncle opened his trunk, took out his fishing-tackle, and, without saying a word, sallied forth with some of those truly alarming steps which Daddy Neptune once took when he was in a great hurry to attend to the affair of the siege of Troy. Trout-fishing was my uncle's favourite sport; and, though I always caught two fish to his one, he never would acknowledge my superiority; but puzzled himself often and often to account for such a singular phenomenon.

Following the current of the brook for a mile or two, we retraced many of our old haunts, and told a hundred adventures which had befallen us at different times. It was like snatching the hour-glass of time, inverting it, and rolling back again the sands that had marked the lapse of years. At length the shadows began to lengthen, the south-wind gradually settled into a perfect calm, the sun threw his rays through the trees on the hill-tops in golden lustre, and a kind of Sabbath stillness pervaded the whole valley, indicating that the hour was fast approaching which was to relieve for a while the farmer from his rural labour, the ox from his toil, the school-urchin from his primer, and bring the loving ploughman home to the feet of his blooming dairymaid.

As we were watching in silence the last rays of the sun, beaming their farewell radiance on the high hills at a distance, my uncle exclaimed, in a kind of half-desponding tone, while he rested his arm over an old tree that had fallen—"I know not how it is, my dear Launce, but such an evening, and such a still quiet scene as this, always make me a little sad; and it is, at such a time, I am most apt to look forward with regret to the period when this farm, on which "I have been young, but now am old," and every object around me that is endeared by long acquaintance,—when all these and I must shake hands and part. I have no fear of death, for my life has afforded but little temptation to wickedness; and when I die, I hope to leave behind me more substantial proofs of virtue than will be found in my epitaph, and more lasting memorials than churches built or hospitals endowed; with wealth wrung from the hard hand of poverty by an unfeeling landlord or unprincipled knave;—but still, when I pass such a day as this and contemplate such a scene, I cannot help feeling a latent wish to linger yet a little longer in this peaceful asylum; to enjoy a little more sunshine in this world, and to have a few more fishing-matches with my boy." As he ended he raised his hand a little from the fallen tree, and dropping it languidly by his side, turned himself towards home. The sentiment, the look, the action, all seemed to be prophetic. And so they were, for when I shook him by the hand and bade him farewell the next morning—it was for the last time!

He died a bachelor, at the age of sixty-three, though he had been all his life trying to get married; and always thought himself on the point of accomplishing his wishes. His disappointments were not owing either to the deformity of his mind or person; for in his youth he was reckoned handsome, and I myself can witness for him that he had as kind a heart as ever was fashioned by heaven; neither were they owing to his poverty,—which sometimes stands in an honest man's way;—for he was born to the inheritance of a small estate which was sufficient to establish his claim to the title of "one well-to-do in the world." The truth is, my uncle had a prodigious antipathy to doing things in a hurry.—"A man should consider," said he to me once—"that he can always get a wife, but cannot always get rid of her. For my part," continued he, "I am a young fellow, with the world before me,"—he was but about forty!—"and am resolved to look sharp, weigh matters well, and know what's what, before I marry:—in short, Launce, *I don't intend to do the thing in a hurry, depend upon it.*" On this whim-wham, he proceeded: he began with young girls, and ended with widows. The girls he courted until they grew old maids, or married out of pure apprehension of incurring certain penalties hereafter; and the widows not having quite as much patience, generally, at the end of a year, while the good man thought himself in the high road to success, married some *harum-scarum* young fellow, who had not such an antipathy *to doing things in a hurry.*

My uncle would have inevitably sunk under these repeated disappointments—for he did not want sensibility—had he not hit upon a discovery which set all to rights at once. He consoled his vanity,—for he was a little vain, and soothed his pride, which was his master-passion,—by telling his friends very significantly, while his eye would flash triumph, "*that he might have had her.*"—Those who know how much of the bitterness of disappointed affection arises from wounded vanity and exasperated pride, will give my uncle credit for this discovery.

My uncle had been told by a prodigious number of married men, and had read in an innumerable quantity of books, that a man could not possibly be happy except in the married state; so he determined at an early age to marry, that he might not lose his only chance for happiness. He accordingly forthwith paid his addresses to the daughter of a neighbouring gentleman farmer, who was reckoned the beauty of the whole world; a phrase by which the honest country people mean nothing more than the circle of their acquaintance, or that territory of land which is within sight of the smoke of their own hamlet.

This young lady, in addition to her beauty, was highly accomplished, for she had spent five or six months at a boarding-school in town; where she learned to work pictures in satin, and paint sheep that might be mistaken for wolves; to hold up her head, sit straight in her chair, and to think every species of useful acquirement beneath her attention. When she returned home, so completely had she forgotten every thing she knew before, that on seeing one of the maids milking a cow, she asked her father, with an air of most enchanting ignorance, "what that odd-looking thing was doing to that queer animal?" The old man shook his head at this; but the mother was delighted at these symptoms of gentility, and so enamoured of her daughter's accomplishments that she actually got framed a picture worked in satin by the young lady. It represented the Tomb Scene in Romeo and Juliet. Romeo was dressed in an orange-coloured cloak, fastened round his neck with a large golden clasp; a white satin tamboured waistcoat, leather breeches, blue silk stockings, and white topt boots. The amiable Juliet shone in a flame-coloured gown, most gorgeously bespangled with silver stars, a high-crowned muslin cap that reached to the top of the tomb;—on her feet she wore a pair of short-quartered, high-heeled shoes, and her waist was the exact fac-simile of an inverted sugar-loaf. The head of the "noble county Paris" looked like a chimney-sweeper's brush that had lost its handle; and the cloak of the good Friar hung about him as gracefully as the armour of a rhinoceros. The good lady considered this picture as a splendid proof of her daughter's accomplishments, and hung it up in the best parlour, as an honest tradesman does his certificate of admission into that enlightened body yclept the Mechanic Society.

With this accomplished young lady then did my uncle John become deeply enamoured, and as it was his first love, he determined to bestir himself in an extraordinary manner. Once at least in a fortnight, and generally on a Sunday evening, he would put on his leather breeches, for he was a great beau, mount his gray horse Pepper, and ride over to see Miss Pamela, though she lived upwards of a mile off, and he was obliged to pass close by a church-yard, which at least a hundred creditable persons would swear was haunted!—Miss Pamela could not be insensible to such proofs of attachment, and accordingly received him with considerable kindness; her mother always left the room when he came, and my uncle had as good as made a declaration, by saying one evening, very significantly, "that he believed that he should soon change his condition;" when, some how or other, he began to think he was *doing things in too great a hurry*, and that it was high time to consider; so he considered near a month about it, and there is no saying how much longer he might have spun the thread of his doubts had he not been roused from this state of indecision by the news that his mistress had married an attorney's apprentice whom she had seen the Sunday before at church; where he had excited the applause of the whole congregation by the invincible gravity with which he listened to a Dutch sermon. The young people in the neighbourhood laughed a good deal at my uncle on the occasion, but he only shrugged his shoulders, looked mysterious, and replied, "*Tut, boys! I might have had her.*"

NOTE BY WILLIAM WIZARD, ESQ.

Our publisher, who is busily engaged in printing a celebrated work, which is perhaps more generally read in this city than any other book, not excepting the Bible; —I mean the New York Directory—has begged so hard that we will not overwhelm him with too much of a good thing, that we have, with Langstaff's approbation, cut short the residue of uncle John's amours. In all probability it will be given in ?,ture number, whenever Launcelot is in the humour for it—he is such an odd— num—for fear of another suspension.

NO. XII.—SATURDAY, JUNE 27, 1807.

FROM MY ELBOW-CHAIR.

Some men delight in the study of plants, in the dissection of a leaf, or the contour and complexion of a tulip;—others are charmed with the beauties of the feathered race, or the varied hues of the insect tribe. A naturalist will spend hours in the fatiguing pursuit of a butterfly, and a man of the ton will waste whole years in the chase of a fine lady. I feel a respect for their avocations, for my own are somewhat similar. I love to open the great volume of human character:—to me the examination of a beau is more interesting than that of a Daffodil or Narcissus; and I feel a thousand times more pleasure in catching a new view of human nature, than in kidnapping the most gorgeous butterfly,—even an Emperor of Morocco himself!

In my present situation I have ample room for the indulgence of this taste; for, perhaps, there is not a house in this city more fertile in subjects for the anatomist of human character, than my cousin Cockloft's. Honest Christopher, as I have before mentioned, is one of those hearty old cavaliers who pride themselves upon keeping up the good, honest, unceremonious hospitality of old times.—He is never so happy as when he has drawn about him a knot of sterling-hearted associates, and sits at the head of his table dispensing a warm, cheering welcome to all. His countenance expands at every glass and beams forth emanations of hilarity, benevolence, and good-fellowship, that inspire and gladden every guest around him. It is no wonder, therefore, that such excellent social qualities should attract a host of friends and guests; in fact, my cousin is almost overwhelmed with them; and they all, uniformly, pronounce old Cockloft to be one of the finest old fellows in the world. His wine also always comes in for a good share of their approbation; nor do they forget to do honour to
at

Mrs. Cockloft's cookery, pronouncing it to be modelled after the most approved recipes of Heliogabulus and Mrs. Glasse. The variety of company thus attracted is particularly pleasing to me; for, being considered a privileged person in the family, I can sit in a corner, indulge in my favourite amusement of observation, and retreat to my elbow-chair, like a bee to his hive, whenever I have collected sufficient food for meditation.

Will Wizard is particularly efficient in adding to the stock of originals which frequent our house: for he is one of the most inveterate hunters of oddities I ever knew; and his first care, on making a new acquaintance, is to gallant him to old Cockloft's, where he never fails to receive the freedom of the house in a pinch from his gold box. Will has, without exception, the queerest, most eccentric, and indescribable set of intimates that ever man possessed; how he became acquainted with them I cannot conceive, except by supposing there is a secret attraction or unintelligible sympathy that unconsciously draws together oddities of every soil.

Will's great crony for some time was TOM STRADDLE, to whom he really took a great liking. Straddle had just arrived in an importation of hardware, fresh from the city of Birmingham, or rather, as the most learned English would call it, *Brummagem*, so famous for its manufactories of gimblets, pen-knives, and pepper-boxes; and where they make buttons and beaux enough to inundate our whole country. He was a young man of considerable standing in the manufactory at Birmingham, sometimes had the honour to hand his master's daughter into a tim-whiskey, was the oracle of the tavern he frequented on Sundays, and could beat all his associates, if you would take his word for it, in boxing, beer-drinking, jumping over chairs, and imitating cats in a gutter and opera singers. Straddle was, moreover, a member of a Catch-club, and was a great hand at ringing bob-majors; he was, of course, a complete connoisseur of music, and entitled to assume that character at all performances in the art. He was likewise a member of a Spouting-club, had seen a company of strolling actors perform in a barn, and had even, like Abel Drugger, "enacted" the part of Major Sturgeon with considerable applause; he was consequently a profound critic, and fully authorized to turn up his nose at any American performances.—He had twice partaken of annual dinners, given to the head manufacturers of Birmingham, where he had the good fortune to get a taste of turtle and turbot; and a smack of Champaign and Burgundy; and he had heard a vast deal of the roast beef of Old England; he was therefore epicure sufficient to d——n every dish, and every glass of wine, he tasted in America; though at the same time he was as voracious an animal as ever crossed the Atlantic. Straddle had been splashed half a dozen times by the carriages of nobility, and had once the superlative felicity of being kicked out of doors by the footman of a noble Duke; he could, therefore, talk of nobility and despise the untitled plebeians of America. In short, Straddle was one of those dapper, bustling, florid, round, self-important "*gemmen*" who bounce upon us half beau, half button-maker; undertake to give us the true polish of the *bon-ton*, and endeavour to inspire us with a proper and dignified contempt of our native country.

Straddle was quite in raptures when his employers determined to send him to America as an agent. He considered himself as going among a nation of barbarians, where he would be received as a prodigy; he anticipated, with a proud satisfaction, the bustle and confusion his arrival would occasion; the crowd that would throng to gaze at him as he passed through the streets; and had little doubt but that he should occasion as much curiosity as an Indian-chief or a Turk in the streets of Birmingham. He had heard of the beauty of our women, and chuckled at the thought of how completely he should eclipse their unpolished beaux, and the number of despairing lovers that would mourn the hour of his arrival. I am even informed by Will Wizard that he put good store of beads, spike-nails, and looking-glasses in his trunk to win the affections of the fair ones as they paddled about in their bark canoes;—the reason Will gave for this error of Straddle's, respecting our ladies, was, that he had read in Guthrie's Geography that the aborigines of America were all savages, and not exactly understanding the word aborigines, he applied to one of his fellow apprentices, who assured him that it was the Latin word for inhabitants.

Wizard used to tell another anecdote of Straddle, which always put him in a passion; Will swore that the captain of the ship told him, that when Straddle heard they were off the banks of Newfoundland, he insisted upon going on shore there to gather some good cabbages, of which he was excessively fond; Straddle, however, denied all this, and declared it to be a mischievous *quiz* of Will Wizard; who indeed often made himself merry at his expense. However this may be, certain it is, he kept his tailor and shoemaker constantly employed for a month before his departure; equipped himself with a smart crooked stick about eighteen inches long, a pair of breeches of most unheard-of length, a little short pair of Hoby's white-topped boots, that seemed to stand on tip-toe to reach his breeches, and his hat had the true trans-atlantic declination towards his right ear. The fact was, nor did he make any secret of it—he was determined to "*astonish the natives a few!*"

Straddle was not a little disappointed on his arrival, to find the Americans were rather more civilized than he had imagined;—he was suffered to walk to his lodgings unmolested by a crowd, and even unnoticed by a single individual;—no love-letters came pouring in upon him; no rivals lay in wait to assassinate him; his very dress excited no attention, for there were many fools dressed equally ridiculously with himself. This was mortifying indeed to an aspiring youth, who had come out with the idea of astonishing and captivating. He was equally unfortunate in his pretensions to the character of critic, connoisseur, and boxer; he condemned our whole dramatic corps, and everything appertaining to the theatre; but his critical abilities were ridiculed—he found fault with old Cockloft's dinner, not even sparing his wine, and was never invited to the house afterwards;—he scoured the streets at night, and was cudgelled by a sturdy watchman;—he hoaxed an honest mechanic, and was soundly kicked. Thus disappointed in all his attempts at notoriety, Straddle hit on the expedient which was resorted to by the *Giblets*—he determined to take the town by storm.—He accordingly bought horses and equipages, and forthwith made a furious dash at style in a gig and tandem.

As Straddle's finances were but limited, it may easily be supposed that his fashionable career infringed a little upon his consignment, which was indeed the case, for, to use a true cockney phrase, *Brummagem suffered*. But this was a circumstance that made little impression upon Straddle, who was now a lad of spirit, and lads of spirit always despise the sordid cares of keeping another man's money. Suspecting this circumstance, I never could witness any of his exhibitions of style, without some whimsical association of ideas. Did he give an entertainment to a host of guzzling friends, I immediately fancied them gormandizing heartily at the expense of poor Birmingham, and swallowing a consignment of hand-saws and razors. Did I behold him dashing through Broadway in his gig, I saw him, "in my mind's eye," driving tandem on a nest of tea-boards;

nor could I ever contemplate his cockney exhibitions of horsemanship, but my mischievous imagination would picture him spurring a cask of hardware like rosy Bacchus bestriding a beer barrel, or the little gentleman who bestraddles the world in the front of Hutching's almanac.

Straddle was equally successful with the Giblets, as may well be supposed; for though pedestrian merit may strive in vain to become fashionable in Gotham, yet a candidate in an equipage is always recognized, and like Philip's ass, laden with gold, will gain admittance every where. Mounted in his curricle or his gig, the candidate is like a statue elevated on a high pedestal; his merits are discernible from afar, and strike the dullest optics. Oh! Gotham, Gotham! most enlightened of cities!—how does my heart swell with delight when I behold your sapient inhabitants lavishing their attention with such wonderful discernment!

Thus Straddle became quite a man of ton, and was caressed, and courted, and invited to dinners and balls. Whatever was absurd and ridiculous in him before, was now declared to be the style. He criticised our theatre, and was listened to with reverence. He pronounced our musical entertainments barbarous; and the judgment of Apollo himself would not have been more decisive. He abused our dinners; and the god of eating, if there be any such deity, seemed to speak through his organs. He became at once a man of taste, for he put his malediction on every thing; and his arguments were conclusve, for he supported every assertion with a bet. He was likewise pronounced, by the learned in the fashionable world, a young man of great research and deep observation; for he had sent home, as natural curiosities, an ear of Indian corn, a pair of moccasons, a belt of wampum, and a four-leaved clover. He had taken great pains to enrich this curious collection with an Indian, and a cataract, but without success. In fine, the people talked of Straddle and his equipage, and Straddle talked of his horses, until it was impossible for the most critical observer to pronounce, whether Straddle or his horses were most admired, or whether Straddle admired himself or his horses most.

Straddle was now in the zenith of his glory. He swaggered about parlours and drawing-rooms with the same unceremonious confidence he used to display in the taverns at Birmingham. He accosted a lady as he would a bar-maid, and this was pronounced a certain proof that he had been used to better company in Birmingham. He became the great man of all the taverns between New-York and Harlem, and no one stood a chance of being accommodated, until Straddle and his horses were perfectly satisfied. He d——d the landlords and waiters, with the best air in the world, and accosted them with the true gentlemanly familiarity. He staggered from the dinner table to the play, entered the box like a tempest, and staid long enough to be bored to death, and to bore all those who had the misfortune to be near him. From thence he dashed off to a ball, time enough to flounder through a cotillion, tear half a dozen gowns, commit a number of other depredations, and make the whole company sensible of his infinite condescension in coming amongst them. The people of Gotham thought him a prodigious fine fellow; the young bucks cultivated his acquaintance with the most persevering assiduity, and his retainers were sometimes complimented with a seat in his curricle, or a ride on one of his fine horses. The belles were delighted with the attentions of such a fashionable gentleman, and struck with astonishment at his learned distinctions between wrought scissors and those of cast-steel; together with his profound dissertations on buttons and horse-flesh. The rich merchants courted his acquaintance because he was an Englishman, and their wives treated him with great deference, because he had come from beyond seas. I cannot help here observing, that your salt water is a marvellous great sharpener of men's wits, and I intend to recommend it to some of my acquaintances in a particular essay.

Straddle continued his brilliant career for only a short time. His prosperous journey over the turnpike of fashion was checked by some of those stumbling-blocks in the way of aspiring youth, called creditors—or duns;—a race of people, who, as a celebrated writer observes, "are hated by gods and men." Consignments slackened, whispers of distant suspicion floated in the dark, and those pests of society, the tailors and shoemakers, rose in rebellion against Straddle. In vain were all his remonstrances, in vain did he prove to them that though he had given them no money, yet he had given them more custom, and as many promises, as any young man in the city. They were inflexible, and the signal of danger being given, a host of other prosecutors pounced upon his back. Straddle saw there was but one way for it; he determined to do the thing genteelly, to go to smash like a hero, and dashed into the limits in high style, being the fifteenth gentleman I have known to drive tandem to the—*ne plus ultra*—the d——l.

Unfortunate Straddle! may thy fate be a warning to all young gentlemen who come out from Birmingham to astonish the natives!—I should never have taken the trouble to dilineate his character had he not been a genuine cockney, and worthy to be the representative of his numerous tribe. Perhaps my simple countrymen may hereafter be able to distinguish between the real English gentleman, and individuals of the cast I have heretofore spoken of, as mere mongrels, springing at one bound from contemptible obscurity at home, to day-light and splendour in this good-natured land. The true-born and true-bred English gentleman is a character I hold in great respect; and I love to look back to the period when our forefathers flourished in the same generous soil, and hailed each other as brothers. But the cockney!—when I contemplate him as springing too from the same source, I feel ashamed of the relationship, and am tempted to deny my origin. In the character of Straddle is traced the complete outline of a true cockney, of English growth, and a descendant of that individual facetious character mentioned by Shakspeare, "*who in pure kindness to his horse, buttered his hay.*"

THE STRANGER AT HOME; OR, A TOUR IN BROADWAY.

BY JEREMY COCKLOFT, THE YOUNGER.

PREFACE.

YOUR learned traveller begins his travels at the commencement of his journey; others begin theirs at the end; and a third class begin any how and any where, which I think is the true way. A late facetious writer begins what he calls "a Picture of New York," with a particular description of Glen's Falls, from whence with admirable dexterity he makes a digression to the celebrated Mill Rock, on Long-Island! Now this is what I like; and I intend, in my present tour, to digress as often and as long as I please. If, therefore, I choose to make a hop, skip, and jump, to China, or New-Holland, or Terra Incognita, or Communipaw, I can produce a host of examples to justify me, even in books that have been praised by the English reviewers, whose *fiat* being all that is necessary to give books a currency in this country, I am determined, as soon as I finish my edition of travels in seventy-five volumes, to transmit it forthwith to them for judgment. If these transatlantic censors praise it, I have no fear of its success in this country, where their approbation gives, like the tower stamp, a fictitious value, and makes tinsel and wampum pass current for classic gold.

Chapter I.

BATTERY—flag-staff kept by Louis Keaffee—Keaffee maintains two spy-glasses by subscriptions—merchants pay two shillings a-year to look through them at the signal poles on Staten-Island—a very pleasant prospect; but not so pleasant as that from the hill of Howth—quere, ever been there?—Young seniors go down to the flag-staff to buy peanuts and beer, after the fatigue of their morning studies, and sometimes to play at ball, or some other innocent amusement—digression to the Olympic, and Isthmian games, with a description of the Isthmus of Corinth, and that of Darien: to conclude with a dissertation on the Indian custom of offering a whiff of tobacco smoke to their great spirit, Areskou.—Return to the battery—delightful place to indulge in the luxury of sentiment—How various are the mutations of this world! but a few days, a few hours—at least not above two hundred years ago, and this spot was inhabited by a race of aborigines, who dwelt in bark huts, lived upon oysters and Indian corn, danced buffalo dances, and were lords "of the fowl and the brute"—but the spirit of time and the spirit of brandy have swept them from their ancient inheritance; and as the white wave of the ocean, by its ever toiling assiduity, gains on the brown land, so the white man, by slow and sure degrees, has gained on the brown savage, and dispossessed him of the land of his forefathers.—Conjectures on the first peopling of America—different opinions on that subject, to the amount of near one hundred—opinion of Augustine Torniel—that they are the descendants of Shem and Japheth, who came by the way of Japan to America—Juffridius Petri says they came from Friezeland, mem. cold journey.—Mons. Charron says they are descended from the Gauls—bitter enough.—A. Milius, from the Celtæ—Kircher, from the Egyptians—L'Compte, from the Phenicians

—Lescarbot, from the Canaanites, alias the Anthropophagi—Brerewood from the Tartars—Grotius, from the Norwegians—and Linkum Fidelius has written two folio volumes to prove that America was first of all peopled either by the Antipodeans or the Cornish miners, who, he maintains, might easily have made a subterraneous passage to this country, particularly the antipodeans, who, he asserts, can get along under ground as fast as moles—quere,'which of these is in the right, or are they all wrong?—For my part, I don't see why America had not as good a right to be peopled at first, as any little contemptible country in Europe, or Asia, and I am determined to write a book at my first leisure, to prove that Noah was born here—and that so far is America from being indebted to any other country for inhabitants, that they were every one of them peopled by colonies from her!—mem. battery a very pleasant place to walk on a Sunday evening—not quite genteel though—everybody walks there, and a pleasure, however genuine, is spoiled by general participation—the fashionable ladies of New-York turn up their noses if you ask them to walk on the battery on Sunday—quere, have they scruples of conscience, or scruples of delicacy?—neither—they have only scruples of gentility, which are quite different things.

Chapter II.

Custom-house—origin of duties on merchandise—this place much frequented by merchants—and why?—different classes of merchants—importers—a kind of nobility—wholesale merchants—have the privilege of going to the city assembly!—Retail traders cannot go to the assembly.—Some curious speculations on the vast distinction betwixt selling tape by the piece or by the yard.—Wholesale merchants look down upon the retailers, who in return look down upon the green-grocers, who look down upon the market women, who don't care a straw about any of them.—Origin of the distinctions of rank—Dr. Johnson once horribly puzzled to settle the point of precedence between a louse and a flea—good hint enough to humble, purse-proud arrogance.—Custom-house partly used as a lodging house for the pictures belonging to the academy of arts—couldn't afford the statues house-room, most of them in the cellar of the City-hall—poor place for the gods and goddesses—after Olympus.—Pensive reflections on the ups and downs of life—Apollo, and the rest of the set, used to cut a great figure in days of yore.—Mem. every dog has his day—sorry for Venus, though, poor wench, to be cooped up in a cellar with not a single grace to wait on her!—Eulogy on the gentlemen of the academy of arts, for the great spirit with which they began the undertaking, and the perseverance with which they have pursued it.—It is a pity, however, they began at the wrong end—maxim—If you want a bird and a cage, always buy the cage first—hem! a word to the wise?

Chapter III.

BOWLING-GREEN—fine place for pasturing cows—a perquisite of the late corporation—formerly ornamented with a statue of George the 3d—people pulled it down in the war to make bullets—great pity, as it might have been given to the academy—it would have become a cellar as well as any other. —Broadway—great difference in the gentility of streets—a man who resides in Pearl-street or Chatham-row, derives no kind of dignity from his domicil; but place him in a certain part of Broadway, any where between the battery and Wall-street, and he straightway becomes entitled to figure in the beau monde, and strut as a person of prodigious consequence!—Quere, whether there is a degree of purity in the air of that quarter which changes the gross particles of vulgarity into gems of refinement and polish?—A question to be asked, but not to be answered—Wall-street—City-hall, famous place for catchpoles, deputy-sheriffs, and young lawyers; which last attend the courts, not because they have business there but because they have no business any where else. My blood always curdles when I see a catch-pole, they being a species of vermin, who feed and fatten on the common wretchedness of mankind, who trade in misery, and in becoming the executioners of the law, by their oppression and villainy, almost counterbalance all the benefits which are derived from its salutary regulations —Story of Quevedo about a catch-pole possessed by a devil, who, on being interrogated, declared that he did not come there voluntarily, but by compulsion; and that a decent devil would never, of his own free will enter into the body of a catch-pole; instead, therefore, of doing him the injustice to say that here was a catch-pole be-deviled, they should say, it was a devil be-catch-poled; that being in reality the truth—

Wonder what has become of the old crier of the court, who used to make more noise in preserving silence than the audience did in breaking it—if a man happened to drop his cane, the old hero would sing out "silence!" in a voice that emulated the "wide-mouthed thunder"—On inquiring, found he had retired from business to enjoy *otium cum dignitate*, as many a great man had done before—Strange that wise men, as they are thought, should toil through a whole existence merely to enjoy a few moments of leisure at last!—why don't they begin to be easy at first, and not purchase a moment's pleasure with an age of pain?—mem. posed some of the jockeys—eh!

CHAPTER IV.

BARBER'S pole; three different orders of *shavers* in New York—those who shave *pigs;* N. B.—freshmen and sophomores, —those who cut beards, and those who *shave notes of hand;* the last are the most respectable, because, in the course of a year, they make more money, and that *honestly*, than the whole corps of other *shavers* can do in half a century; besides, it would puzzle a common barber to ruin any man, except by cutting his throat; whereas your higher order of *shavers*, your true blood-suckers of the community, seated snugly behind the curtain, in watch for prey, live on the vitals of the unfortunate, and grow rich on the ruins of thousands.—Yet this last class of *barbers* are held in high respect in the world; they never offend against the decencies of life, go often to church, look down on honest poverty walking on foot, and call themselves gentlemen; yea, men of honour!—Lottery offices— another set of capital shavers!—licensed gambling houses!— good things enough though, as they enable a few *honest, industrious gentlemen* to humbug the people—according to law; —besides, if the people will be such fools, whose fault is it but their own if they get *bit?*—Messrs. Paff—beg pardon for putting them in bad company, because they are a couple of fine fellows —mem. to recommend Michael's antique snuff box to all amateurs *in the art.*—Eagle singing Yankee-doodle—N. B.—Buffon, Penant, and the rest of the naturalists, all *naturals* not to know the eagle was a singing bird; Linkum Fidelius knew better, and gives a long description of a bald eagle that serenaded him once in Canada;—digression: particular account of the Canadian Indians;—story about Areskou learning to make fishing nets of a spider—don't believe it though, because, according to Linkum, and many other learned authorities, Areskou is the same as *Mars*, being derived from his Greek names of *Ares;* and if so, he knew well enough what a *net* was without consulting a spider;—story of Arachne being changed into a spider as a reward for having hanged herself;—derivation of the word spinster from spider;—Colophon, now Altobosco, the birthplace of Arachne, remarkable for a famous breed of spiders to this day;—mem.—nothing like a little scholarship—make the *ignoramus*, viz., the majority of my readers, stare like wild pigeons;—return to New-York a short cut—meet a dashing belle, in a little thick white veil—tried to get a peep at her face—saw she squinted a little—thought so at first; —never saw a face covered with a veil that was worth looking at;—saw some ladies holding a conversation across the street about going to church next Sunday—talked so loud they frightened a cartman's horse, who ran away, and overset a basket of gingerbread with a little boy under it;—mem.—I don't much see the use of speaking-trumpets now-a-days.

Chapter V.

Bought a pair of gloves; dry-good stores the genuine schools of politeness—true Parisian manners there--got a pair of gloves and a pistareen's worth of bows for a dollar—dog cheap! —Courtlandt-street corner—famous place to see the belles go by —quere, ever been shopping with a lady?—some account of it— ladies go into all the shops in the city to buy a pair of gloves— good way of spending time, if they have nothing else to do.— Oswego-market—looks very much like a triumphal arch—some account of the manner of erecting them in ancient times;—digression to the *arch*-duke Charles, and some account of the ancient Germans.—N. B.—quote Tacitus on this subject.—Particular description of market-baskets, butcher's blocks, and wheelbarrows;—mem. queer things run upon one wheel!—Saw a cart-man driving full-tilt through Broadway—ran over a child—good enough for it—what business had it to be in the way?—Hint concerning the laws against pigs, goats, dogs, and cartmen—grand apostrophe to the sublime science of jurisprudence;—comparison between legislators and tinkers; quere, whether it requires greater ability to mend a law than to mend a kettle?—inquiry into the utility of making laws that are broken a hundred times a day with impunity;—my lord Coke's opinion on the subject;—my lord a very great man—so was lord Bacon: good story about a criminal named Hog claiming relationship with him.—Hogg's porter-house;—great haunt of Will Wizard; Will put down there one night by a sea-captain, in an argument concerning the era of the Chinese empire Whangpo;—Hogg's capital place for hearing the same stories, the same jokes, and the same songs every night in the year—mem. except Sunday nights; fine school for young politicians too—some of the longest and thickest heads in the city come there to settle the nation.—Scheme of *Ichabod Fungus* to restore the balance of Europe;—digression;—some account of the balance of Europe; comparison between it and a pair of scales, with the Emperor Alexander in one and the Emperor Napoleon in the other: fine fellows—both of a weight, can't tell which will kick the beam:—mem. don't care much either—nothing to me:—*Ichabod* very unhappy about it—thinks Napoleon has an eye on this country—capital place to pasture his horses, and provide for the rest of his family:—Dey-street—ancient Dutch name of it, signifying murderers' valley, formerly the site of a great peach orchard; my grandmother's history of the famous *Peach war*—arose from an Indian stealing peaches out of this orchard; good cause as need be for a war; just as good as the balance of power. Anecdote of a war between two Italian states about a bucket; introduce some capital new truisms about the folly of mankind, the ambition of kings, potentates, and princes; particularly Alexander, Cæsar, Charles the XIIth, Napoleon, little King Pepin, and the great Charlemagne.—Conclude with an exhortation to the present race of sovereigns to keep the king's peace and abstain from all those deadly quarrels which produce battle, murder, and sudden death: mem. ran my nose against a lamp-post—conclude in great dudgeon.

FROM MY ELBOW-CHAIR.

OUR cousin Pindar, after having been confined for some time past with a fit of the gout, which is a kind of keepsake in our family, has again set his mill going, as my readers will perceive. On reading his piece I could not help smiling at the high compliments which, contrary to his usual style, he has lavished on the dear sex. The old gentleman, unfortunately observing my merriment, stumped out of the room with great vociferation of crutch, and has not exchanged three words with me since. I expect every hour to hear that he has packed up his movables, and, as usual in all cases of disgust, retreated to his old country house.

Pindar, like most of the old Cockloft heroes, is wonderfully susceptible to the genial influence of warm weather. In winter he is one of the most crusty old bachelors under heaven, and is wickedly addicted to sarcastic reflections of every kind; particularly on the little enchanting foibles and whim-whams of women. But when the spring comes on, and the mild influence of the sun releases nature from her icy fetters, the ice of his bosom dissolves into a gentle current which reflects the bewitching qualities of the fair; as in some mild clear evening, when nature reposes in silence, the stream bears in its pure bosom all the starry magnificence of heaven. It is under the control of this influence he has written his piece; and I beg the ladies, in the plenitude of their harmless conceit, not to flatter themselves that because the good Pindar has suffered them to escape his censures he had nothing more to censure. It is but sunshine and zephyrs which have wrought this wonderful change; and I am much mistaken if the first north-easter don't convert all his good nature into most exquisite spleen.

FROM THE MILL OF PINDAR COCKLOFT, ESQ.

How often I cast my reflections behind,
And call up the days of past youth to my mind,
When folly assails in habiliments new,
When fashion obtrudes some fresh whim-wham to view;
When the foplings of fashion bedazzle my sight,
Bewilder my feelings—my senses benight;
I retreat in disgust from the world of to-day,
To commune with the world that has moulder'd away;
To converse with the shades of those friends of my love,
Long gather'd in peace to the angels above.
In my rambles through life should I meet with annoy,
From the bold beardless stripling—the turbid pert boy,
One rear'd in the mode lately reckon'd genteel,
Which neglecting the head, aims to perfect the heel;

Which completes the sweet fopling while yet in his teens,
And fits him for fashion's light changeable scenes;
Proclaims him a man to the near and the far,
Can he dance a cotillion or smoke a segar;
And though brainless and vapid as vapid can be,
To routs and to parties pronounces him free:—
Oh, I think on the beaux that existed of yore,
On those rules of the *ton* that exist now no more!
   I recall with delight how each yonker at first
In the cradle of science and virtue was nursed:
—How the graces of person and graces of mind,
The polish of learning and fashion combined,
Till softened in manners and strengthened in head,
By the classical lore of the living and dead,
Matured in his person till manly in size,
He *then* was presented a beau to our eyes!
   My nieces of late have made frequent complaint
That they suffer vexation and painful constraint
By having their circles too often distrest
By some three or four goslings just fledged from the nest,
Who, propp'd by the credit their fathers sustain,
Alike tender in years and in person and brain,
But plenteously stock'd with that substitute, brass,
For true wits and critics would anxiously pass.
They complain of that empty sarcastical slang,
So common to all the coxcombical gang,
Who the fair with their shallow experience vex,
By thrumming for ever their weakness of sex;
And who boast of themselves, when they talk with proud air
Of Man's mental ascendancy over the fair.
   'Twas thus the young owlet produced in the nest,
Where the eagle of Jove her young eaglets had prest,
Pretended to boast of his royal descent,
And vaunted that force which to eagles is lent.
Though fated to shun with his dim visual ray,
The cheering delights and the brilliance of day;
To forsake the fair regions of æther and light,
For dull moping caverns of darkness and night:
Still talk'd of that eagle-like strength of the eye,
Which approaches unwinking the pride of the sky,
Of that wing which unwearied can hover and play
In the noon-tide effulgence and torrent of day.

Dear girls, the sad evils of which ye complain,
Your sex must endure from the feeble and vain,
'Tis the commonplace jest of the nursery scape-goat,
'Tis the commonplace ballad that croaks from his throat;
He knows not that nature—that polish decrees,
That women should always endeavour to please.
That the law of their system has early imprest
The importance of fitting themselves to each guest;
And, of course, that full oft when ye trifle and play,
'Tis to gratify triflers who strut in your way.
The child might as well of its mother complain,
As wanting true wisdom and soundness of brain:
Because that, at times, while it hangs on her breast,
She with "lulla-by-baby" beguiles it to rest.
'Tis its weakness of mind that induces the strain,
For wisdom to infants is prattled in vain.
 'Tis true at odd times, when in frolicsome fit,
In the midst of his gambols, the mischievous wit
May start some light foible that clings to the fair
Like cobwebs that fasten to objects most rare,—
In the play of his fancy will sportively say
Some delicate censure that pops in his way,
He may smile at your fashions, and frankly express
His dislike of a dance, or a flaming red dress;
Yet he blames not your want of man's physical force,
Nor complains though ye cannot in Latin discourse.
He delights in the language of nature ye speak,
Though not so refined as true classical Greek.
He remembers that Providence never design'd
Our females like suns to bewilder and blind;
But like the mild orb of pale ev'ning serene,
Whose radiance illumines, yet softens the scene,
To light us with cheering and welcoming ray,
Along the rude path when the sun is away.
 I own in my scribblings I lately have nam'd
Some faults of our fair which I gently have blam'd,
But be it for ever by all understood
My censures were only pronounc'd for their good.
I delight in the sex, 'tis the pride of my mind
To consider them gentle, endearing, refin'd;
As our solace below in the journey of life,
To smooth its rough passes;—to soften its strife:

As objects intended our joys to supply,
And to lead us in love to the temples on high.
How oft have I felt, when two lucid blue eyes,
As calm and as bright as the gems of the skies,
Have beam'd their soft radiance into my soul,
Impress'd with an awe like an angel's control!
   Yes, fair ones, by this is for ever defin'd
The fop from the man of refinement and mind;
The latter believes ye in bounty were given
As a bond upon earth of our union with heaven:
And if ye are weak, and are frail, in his view,
'Tis to call forth fresh warmth and his fondness renew.
'Tis his joy to support these defects of your frame,
And his love at your weakness redoubles its flame:
He rejoices the gem is so rich and so fair,
And is proud that it claims his protection and care.

NO. XIII.—FRIDAY, AUGUST 14, 1807.

FROM MY ELBOW-CHAIR.

I WAS not a little perplexed, a short time since, by the eccentric conduct of my knowing coadjutor, Will Wizard. For two or three days, he was completely in a quandary. He would come into old Cockloft's parlour ten times a day, swinging his ponderous legs along with his usual vast strides, clap his hands into his sides, contemplate the little shepherdesses on the mantel-piece for a few minutes, whistling all the while, and then sally out full sweep, without uttering a word. To be sure, a pish or a pshaw occasionally escaped him; and he was observed once to pull out his enormous tobacco-box, drum for a moment upon its lid with his knuckles, and then return it into his pocket without taking a quid:—'twas evident Will was full of some mighty idea:—not that his restlessness was any way uncommon; for I have often seen Will throw himself almost into a fever of heat and fatigue—doing nothing. But his inflexible taciturnity set the whole family, as usual a wondering: as Will seldom enters the house without giving one of his "one thousand and one" stories. For my part, I began to think that the late *fracas* at Canton had alarmed Will for the safety of his friends Kinglun, Chinqua, and Consequa; or, that something had gone wrong in the alterations of the theatre—or that some new outrage at Norfolk had put him in a orry; in short, I did not know what to think; for Will is such an universal busy-body, and meddles so much in every thing going forward, that you might as well attempt to conjecture what is going on in the north star, as in his precious pericranium. Even Mrs. Cockloft, who, like a worthy woman as she is, seldom troubles herself about any thing in this world —saving the affairs of her household, and the correct deportment of her female friends—was struck with the mystery of

Will's behaviour. She happened, when he came in and went out the tenth time, to be busy darning the bottom of one of the old red damask chairs; and notwithstanding this is to her an affair of vast importance, yet she could not help turning round and exclaiming, "I wonder what can be the matter with Mr. Wizard?" "Nothing," replied old Christopher, "only we shall have an eruption soon." The old lady did not understand a word of this, neither did she care; she had expressed her wonder; and that, with her, is always sufficient.

I am so well acquainted with Will's peculiarities that I can tell, even by his whistle, when he is about an essay for our paper as certainly as a weather wiseacre knows that it is going to rain when he sees a pig run squeaking about with his nose in the wind. I, therefore, laid my account with receiving a communication from him before long; and sure enough, the evening before last I distinguished his free-mason knock at my door. I have seen many wise men in my time, philosophers, mathematicians, astronomers, politicians, editors and almanac makers; but never did I see a man look half so wise as did my friend Wizard on entering the room. Had Lavater beheld him at that moment he would have set him down, to a certainty, as a fellow who had just discovered the longitude or the philosopher's stone.

Without saying a word, he handed me a roll of paper; after which he lighted his segar, sat down, crossed his legs, folded his arms, and elevating his nose to an angle of about forty-five degrees, began to smoke like a steam engine;—Will delights in the picturesque. On opening his budget, and perceiving the motto, it struck me that Will had brought me one of his confounded Chinese manuscripts, and I was forthwith going to dismiss it with indignation; but accidentally seeing the name of our oracle, the sage Linkum, of whose inestimable folios we pride ourselves upon being the sole possessors, I began to think the better of it, and looked round to Will to express my approbation. I shall never forget the figure he cut at that moment! He had watched my countenance, on opening his manuscript, with the argus eyes of an author: and perceiving some tokens of disapprobation, began, according to custom, to puff away at his segar with such vigour that in a few minutes he had entirely involved himself in smoke: except his nose and one foot, which were just visible, the latter wagging with great velocity. I believe I have hinted before—at least I ought to have done so—that Will's nose is a very goodly nose; to which it may be as well to add, that in his voyages under the tropics, it has acquired a copper complexion, which renders it very brilliant and luminous. You may imagine what a sumptuous appearance it made, projecting boldly, like the celebrated *promontorium nasidium* at Samos with a light-house upon it, and surrounded on all sides with smoke and vapour. Had my gravity been like the Chinese philosopher's "within one degree of absolute frigidity," here would have been a trial for it.—I could not stand it, but burst into such a laugh as I do not indulge in above once in a hundred years;—this was too much for Will; he emerged from his cloud, threw his segar into the fire-place, and strode out of the room, pulling up his breeches, muttering something which, I verily believe, was nothing more than a horrible long Chinese malediction.

He, however, left his manuscript behind him, which I now give to the world. Whether he is serious on the occasion, or only bantering, no one, I believe, can tell: for, whether in speaking or writing, there is such an invincible gravity in his demeanour and style, that even I, who have studied him as closely as an antiquarian studies an old manuscript or inscription, am frequently at a loss to know what the rogue would be at. I have seen him indulge in his favourite amusement of quizzing for hours together, without any one having the least suspicion of the matter, until he would suddenly twist his phiz into an expression that baffles all description, thrust his tongue in his cheek and blow up in a laugh almost as loud as the shout of the Romans on a certain occasion; which honest Plutarch avers frightened several crows to such a degree that they fell down stone dead into the Campus Martius. Jeremy Cockloft the younger, who like a true modern philosopher delights in experiments that are of no kind of use, took the trouble to measure one of Will's risible explosions, and declared to me that, according to accurate measurement, it contained thirty feet square of solid laughter:—what will the professors say to this?

PLANS FOR DEFENDING OUR HARBOUR.

BY WILLIAM WIZARD, ESQ.

Long-fong teko buzz tor-pe-do,
Fudge———— —*Confucius.*
We'll blow the villains all sky high;
But do it with econo————my. —*Link. Fid.*

SURELY never was a town more subject to mid-summer fancies and dog-day whim-whams, than this most excellent of cities;—our notions, like our diseases, seem all epidemic; and no sooner does a new disorder or a new freak seize one individual but it is sure to run through all the community. This is particularly the case when the summer is at the hottest, and every body's head is in a vertigo and his brain in a ferment; 'tis absolutely necessary then the poor souls should have some bubble to amuse themselves with, or they would certainly run mad. Last year the poplar worm made its appearance most fortunately for our citizens; and every body was so much in horror of being poisoned, and devoured; and so busied in making humane experiments on cats and dogs, that we got through the summer quite comfortably;—the cats had the worst of it; —every mouser of them was shaved, and there was not a whisker to be seen in the whole sisterhood. This summer every body has had full employment in planning fortifications for our harbour. Not a cobbler or tailor in the city but has left his awl and his thimble, become an engineer outright, and aspired most magnanimously to the building of forts and destruction of navies!—heavens! as my friend Mustapha would say, on what a great scale is every thing in this country!

Among the various plans that have been offered, the most conspicuous is one devised and exhibited, as I am informed, by that notable confederacy, THE NORTH RIVER SOCIETY.

Anxious to redeem their reputation from the foul suspicions that have for a long time overclouded it, these aquatic incendiaries have come forward, at the present alarming juncture, and announced a most potent discovery which is to guarantee our port from the visits of any foreign marauders. The society have, it seems, invented a cunning machine, shrewdly yclep'd a *Torpedo;* by which the stoutest line of battle ship, even a

Santissima Trinidada, may be caught napping and decomposed in a twinkling; a kind of sub-marine powder-magazine to swim under water, like an aquatic mole, or water rat, and destroy the enemy in the moments of unsuspicious security.

This straw tickled the noses of all our dignitaries wonderfully; for to do our government justice, it has no objection to injuring and exterminating its enemies in any manner—provided the thing can be done economically.

It was determined the experiment should be tried, and an old brig was purchased, for not more than twice its value, and delivered over into the hands of its tormentors, the North River Society, to be tortured, and battered, and annihilated, *secundum artem*. A day was appointed for the occasion, when all the good citizens of the wonder-loving city of Gotham were invited to the blowing up; like the fat inn-keeper in Rabelais, who requested all his customers to come on a certain day and see him burst.

As I have almost as great a veneration as the good Mr. Walter Shandy for all kinds of experiments that are ingeniously ridiculous, I made very particular mention of the one in question, at the table of my friend Christopher Cockloft; but it put the honest old gentleman in a violent passion. He condemned it in toto, as an attempt to introduce a dastardly and exterminating mode of warfare. "Already have we proceeded far enough," said he, "in the science of destruction; war is already invested with sufficient horrors and calamities, let us not increase the catalogue; let us not by these deadly artifices provoke a system of insidious and indiscriminate hostility, that shall terminate in laying our cities desolate, and exposing our women, our children, and our infirm to the sword of pitiless recrimination." Honest old cavalier!—it was evident he did not reason as a true politician,—but he felt as a Christian and philanthropist; and that was, perhaps, just as well.

It may be readily supposed, that our citizens did not refuse the invitation of the society to the blow-up; it was the first naval action ever exhibited in our port, and the good people all crowded to see the British navy blown up in effigy. The young ladies were delighted with the novelty of the show, and declared that if war could be conducted in this manner, it would become a fashionable amusement; and the destruction of a fleet be as pleasant as a ball or a tea-party. The old folk were equally pleased with the spectacle,—because it cost them nothing. Dear souls, how hard was it they should be disappointed!

the brig most obstinately refused to be decomposed; the dinners grew cold, and the puddings were over-boiled, throughout the renowned city of Gotham: and its sapient inhabitants, like the honest Strasburghers, from whom most of them are doubtless descended, who went out to see the courteous stranger and his nose, all returned home after having threatened to pull down the flag-staff by way of taking satisfaction for their disappointment. By the way, their is not an animal in the world more discriminating in its vengeance than a free-born mob.

In the evening I repaired to friend Hogg's to smoke a sociable segar, but had scarcely entered the room when I was taken prisoner by my friend, Mr. Ichabod Fungus; who, I soon saw was at his usual trade of prying into mill-stones. The old gentleman informed me, that the brig had actually blown up, after a world of manœuvring, and had nearly blown up the society with it; he seemed to entertain strong doubts as to the objects of the society in the invention of these infernal machines;—hinted a suspicion of their wishing to set the river on fire, and that he should not be surprised on waking one of these mornings to find the Hudson in a blaze. "Not that I disapprove of the plan," said he, "provided it has the end in view which they profess; no, no, an excellent plan of defence; —no need of batteries, forts, frigates, and gun-boats; observe, sir, all that's necessary is that the ships must come to anchor in a convenient place;—watch must be asleep, or so complacent as not to disturb any boats paddling about them—fair wind and tide—no moonlight—machines well-directed—musn't flash in the plan—bang's the word, and the vessel's blown up in a moment!" "Good," said I, "you remind me of a lubberly Chinese who was flogged by an honest captain of my acquaintance, and who, on being advised to retaliate, exclaimed—'Hi yah! s'pose two men hold fast him captain, den very mush me bamboo he!'"

The old gentleman grew a little crusty, and insisted that I did not understand him;—all that was requisite to render the effect certain was, that the enemy should enter into the project; or, in other words, be agreeable to the measure; so that if the machine did not come to the ship, the ship should go to the machine; by which means he thought the success of the machine would be inevitable—provided it struck fire. "But do not you think," said I, doubtingly, "that it would be rather difficult to persuade the enemy into such an agreement?—Some people have an invincible antipathy to being blown up." "Not at all, not at all," replied he, triumphantly; "got an excellent notion for that;—do with them as we have done with the brig; buy all the vessels we mean to destroy, and blow 'em up as best suits our convenience. I have thought deeply on that subject and have calculated to a certainty, that if our funds hold out we may in this way destroy the whole British navy—by contract."

By this time all the quidnuncs of the room had gathered around us, each pregnant with some mighty scheme for the salvation of his country.—One pathetically lamented that we had no such men among us as the famous Toujoursdort and Grossitout; who, when the celebrated captain Tranchemont made war against the city of Kalacahabalaba, utterly discomfited the great king Bigstaff, and blew up his whole army by sneezing.—Another imparted a sage idea, which seems to have occupied more heads than one; that is, that the best way of fortifying the harbour was to ruin it at once; choke the channel with rocks and blocks; strew it with *chevaux-de-frises* and torpedoes; and make it like a nursery-garden, full of men-traps and spring-guns. No vessel would then have the temerity to enter our harbour; we should not even dare to navigate it ourselves. Or if no cheaper way could be devised, let Governor's Island be raised by levers and pulleys—floated with empty casks, &c., towed down to the Narrows, and dropped plump in the very mouth of the harbour!—"But," said I, "would not the prosecution of these whim-whams be rather expensive and dilatory?"——"Pshaw!" cried the other—"what's a million of money to an experiment; the true spirit of our economy requires that we should spare no expense in discovering the cheapest mode of defending ourselves; and then if all these modes should fail, why, you know the worst we have to do is to return to the old-fashioned hum-drum mode of forts and batteries." "By which time," cried I, "the arrival of the enemy may have rendered their erection superfluous."

A shrewd old gentleman, who stood listening by, with a mischievously equivocal look, observed that the most effectual mode of repulsing a fleet from our ports would be to administer them a proclamation from time to time, till it operated.

Unwilling to leave the company without demonstrating my patriotism and ingenuity, I communicated a plan of defence; which, in truth, was suggested long since by that infallible oracle MUSTAPHA, who had as clear a head for cobweb-weaving as ever dignified the shoulders of a projector. He thought the most effectual mode would be to assemble all the *slang-whangers*, great and small, from all parts of the state, and marshal them at the battery; where they should be exposed, point blank, to the enemy, and form a tremendous body of scolding infantry; similar to the *poissards* or doughty champions of Billingsgate. They should be exhorted to fire away, without pity or remorse, in sheets, half-sheets, columns, hand-bills, or squibs; great canon, little canon, pica, german-text, stereotype, and to run their enemies through and through with sharp-pointed italics. They should have orders to show no quarter—to blaze away in their loadest epithets——"*miscreants!*" "*murderers!*" "*barbarians!*" "*pirates!*" "*robbers!*" "BLACKGUARDS!" and to do away all fear of consequences, they should be guaranteed from all dangers of pillory, kicking, cuffing, nose-pulling, whipping-post, or prosecution for libels. If, continued Mustapha, you wish men to fight well and valiantly, they must be allowed those weapons they have been used to handle. Your countrymen are notoriously adroit in the management of the tongue and the pen, and conduct all their battles by speeches or newspapers. Adopt, therefore, the plan I have pointed out; and rely upon it that let any fleet, however large, be but once assailed by this battery of slang-whangers, and if they have not entirely lost the sense of hearing, or a regard for their own characters and feelings, they will, at the very first fire, slip their cables and retreat with as much precipitation as if they had unwarily entered into the atmosphere of the *Bohan upas*. In this manner may your wars be conducted with proper economy; and it will cost no more to drive off a fleet than to write up a party, or write down a bashaw with three tails.

 The sly old gentleman, I have before mentioned, was highly delighted with this plan; and proposed, as an improvement, that mortars should be placed on the battery, which, instead of throwing shells and such trifles, might be charged with newspapers, Tammany addresses, etc., by way of red-hot shot, which would undoubtedly be very potent in blowing up any powder-magazine they might chance to come in contact with. He concluded by informing the company, that in the course of a few evenings he would have the honour to present them with a scheme for loading certain vessels with newspapers, resolutions of "numerous and respectable meetings," and other combustibles, which vessels were to be blown directly in the midst of the enemy by the bellows of the slang-whangers; and he was much mistaken if they would not be more fatal than fire-ships, bomb-ketches, gun-boats, or even torpedoes.

These are but two or three specimens of the nature and efficacy of the innumerable plans with which this city abounds. Every body seems charged to the muzzle with gunpowder,—every eye flashes fireworks and torpedoes, and every corner is occupied by knots of inflammatory projectors; not one of whom but has some preposterous mode of destruction which he has proved to be infallible by a previous experiment in a tub of water!

Even Jeremy Cockloft has caught the infection, to the great annoyance of the inhabitants of Cockloft-hall, whither he retired to make his experiments undisturbed. At one time all the mirrors in the house were unhung,—their collected rays thrown into the hot-house, to try Archimedes' plan of burning glasses; and the honest old gardener was almost knocked down by what he mistook for a stroke of the sun, but which turned out to be nothing more than a sudden attack of one of these tremendous jack-o'-lanterns. It became dangerous to walk through the court-yard for fear of an explosion; and the whole family was thrown into absolute distress and consternation by a letter from the old housekeeper to Mrs. Cockloft; informing her of his having blown up a favourite Chinese gander, which I had brought from Canton, as he was majestically sailing in the duck-pond.

"In the multitude of counsellors there is safety;"—if so, the defenceless city of Gotham has nothing to apprehend;—but much do I fear that so many excellent and infallible projects will be presented, that we shall be at a loss which to adopt; and the peaceable inhabitants fare like a famous projector of my acquaintance, whose house was unfortunately plundered while he was contriving a patent lock to secure his door.

FROM MY ELBOW-CHAIR.

A RETROSPECT; OR, "WHAT YOU WILL."

LOLLING in my elbow-chair this fine summer noon, I feel myself insensibly yielding to that genial feeling of indolence the season is so well fitted to inspire. Every one who is blessed with a little of the delicious languor of disposition that delights in repose, must often have sported among the fairy scenes, the golden visions, the voluptuous reveries, that swim before the imagination at such moments, and which so much resemble those blissful sensations a Mussulman enjoys after his favourite indulgence of opium, which Will Wizard declares can be compared to nothing but "swimming in an ocean of peacocks' feathers. In such a mood, every body must be insensible it would be idle and unprofitable for a man to send his wits a-gadding on a voyage of discovery into futurity; or even to trouble himself with a laborious investigation of what is actually passing under his eye. We are at such times more disposed to resort to the pleasures of memory than to those of the imagination; and, like the wayfaring traveller, reclining for a moment on his staff, had rather contemplate the ground we have travelled, than the region which is yet before us.

I could here amuse myself and stultify my readers with a most elaborate and ingenious parallel between authors and travellers; but in this balmy season which makes men stupid and dogs mad, and when doubtless many of our most strenuous admirers have great difficulty in keeping awake through the day, it would be cruel to saddle them with the formidable difficulty of putting two ideas together and drawing a conclusion; or in the learned phrase, forging *syllogisms in Baroco:*—a terrible undertaking for the dog days! to say the truth, my observations were only intended to prove that this, of all others, is the most auspicious moment, and my present, the most favourable mood for indulging in a restrospect. Whether, like certain great personages of the day, in attempting to prove one thing, I have exposed another; or whether, like certain other great personages, in attempting to prove a great deal, I have proved nothing at all, I leave to my readers to decide; provided they have the power and inclination so to do; but a RETROSPECT will I take notwithstanding.

I am perfectly aware that in doing this I shall lay myself open to the charge of imitation, than which a man might be better accused of downright house-breaking; for it has been a standing rule with many of my illustrious predecessors, occasionally, and particularly at the conclusion of a volume, to look over their shoulder and chuckle at the miracles they had achieved. But as I before professed, I am determined to hold myself entirely independent of all manner of opinions and criticisms as the only method of getting on in this world in any thing like a straight line. True it is, I may sometimes seem to angle a little for the good opinion of mankind by giving them some excellent reasons for doing unreasonable things; but this is merely to show them, that although I may occasionally go wrong, it is not for want of knowing how to go right; and here I will lay down a maxim, which will for ever entitle me to the gratitude of my inexperienced readers, namely, that a man always gets more credit in the eyes of this naughty world for sinning wilfully, than for sinning through sheer ignorance.

It will doubtless be insisted by many ingenious cavillers, who will be meddling with what does not at all concern them, that this retrospect should have been taken at the commencement of our second volume; it is usual, I know: moreover, it is natural. So soon as a writer has once accomplished a volume, he forthwith becomes wonderfully increased in altitude! he steps upon his book as upon a pedestal, and is elevated in proportion to its magnitude. A duodecimo makes him one inch taller; an octavo, three inches, a quarto, six:—but he who has made out to swell a folio, looks down upon his fellow-creatures from such a fearful height that, ten to one, the poor man's head is turned for ever afterwards. From such a lofty situation, therefore, it is natural an author should cast his eyes behind; and having reached the first landing place on the stairs of immortality, may reasonably be allowed to plead his privilege to look back over the height he has ascended. I have deviated a little from this venerable custom, merely that our retrospect might fall in the dog days—of all days in the year most congenial to the indulgence of a little self-sufficiency; inasmuch as people have then little to do but to retire within the sphere of self, and make the most of what they find there.

Let it not be supposed, however, that we think ourselves a whit the wiser or better since we have finished our volume than we were before; on the contrary, we seriously assure our readers that we were fully possessed of all the wisdom and morality it contains at the moment we commenced writing. It is the world which has grown wiser,—not us; we have thrown our mite into the common stock of knowledge, we have shared our morsel with the ignorant multitude; and so far from elevating ourselves above the world, our sole endeavor has been to raise the world to our own level, and make it as wise as we, its disinterested benefactors.

To a moral writer like myself, who, next to his own comfort and entertainment, has the good of his fellow-citizens at heart, a retrospect is but a sorry amusement. Like the industrious husbandman, he often contemplates in silent disappointment his labours wasted on a barren soil, or the seeds he has carefully sown, choked by a redundancy of worthless weeds. I expected long ere this to have seen a complete reformation in manner and morals, achieved by our united efforts. My fancy echoed to the applauding voices of a retrieved generation; I anticipated, with proud satisfaction, the period, not far distant, when our work would be introduced into the academies with which every lane and alley of our cities abounds; when our precepts would be gently inducted into every unlucky urchin by force of birch, and my iron-bound physiogomy, as taken by Will Wizard, be as notorious as that of Noah Webster, junr. Esq., or his no less renowned predecessor, the illustrious Dilworth, of spelling-book immortality. But, well-a-day! to let my readers into a profound secret—the expectations of man are like the varied hues that tinge the distant prospect; never to be realized, never to be enjoyed but in perspective. Luckless Launcelot, that the humblest of the many air castles thou hast erected should prove a "baseless fabric!" Much does it grieve me to confess, that after all our lectures, and excellent admonitions, the people of NEW-YORK are nearly as much given to backsliding and ill-nature as ever; they are just as much abandoned to dancing, and tea-drinking; and as to scandal, Will Wizard informs me that, by a rough computation, since the last cargo of gunpowder-tea from Canton, no less than eighteen characters have been blown up, besides a number of others that have been wofully shattered.

The ladies still labour under the same scarcity of muslins, and delight in flesh-coloured silk stockings; it is evident, however, that our advice has had very considerable effect on them, as they endeavour to act as opposite to it as possible; this being what Evergreen calls female independence. As to the Straddles, they abound as much as ever in Broadway, particularly on Sundays; and Wizzard roundly asserts that he supped in company with a knot of them a few evenings since, when they liquidated a whole Birmingham consignment, in a batch of imperial champaign. I have, furthermore, in the course of a month past, detected no less than three Giblet families making their first onset towards style and gentility in the very manner we have heretofore reprobated. Nor have our utmost efforts been able to check the progress of that alarming epidemic, the rage for punning, which, though doubtless originally intended merely to ornament and enliven conversation by little sports of fancy, threatens to overrun and poison the whole, like the baneful ivy which destroys the useful plant it first embellished. Now I look upon an habitual punster as a depredator upon conversation; and I have remarked sometimes one of these offenders, sitting silent on the watch for an hour together until some luckless wight, unfortunately for the ease and quiet of the company, dropped a phrase susceptible of a double meaning;—when——pop, our punster would dart out like a veteran mouser from her covert, seize the unlucky word, and after worrying and mumbling at it until it was capable of no further marring, relapse again into silent watchfulness, and lie in wait for another opportunity.—Even this might be borne with, by the aid of a little philosophy; but the worst of it is, they are not content to manufacture puns and laugh heartily at them themselves; but they expect we should laugh with them;—which I consider as an intolerable hardship, and a flagrant imposition on good-nature. Let those gentlemen fritter away conversation with impunity, and deal out their wits in sixpenny bits if they please; but I beg I may have the choice of refusing currency to their small change. I am seriously afraid, however, that our junto is not quite free from the infection; nay, that it has even approached so near as to menace the tranquillity of my elbow-chair: for, Will Wizzard, as we were in caucus the other night, absolutely electrified Pindar and myself with a most palpable and perplexing pun; had it been a torpedo, it could not have more discomposed the fraternity. Sentence of banishment was unanimously decreed; but on his confessing that, like many celebrated wits, he was merely retailing other men's wares on commission, he was for that once forgiven on condition of refraining from such diabolical practices in future. Pindar is particularly outrageous against punsters; and quite astonished and put me to a nonplus a day or two since, by asking abruptly "whether I thought a punster could be a good Christain?" He followed up his question triumphantly by offering to prove, by sound logic and historical fact, that the Roman empire owed its decline and fall to a pun; and that nothing tended so much to demoralize the French nation, as their abominable rage for *jeux de mots*.

But what, above every thing else, has caused me much vexation of spirit, and displeased me most with this stiff-necked nation, is, that in spite of all the serious and profound censures of the sage Mustapha, in his various letters—they *will talk!*—they will still wag their tongues, and chatter like very slang-whangers! this is a degree of obstinacy incomprehensible in the extreme; and is another proof how alarming is the force of habit, and how difficult it is to reduce beings, accustomed to talk, to that state of silence which is the very acme of human wisdom.

We can only account for these disappointments in our moderate and reasonable expectations, by supposing the world so deeply sunk in the mire of delinquency, that not even Hercules, were he to put his shoulder to the axletree, would be able to extricate it. We comfort ourselves, however, by the reflection that there are at least three good men left in this degenerate age to benefit the world by example should precept ultimately fail. And borrowing, for once, an example from certain sleepy writers, who, after the first emotions of surprise in finding their invaluable effusions neglected or despised, console themselves with the idea that 'tis a stupid age, and look forward to posterity for redress;—we bequeath our volume to future generations,—and much good may it do them. Heaven grant they may be able to read it! for, if our fashionable mode of education continues to improve, as of late, I am under serious apprehensions that the period is not far distant when the discipline of the dancing master will supersede that of the grammarian; crotchets and quavers supplant the alphabet; and the heels, by an antipodean manœuvre, obtain entire pre-eminence over the head. How does my heart yearn for poor dear posterity, when this work shall become as unintelligible to our grandchildren as it seems to be to their grandfathers and grandmothers.

In fact, for I love to be candid, we begin to suspect that many people read our numbers merely for their amusement, without paying any attention to the serious truths conveyed in every page. Unpardonable want of penetration! not that we wish to restrict our readers in the article of laughing, which we consider as one of the dearest prerogatives of man, and the distinguishing characteristic which raises him above all other animals: let them laugh, therefore, if they will, provided they profit at the same time, and do not mistake our object. It is one of our indisputable facts that it is easier to laugh ten follies out of countenance than to coax, reason or flog a man out of one. In this odd, singular, and indescribable age, which is neither the age of gold, silver, iron, brass, chivalry, or *pills*, as Sir John Carr asserts, a grave writer who attempts to attack folly with the heavy artillery of moral reasoning, will fare like Smollet's honest pedant, who clearly demonstrated by angles, &c., after the manner of Euclid, that it was wrong to do evil;—and was laughed at for his pains. Take my word for it, a little well-applied ridicule, like Hannibal's application of vinegar to rocks, will do more with certain hard heads and obdurate hearts, than all the logic or demonstrations in Longinus or Euclid. But the people of Gotham, wise souls, are so much accustomed to see morality approach them clothed in formidable wigs and sable garbs, "with leaden eye that loves the ground," that they can never recognize her when, drest in gay attire, she comes tripping towards them with smiles and sunshine in her countenance.—Well, let the rogues remain in happy ignorance, for "ignorance is bliss," as the poets say;—and I put as implicit faith in poetry as I do in the almanac or in the newspaper;—we will improve them, without their being the wiser for it, and they shall become better in spite of their teeth, and without their having the least suspicion of the reformation working within them.

Among all our manifold grievances, however, still some small but vivid rays of sunshine occasionally brighten along our path; cheering our steps, and inviting us to persevere.

The public have paid some little regard to a few articles of our advice;—they have purchased our numbers freely;—so much the better for our publisher;—they have read them attentively;—so much the better for themselves. The melancholy fate of my dear aunt Charity has had a wonderful effect; and I have now before me a letter from a gentleman who lives opposite to a couple of old ladies, remarkable for the interest they took in his affairs;—his apartments were absolutely in a state of blockade, and he was on the point of changing his lodgings, or capitulating, until the appearance of our ninth number, which he immediately sent over with his compliments;—the good ladies took the hint, and have scarcely appeared at their window since. As to the wooden gentlemen, our friend Miss Sparkle assures me, they are wonderfully improved by our criticisms, and sometimes venture to make a remark, or attempt a pun in company, to the great edification of all who happen to understand them. As to red shawls, they are entirely discarded from the fair shoulders of our ladies— ever since the last importation of finery;—nor has any lady, since the cold weather, ventured to expose her elbows to the admiring gaze of scrutinizing passengers. But there is one victory we have achieved which has given us more pleasure than to have written down the whole administration: I am assured, from unquestionable authority, that our young ladies, doubtless in consequence of our weighty admonition, have not once indulged in that intoxicating, inflammatory, and whirligig dance, the waltz—ever since hot weather commenced. True it is, I understand, an attempt was made to exhibit it by some of the sable fair ones at the last African ball, but it was highly disapproved of by all the respectable elderly ladies present.

These are sweet sources of comfort to atone for the many wrongs and misrepresentations heaped upon us by the world; —for even we have experienced its ill-nature. How often have we heard ourselves reproached for the insidious applications of the uncharitable!—how often have we been accused of emotions which never found an entrance into our bosoms!—how often have our sportive effusions been wrested to serve the purposes of particular enmity and bitterness!—Meddlesome spirits! little do they know our disposition; we "lack gall" to wound the feelings of a single innocent individual; we can even forgive them from the very bottom of our souls; may they meet as ready a forgiveness from their own consciences! like true and independent bachelors, having no domestic cares to interfere with our general benevolence, we consider it incumbent upon us to watch over the welfare of society; and although we are indebted to the world for little else than left-handed favours, yet we feel a proud satisfaction in requiting evil with good, and the sneer of illiberality with the unfeigned smile of good humour. With these mingled motives of selfishness and philanthropy we commenced our work, and if we cannot solace ourselves with the consciousness of having done much good! yet there is still one pleasing consolation left, which the world can neither give nor take away. There are moments,—lingering moments of listless indifference and heavy-hearted despondency,—when our best hopes and affections slipping, as they sometimes will, from their hold on those objects to which they usually cling for support, seem abandoned on the wide waste of cheerless existence, without a place to cast anchor; without a shore in view to excite a single wish, or to give a momentary interest to contemplation. We look back with delight upon many of these moments of mental gloom, whiled away by the cheerful exercise of our pen, and consider every such triumph over the spleen as retarding the furrowing hand of time in its insidious encroachments on our brows. If, in addition to our own amusements, we have, as we jogged carelessly laughing along, brushed away one tear of dejection and called forth a smile in its place —if we have brightened the pale countenance of a single child of sorrow—we shall feel almost as much joy and rejoicing as a slang-whanger does when he bathes his pen in the heart's blood of a patron and benefactor; or sacrifices one more illustrious victim on the altar of party animosity.

TO READERS AND CORRESPONDENTS.

IT is our misfortune to be frequently pestered, in our peregrinations about this blessed city, by certain critical gad-flies; who buzz around and merely attack the skin, without ever being able to penetrate the body. The reputation of our promising *protégé* Jeremy Cockloft the younger, has been assailed by these skin-deep critics; they have questioned his claims to originality, and even hinted that the ideas for his New-Jersey Tour were borrowed from a late work entitled "MY POCKETBOOK." As there is no literary offence more despicable in the eyes of the trio than borrowing, we immediately called Jeremy to an account: when he proved, by the dedication of the work in question, that it was first published in London in March, 1807—and that his "Stranger in New-Jersey" had made its appearance on the 24th of the preceding February.

We were on the point of acquitting Jeremy with honour on the ground that it was impossible, knowing as he is, to borrow from a foreign work one month before it was in existence; when Will Wizard suddenly took up the cudgels for the critics, and insisted that nothing was more probable; for he recollected reading of an ingenious Dutch author who plainly convicted the ancients of stealing from his labours!——So much for criticism.

WE have received a host of friendly and admonitory letters from different quarters, and among the rest a very loving epistle from Georgetown, Columbia, signed Teddy M'Gundy, who addresses us by the name of Saul M'Gundy, and insists that we are descended from the same Irish progenitors, and nearly related. As friend Teddy seems to be an honest, merry rogue, we are sorry that we cannot admit his claims to kindred; we thank him, however, for his good-will, and should he ever be inclined to favour us with another epistle, we will hint to him, and, at the same time, to our other numerous correspondents, that their communications will be infinitely more acceptable, if they will just recollect Tom Shuffleton's advice, "pay the post-boy, Muggins."

NO. XIV.—SATURDAY, SEPT. 16, 1807.

LETTER FROM MUSTAPHA RUB-A-DUB KELI KHAN,

TO·ASEM HACCHEM, PRINCIPAL SLAVE-DRIVER TO HIS HIGHNESS THE BASHAW OF TRIPOLI.

HEALTH and joy to the friend of my heart!—May the angel of peace ever watch over thy dwelling, and the star of prosperity shed its benignant lustre on all thy undertakings. Far other is the lot of thy captive friend;—his brightest hopes extend but to a lengthened period of weary captivity, and memory only adds to the measure of his griefs, by holding up a mirror which reflects with redoubled charms the hours of past felicity. In midnight slumbers my soul holds sweet converse with the tender objects of its affections;—it is then the exile is restored to his country;—it is then the wide waste of waters that rolls between us disappears, and I clasp to my bosom the companion of my youth; I awake and find it is but a vision of the night. The sigh will rise,—the tear of dejection will steal down my cheek:—I fly to my pen, and strive to forget myself, and my sorrows, in conversing with my friend.

In such a situation, my good Asem, it cannot be expected that I should be able so wholly to abstract myself from my own feelings, as to give thee a full and systematic account of the singular people among whom my disastrous lot has been cast. I can only find leisure, from my own individual sorrows, to entertain thee occasionally with some of the most prominent features of their character; and now and then a solitary picture of their most preposterous eccentricities.

I have before observed, that among the distinguishing characteristics of the people of this logocracy, is their invincible love of talking; and, that I could compare the nation to nothing but a mighty wind-mill. Thou art doubtless at a loss to conceive how this mill is supplied with grist; or, in other words, how it is possible to furnish subjects to supply the perpetual motion of so many tongues.

The genius of the nation appears in its highest lustre in this particular in the discovery, or rather the application, of a subject which seems to supply an inexhaustible mine of words. It is nothing more, my friend, than POLITICS; a word which, I declare to thee, has perplexed me almost as much as the redoubtable one of economy. On consulting a dictionary of this language, I found it denoted the science of government; and the relations, situations, and dispositions of states and empires. —Good, thought I, for a people who boast of governing themselves there could not be a more important subject of investigation. I therefore listened attentively, expecting to hear from "the most enlightened people under the sun," for so they modestly term themselves, sublime disputations on the science of legislation and precepts of political wisdom that would not have disgraced our great prophet and legislator himself!— but, alas, Asem! how continually are my expectations disappointed! how dignified a meaning does this word bear in the dictionary;—how despicable its common application; I find it extending to every contemptible discussion of local animosity, and every petty altercation of insignificant individuals. It embraces, alike, all manner of concerns; from the organization of a divan, the election of a bashaw, or the levying of an army, to the appointment of a constable, the personal disputes of two miserable slang-whangers, the cleaning of the streets, or the economy of a dirt-cart. A couple of politicians will quarrel, with the most vociferous pertinacity, about the character of a bum-bailiff whom nobody cares for; or the deportment of a little great man whom nobody knows; – and this is called talking politics; nay! it is but a few days since that I was annoyed by a debate between two of my fellow-lodgers, who were magnanimously employed in condemning a luckless wight to infamy, because he chose to wear a red coat, and to entertain certain erroneous opinions some thirty years ago. Shocked at their illiberal and vindictive spirit, I rebuked them for thus indulging in slander and uncharitableness, about the colour of a coat; which had doubtless for many years been worn out; or the belief in errors, which, in all probability, had been long since atoned for and abandoned; but they justified themselves by alleging that they were only engaged in politics, and exerting that liberty of speech, and freedom of discussion, which was the glory and safeguard of their national independence. "Oh, Mahomet!" thought I, "what a country must that be, which builds its political safety on ruined characters and the persecution of individuals!"

Into what transports of surprise and incredulity am I continually betrayed, as the character of this eccentric people gradually developes itself to my observations. Every new research increases the perplexities in which I am involved, and I am more than ever at a loss where to place them in the scale of my estimation. It is thus the philosopher, in pursuing truth through the labyrinth of doubt, error, and misrepresentation, frequently finds himself bewildered in the mazes of contradictory experience; and almost wishes he could quietly retrace his wandering steps, steal back into the path of honest ignorance, and jog on once more in contented indifference.

How fertile in these contradictions is this extensive logocracy! Men of different nations, manners, and languages live in this country in the most perfect harmony; and nothing is more common than to see individuals, whose respective governments are at variance, taking each other by the hand and exchanging the offices of friendship. Nay, even on the subject of religion, which, as it affects our dearest interests, our earliest opinions and prejudices, some warmth and heart-burnings might be excused, which, even in our enlightened country, is so fruitful in difference between man and man!—even religion occasions no dissension among these people; and it has even been discovered by one of their sages that believing in one God or twenty Gods "neither breaks a man's leg nor picks his pocket." The idolatrous Persian may here bow down before his everlasting fire, and prostrate himself towards the glowing east. The Chinese may adore his Fo, or his Josh; the Egyptian his stork; and the Mussulman practise, unmolested, the divine precepts of our immortal prophet. Nay, even the forlorn, abandoned Atheist, who lies down at night without committing himself to the protection of heaven, and rises in the morning without returning thanks for his safety;—who hath no deity but his own will;—whose soul, like the sandy desert, is barren of every flower of hope to throw a solitary bloom over the deal level of sterility and soften the wide extent of desolation;—whose darkened views extend not beyond the horizon that bounds his cheerless existence;—to whom no blissful perspective opens beyond the grave;—even he is suffered to indulge in his desperate opinions, without exciting one other emotion than pity or contempt. But this mild and tolerating spirit reaches not beyond the pale of religion:—once differ in politics, in mere theories, visions, and chimeras, the growth of interest, of folly, or madness, and deadly warfare ensues; every eye flashes fire, every tongue is loaded with reproach, and every heart is filled with gall and bitterness.

At this period several unjustifiable and serious injuries on the part of the barbarians of the British island, have given a new impulse to the tongue and the pen, and occasioned a terrible wordy fever.—Do not suppose, my friend, that I mean to condemn any proper and dignified expression of resentment for injuries. On the contrary, I love to see a word before a blow: for "in the fulness of the heart the tongue moveth." But my long experience has convinced me that people who talk the most about taking satisfaction for affronts, generally content themselves with talking instead of revenging the insult: like the street women of this country, who, after a prodigious scolding, quietly sit down and fan themselves cool as fast as possible. But to return:—the rage for talking has now, in consequence of the aggressions I alluded to, increased to a degree far beyond what I have observed heretofore. In the gardens of his highness of Tripoli are fifteen thousand beehives, three hundred peacocks, and a prodigious number of parrots and baboons;—and yet I declare to thee, Asem, that their buzzing, and squalling, and chattering is nothing compared to the wild uproar and war of words now raging within the bosom of this mighty and distracted logocracy. Politics pervade every city, every village, every temple, every porterhouse;—the universal question is, "what is the news?"—This is a kind of challenge to political debate; and as no two men think exactly alike, 'tis ten to one but before they finish all the polite phrases in the language are exhausted by way of giving fire and energy to argument. What renders this talking fever more alarming, is that the people appear to be in the unhappy state of a patient whose palate nauseates the medicine best calculated for the cure of his disease, and seem anxious to continue in the full enjoyment of their chattering epidemic. They alarm each other by direful reports and fearful apprehensions; like I have seen a knot of old wives in this country entertain themselves with stories of ghosts and goblins until their imaginations were in a most agonizing panic. Every day begets some new tale, big with agitation; and the busy goddess, rumour, to speak in the poetic language of the Christians, is constantly in motion. She mounts her rattling stage-wagon and gallops about the country, freighted with a load of "hints," "informations," "extracts of letters from respectable gentlemen," "observations of respectable correspondents," and "unquestionable authorities;"—which her high-priests, the slang-whangers, retail to their sapient followers with all the solemnity—and all the authenticity of oracles. True it is, the unfortunate slang-whangers are sometimes at a loss for food to supply this insatiable appetite for intelligence; and are, not unfrequently, reduced to the necessity of manufacturing dishes suited to the taste of the times: to be served up as morning and evening repasts to their disciples.

When the hungry politician is thus full charged with important information, he sallies forth to give due exercise to his tongue; and tells all he knows to everybody he meets. Now it is a thousand to one that every person he meets is just as wise as himself, charged with the same articles of information, and possessed of the same violent inclination to give it vent; for in this country every man adopts some particular slang-whanger as the standard of his judgment, and reads every thing he writes, if he reads nothing else; which is doubtless the reason why the people of this logocracy are so marvelously enlightened. So away they tilt at each other with their borrowed lances, advancing to the combat with the opinions and speculations of their respective slang-whangers, which in all probability are diametrically opposite:—here, then, arises as fair an opportunity for a battle of words as heart could wish; and thou mayest rely upon it, Asem, they do not let it pass unimproved. They sometimes begin with argument; but in process of time, as the tongue begins to wax wanton, other auxiliaries become necessary; recrimination commences; reproach follows close at its heels;—from political abuse they proceed to personal; and thus often is a friendship of years trampled down by this contemptible enemy, this gigantic dwarf of POLITICS, the mongrel issue of grovelling ambition and aspiring ignorance!

There would be but little harm indeed in all this, if it ended merely in a broken head; for this might soon be healed, and the scar, if any remained, might serve as a warning ever after against the indulgence of political intemperance;——at the worst, the loss of such heads as these would be a gain to the nation. But the evil extends far deeper; it threatens to impair all social intercourse, and even to sever the sacred union of family and kindred. The convivial table is disturbed; the cheerful fireside is invaded; the smile of social hilarity is chased away;—the bond of social love is broken by the everlasting intrusion of this fiend of contention, who lurks in the sparkling bowl, crouches by the fireside, growls in the friendly circle, infests every avenue to pleasure; and, like the scowling incubus, sits on the bosom of society, pressing down and smothering every throb and pulsation of liberal philanthropy.

But thou wilt perhaps ask, "What can these people dispute about? one would suppose that being all free and equal, they would harmonize as brothers; children of the same parent, and equal heirs of the same inheritance." This theory is most exquisite, my good friend, but in practice it turns out the very dream of a madman. Equality, Asem, is one of the most consummate scoundrels that ever crept from the brain of a political juggler—a fellow who thrusts his hand into the pocket of honest industry, or enterprising talent, and sqanders their hard-earned profits on profligate idleness or indolent stupidity. There will always be an inequality among mankind so long as a portion of it is enlightened and industrious, and the rest idle and ignorant. The one will acquire a larger share of wealth, and its attendant comforts, refinements, and luxuries of life; and the influence, and power, which those will always possess who have the greatest ability of administering to the necessities of their fellow-creatures. These advantages will inevitably excite envy; and envy as inevitably begets ill-will:—hence arises that eternal warfare, which the lower orders of society are waging against those who have raised themselves by their own merits, or have been raised by the merits of their ancestors, above the common level. In a nation possessed of quick feelings and impetuous passions, the hostility might engender deadly broils and bloody commotions; but here it merely vents itself in high-sounding words, which lead to continual breaches of decorum; or in the insidious assassination o character, and a restless propensity among the base to blacken every reputation which is fairer than their own.

I cannot help smiling sometimes to see the solicitude with which the people of America, so called from the country having been first discovered by Christopher Columbus, battle about them when any election takes place; as if they had the least concern in the matter, or were to be benefited by an exchange of bashaws;—they really seem ignorant that none but the bashaws and their dependants are at all interested in the event; and that the people at large will not find their situation altered in the least. I formerly gave thee an account of an election which took place under my eye.—The result has been that the people, as some of the slang-whangers say, have obtained a glorious triumph; which, however, is flatly denied by the opposite slang-whangers, who insist that their party is composed of the true sovereign people; and that the others are all jacobins, Frenchmen, and Irish rebels. I ought to apprise thee that the last is a term of great reproach here; which, perhaps, thou wouldst not otherwise imagine, considering that it is not many years since this very people were engaged in a revolution; the failure of which would have subjected them to the same ignominious epithet, and a participation in which is now the highest recommendation to public confidence. By Mahomet, but it cannot be denied, that the consistency of this people, like every thing else appertaining to them, is on a prodigious great scale! To return, however, to the event of the election.—The people triumphed, and much good has it done them. I, for my part, expected to see wonderful changes, and most magical metamorphoses. I expected to see the people all rich, that they would be all gentlemen bashaws, riding in their coaches, and faring sumptuously every day; emancipated from toil, and revelling in luxurious ease. Wilt thou credit me, Asem, when I declare to thee that every thing remains exactly in the same state it was before the last wordy campaign?—except a few noisy retainers, who have crept into office, and a few noisy patriots, on the other side, who have been kicked out, there is not the least difference. The labourer toils for his daily support; the beggar still lives on the charity of those who have any charity to bestow; and the only solid satisfaction the multitude have reaped is, that they have got a new governor, or bashaw, whom they will praise, idolize, and exalt for a while; and afterwards, notwithstanding the sterling merits he really possesses, in compliance with immemorial custom, they will abuse, calumniate, and trample him under foot.

Such, my dear Asem, is the way in which the wise people of "the most enlightened country under the sun" are amused with straws and puffed up with mighty conceits; like a certain fish I have seen here, which, having his belly tickled for a short time, will swell and puff himself up to twice his usual size, and become a mere bladder of wind and vanity.

The blessing of a true Mussulman light on thee, good Asem;

ever while thou livest be true to thy prophet; and rejoice, that, though the boasting political chatterers of this logocracy cast upon thy countrymen the ignominious epithet of slaves, thou livest in a country where the people, instead of being at the mercy of a tyrant with a million of heads, have nothing to do but submit to the will of a bashaw of only three tails.

Ever thine, MUSTAPHA.

COCKLOFT HALL.

BY LAUNCELOT LANGSTAFF, ESQ.

THOSE who pass their time immured in the smoky circumference of the city, amid the rattling of carts, the brawling of the multitude, and the variety of unmeaning and discordant sounds that prey insensibly upon the nerves and beget a weariness of the spirits, can alone understand and feel that expansion of the heart, that physical renovation which a citizen experiences when he steals forth from his dusty prison to breathe the free air of heaven and enjoy the clear face of nature. Who that has rambled by the side of one of our majestic rivers at the hour of sunset, when the wildly romantic scenery around is softened and tinted by the voluptuous mist of evening; when the bold and swelling outlines of the distant mountain seem melting into the glowing horizon and a rich mantle of refulgence is thrown over the whole expanse of the heavens, but must have felt how abundant is nature in sources of pure enjoyment; how luxuriant in all that can enliven the senses or delight the imagination. The jocund zephyr, full freighted with native fragrance, sues sweetly to the senses; the chirping of the thousand varieties of insects with which our woodlands abound, forms a concert of simple melody; even the barking of the farm dog, the lowing of the cattle, the tinkling of their bells, and the strokes of the woodman's axe from the opposite shore, seem to partake of the softness of the scene and fall tunefully upon the ear; while the voice of the villager, chanting some rustic ballad, swells from a distance in the semblance of the very music of harmonious love.

At such time I feel a sensation of sweet tranquillity; a hallowed calm is diffused over my senses; I cast my eyes around, and every object is serene, simple, and beautiful; no warring passion, no discordant string there vibrates to the touch of ambition, self-interest, hatred, or revenge;—I am at peace with the whole world, and hail all mankind as friends and brothers.—Blissful moments! ye recall the careless days of my boyhood, when mere existence was happiness, when hope was certainty, this world a paradise, and every woman a ministering angel!—surely man was designed for a tenant of the universe, instead of being pent up in these dismal cages, these dens of strife, disease, and discord. We were created to range the fields, to sport among the groves, to build castles in the air, and have every one of them realized!

A whole legion of reflections like these insinuated themselves into my mind, and stole me from the influence of the cold realities before me, as I took my accustomed walk, a few weeks since, on the battery. Here watching the splendid mutations of one of our summer skies, which emulated the boasted glories of an Italian sun-set, I all at once discovered that it was but to pack up my portmanteau, bid adieu for awhile to my elbow-chair, and in a little time I should be transported from the region of smoke, and noise, and dust, to the enjoyment of a far sweeter prospect and a brighter sky. The next morning I was off full tilt to Cockloft-Hall, leaving my man Pompey to follow at his leisure with my baggage. I love to indulge in rapid transitions, which are prompted by the quick impulse of the moment;—'tis the only mode of guarding against that intruding and deadly foe to all parties of pleasure,—anticipation.

Having now made good my retreat, until the black frosts commence, it is but a piece of civility due to my readers, who I trust are, ere this, my friends, to give them a proper introduction to my present residence. I do this as much to gratify them as myself: well knowing a reader is always anxious to learn how his author is lodged, whether in a garret, a cellar, a hovel, or a palace; at least an author is generally vain enough to think so; and an author's vanity ought sometimes to be gratified; poor vagabond! it is often the only gratification he ever tastes in this world!

COCKLOFT-HALL is the country residence of the family, or rather the paternal mansion; which, like the mother country, sends forth whole colonies to populate the face of the earth. Pindar whimsically denominates it the family hive! and there is at least as much truth as humour in my cousin's epithet;—for many a redundant swarm has it produced. I don't recollect whether I have at any time mentioned to my readers, for I seldom look back on what I have written, that the fertility of the Cocklofts is proverbial. The female members of the family are most incredibly fruitful; and to use a favourite phrase of old Cockloft, who is excessively addicted to backgammon, they seldom fail "to throw doublets every time." I myself have known three or four very industrious young men reduced to great extremities, with some of these capital breeders; heaven smiled upon their union, and enriched them with a numerous and hopeful offspring—who eat them out of doors.

But to return to the hall.—It is pleasantly situated on the bank of a sweet pastoral stream: not so near town as to invite an inundation of unmeaning, idle acquaintance, who come to lounge away an afternoon, nor so distant as to render it an absolute deed of charity or friendship to perform the journey. It is one of the oldest habitations in the country, and was built by my cousin Christopher's grandfather, who was also mine by the mother's side, in his latter days, to form, as the old gentleman expressed himself, "a snug retreat, where he meant to sit himself down in his old days and be comfortable for the rest of his life." He was at this time a few years over four score: but this was a common saying of his, with which he usually closed his airy speculations. One would have thought, from the long vista of years through which he contemplated many of his projects, that the good man had forgot the age of the patriarchs had long since gone by, and calculated upon living a century longer at least. He was for a considerable time in doubt on the question of roofing his house with shingles or slate:—shingles would not last above thirty years! but then they were much cheaper than slates. He settled the matter by a kind of compromise, and determined to build with shingles first; "and when they are worn out," said the old gentleman, triumphantly, "'twill be time enough to replace them with more durable materials!" But his contemplated improvements surpassed every thing; and scarcely had he a roof over his head, when he discovered a thousand things to be arranged before he could "sit down comfortably." In the first place, every tree and bush on the place was cut down or grubbed up by the roots, because they were not placed to his mind; and a vast quantity of oaks, chestnuts, and elms, set out in clumps and rows, and labyrinths, which he observed in about five-and-twenty or thirty years at most, would yield a very tolerable shade, and, moreover, shut out all the surrounding country:

for he was determined, he said, to have all his views on his own land, and be beholden to no man for a prospect. This, my learned readers will perceive, was something very like the idea of Lorenzo de Medici, who gave as a reason for preferring one of his seats above all the others, "that all the ground within view of it was his own:" now, whether my grandfather ever heard of the Medici, is more than I can say; I rather think, however, from the characteristic originality of the Cocklofts, that it was a whim-wham of his own begetting. Another odd notion of the old gentleman was to blow up a large bed of rocks, for the purpose of having a fish-pond, although the river ran at about one hundred yards distance from the house, and was well stored with fish;—but there was nothing, he said, like having things to one's-self. So at it he went with all the ardour of a projector who has just hit upon some splendid and useless whim-wham. As he proceeded, his views enlarged; he would have a summer-house built on the margin of the fish-pond; he would have it surrounded with elms and willows; and he would have a cellar dug under it, for some incomprehensible purpose, which remains a secret to this day. "In a few years," he observed, "it would be a delightful piece of wood and water, where he might ramble on a summer's noon, smoke his pipe, and enjoy himself in his old days:"—thrice honest old soul!—he died of an apoplexy in his ninetieth year, just as he had begun to blow up the fish-pond.

Let no one ridicule the whim-whams of my grandfather.—If—and of this there is no doubt, for wise men have said it—if life is but a dream, happy is he who can make the most of the illusion.

Since my grandfather's death, the hall has passed through the hands of a succession of true old cavaliers, like himself, who gloried in observing the golden rules of hospitality; which, according to the Cockloft principle, consist in giving a guest the freedom of the house, cramming him with beef and pudding, and, if possible, laying him under the table with prime port, claret, or London particular. The mansion appears to have been consecrated to the jolly god, and teems with monuments sacred to conviviality. Every chest of drawers, clothes-press, and cabinet, is decorated with enormous China punch-bowls, which Mrs. Cockloft has paraded with much ostentation, particularly in her favourite red damask bed-chamber, and in which a projector might, with great satisfaction, practise his experiments on fleets, diving-bells, and sub-marine boats.

I have before mentioned cousin Christopher's profound veneration for antique furniture; in consequence of which the old hall is furnished in much the same style with the house in town. Old-fashioned bedsteads, with high testers; massy clothes-presses, standing most majestically on eagles' claws, and ornamented with a profusion of shining brass handles, clasps, and hinges; and around the grand parlour are solemnly arranged a set of high-backed, leather-bottomed, massy, mahogany chairs, that always remind me of the formal long-waisted belles, who flourished in stays and buckram, about the time they were in fashion.

If I may judge from their height, it was not the fashion for gentlemen in those days to loll over the back of a lady's chair, and whisper in her ear what—might be as well spoken aloud;—at least, they must have been Patagonians to have effected it. Will Wizard declares that he saw a little fat German gallant attempt once to whisper Miss Barbara Cockloft in this manner, but being unluckily caught by the chin, he dangled and kicked about for half a minute, before he could find terra firma;—but Will is much addicted to hyperbole, by reason of his having been a great traveller.

But what the Cocklofts most especially pride themselves upon, is the possession of several family portraits, which exhibit as honest a square set of portly, well-fed looking gentlemen, and gentlewomen, as ever grew and flourished under the pencil of a Dutch painter. Old Christopher, who is a complete genealogist, has a story to tell of each; and dilates with copious eloquence on the great services of the general in large sleeves, during the old French war; and on the piety of the lady in blue velvet, who so attentively peruses her book, and was once so celebrated for a beautiful arm: but much as I reverence my illustrious ancestors, I find little to admire in their biography, except my cousin's excellent memory; which is most provokingly retentive of every uninteresting particular.

My allotted chamber in the hall is the same that was occupied in days of yore by my honoured uncle John. The room exhibits many memorials which recall to my remembrance the solid excellence and amiable eccentricities of that gallant old lad. Over the mantel-piece hangs the portrait of a young lady dressed in a flaring, long-waisted, blue-silk gown; be-flowered, and be-furbelowed, and be-cuffed, in a most abundant manner·

she holds in one hand a book, which she very complaisantly neglects to turn and smile on the spectator; in the other a flower, which I hope, for the honour of dame nature, was the sole production of the painter's imagination; and a little behind her is something tied to a blue riband, but whether a little dog, a monkey, or a pigeon, must be left to the judgment of future commentators. The little damsel, tradition says, was my uncle John's third flame; and he would infallibly have run away with her, could he have persuaded her into the measure; but at that time ladies were not quite so easily run away with as Columbine; and my uncle, failing in the point, took a lucky thought; and with great gallantry ran off with her picture, which he conveyed in triumph to Cockloft-hall, and hung up in his bed-chamber as a monument of his enterprising spirit. The old gentleman prided himself mightily on this chivalric manœuvre; always chuckled, and pulled up his stock when he contemplated the picture, and never related the exploit without winding up with—"I might, indeed, have carried off the original, had I chose to dangle a little longer after her chariot-wheels;—for, to do the girl justice, I believe she had a liking for me; but I always scorned to coax, my boy,--always,—'twas my way." My uncle John was of a happy temperament;—I would give half I am worth for his talent at self-consolation.

The Miss Cocklofts have made several spirited attempts to introduce modern furniture into the hall; but with very indifferent success. Modern style has always been an object of great annoyance to honest Christopher; and is ever treated by him with sovereign contempt, as an upstart intruder.—It is a common observation of his, that your old-fashioned substantial furniture bespeaks the respectability of one's ancestors, and indicates that the family has been used to hold up its head for more than the present generation; whereas the fragile appendages of modern style seemed to be emblems of mushroom gentility; and, to his mind, predicted that the family dignity would moulder away and vanish with the finery thus put on of a sudden.—The same whim-wham makes him averse to having his house surrounded with poplars; which he stigmatizes as mere upstarts; just fit to ornament the shingle palaces of modern gentry, and characteristic of the establishments they decorate. Indeed, so far does he carry his veneration for all the antique trumpery, that he can scarcely see the venerable dust brushed from its resting place on the old-fashioned testers; or a gray-bearded spider dislodged from his ancient inheritance without groaning; and I once saw him in a transport of passion on Jeremy's knocking down a mouldering martin-coop with his tennis-ball, which had been set up in the latter days of my grandfather. Another object of his peculiar affection is an old English cherry tree, which leans against a corner of the hall; and whether the house supports it, or it supports the house, would be, I believe, a question of some difficulty to decide. It is held sacred by friend Christopher because he planted and reared it himself, and had once well-nigh broke his neck by a fall from one of its branches. This is one of his favourite stories:—and there is reason to believe, that if the tree was out of the way, the old gentleman would forget the whole affair;—which would be a great pity.—The old tree has long since ceased bearing, and is exceedingly infirm;—every tempest robs it of a limb; and one would suppose from the lamentations of my old friend, on such occasions, that he had lost one of his own. He often contemplates it in a half-melancholy, half-moralizing humour—"together," he says, "have we flourished, and together shall we wither away:—a few years, and both our heads will be laid low; and, perhaps, my mouldering bones may, one day or other, mingle with the dust of the tree I have planted." He often fancies, he says, that it rejoices to see him when he revisits the hall; and that its leaves assume a brighter verdure, as if to welcome his arrival. How whimsically are our tenderest feelings assailed! At one time the old tree had obtruded a withered branch before Miss Barbara's window, and she desired her father to order the gardener to saw it off. I shall never forget the old man's answer, and the look that accompanied it. "What," cried he, "lop off the limbs of my cherry tree in its old age?—why do you not cut off the gray locks of your poor old father?"

Do my readers yawn at this long family detail? They are welcome to throw down our work, and never resume it again. I have no care for such ungratified spirits, and will not throw away a thought on one of them;—full often have I contributed to their amusement, and have I not a right, for once, to consult my own? Who is there that does not fondly turn, at times, to linger round those scenes which were once the haunt of his boyhood, ere his heart grew heavy and his head waxed gray;—and to dwell with fond affection on the friends who have twined themselves round his heart,——mingled in all his enjoyments, ——contributed to all his felicities? If there be any who cannot relish these enjoyments, let them despair;—for they have been so soiled in their intercourse with the world, as to be incapable of tasting some of the purest pleasures that survive the happy period of youth.

To such as have not yet lost the rural feeling, I address this simple family picture; and in the honest sincerity of a warm heart, I invite them to turn aside from bustle, care, and toil, to tarry with me for a season, in the hospitable mansion of the Cocklofts.

I WAS really apprehensive, on reading the following effusion of Will Wizard, that he still retained that pestilent hankering after puns of which we lately convicted him. He, however, declares, that he is fully authorized by the example of the most popular critics and wits of the present age, whose manner and matter he has closely, and he flatters himself successfully, copied in the subsequent essay.

THEATRICAL INTELLIGENCE.

BY WILLIAM WIZARD, ESQ.

THE uncommon healthiness of the season, occasioned, as several learned physicians assure me, by the universal prevalence of the influenza, has encouraged the chieftain of our dramatic corps to marshal his forces, and to commence the campaign at a much earlier day than usual. He has been induced to take the field thus suddenly, I am told, by the invasion of certain foreign marauders, who pitched their tents at Vauxhall-Garden during the warm months; and taking advantage of his army being disbanded and dispersed in summer quarters, committed sad depredations upon the borders of his territories:—carrying off a considerable portion of his winter harvest, and murdering some of his most distinguished characters.

It is true, these hardy invaders have been reduced to great extremity by the late heavy rains, which injured and destroyed much of their camp-equipage; besides spoiling the best part of their wardrobe. Two cities, a triumphal car, and a new moon for Cinderella, together with the barber's boy who was employed every night to powder and make it shine white, have been entirely washed away, and the sea has become very wet and mouldy; insomuch that great apprehensions are entertained that it will never be dry enough for use. Add to this the noble county Paris had the misfortune to tear his corduroy breeches, in the scuffle with Romeo, by reason of the tomb being very wet, which occasioned him to slip; and he and his noble rival possessing but one poor pair of satin ones between them, were reduced to considerable shifts to keep up the dignity of their respective houses. In spite of these disadvantages, and the untoward circumstances, they continued to enact most intrepidly; performing with much ease and confidence, inasmuch as they were seldom pestered with an audience to criticise and put them out of countenance. It is rumoured that the last heavy shower absolutely dissolved the company, and that our manager has nothing further to apprehend from that quarter.

The theatre opened on Wednesday last, with great eclat, as we critics say, and almost vied in brilliancy with that of my superb friend Consequa in Canton; where the castles were all ivory, the sea mother-of-pearl, the skies gold and silver leaf, and the outside of the boxes inlaid with scallop shell-work. Those who want a better description of the theatre, may as well go and see it; and then they can judge for themselves. For the gratification of a highly respectable class of readers, who love to see every thing on paper, I had indeed prepared a circumstantial and truly incomprehensible account of it, such as your traveller always fills his book with, and which I defy the most intelligent architect, even the great Sir Christopher Wren, to understand. I had jumbled cornices, and pilasters, and pillars, and capitals, and trigliphs, and modules, and plinths, and volutes, and perspectives, and foreshortenings, helter-skelter; and had set all the orders of architecture, Doric, Ionic, Corinthian, etc., together by the ears, in order to work out a satisfactory description; but the manager having sent me a polite note, requesting that I would not take off the sharp edge, as he whimsically expresses it, of public curiosity, thereby diminishing the receipts of his house, I have willingly consented to oblige him, and have left my description at the store of our publisher, where any person may see it—provided he applies at a proper hour.

I cannot refrain here from giving vent to the satisfaction I received from the excellent performances of the different actors one and all; and particularly the gentlemen who shifted the scenes, who acquitted themselves throughout with great celerity, dignity, pathos and effect. Nor must I pass over the peculiar merits of my friend JOHN, who gallanted off the chairs and tables in the most dignified and circumspect manner. Indeed, I have had frequent occasion to applaud the correctness with which this gentleman fulfils the parts allotted him, and consider him as one of the best general performers in the company. My friend, the cockney, found considerable fault with the manner in which John shoved a huge rock from behind the scenes; maintaining that he should have put his left foot forward, and pushed it with his right hand, that being the method practised by his contemporaries of the royal theatres, and universally approved by their best critics. He also took exception to John's coat, which he pronounced too short by a foot at least; particularly when he turned his back to the company. But I look upon these objections in the same light as new readings, and insist that John shall be allowed to manœuvre his chairs and tables, shove his rocks, and wear his skirts in that style which his genius best effects. My hopes in the rising merit of this favourite actor daily increase; and I would hint to the manager the propriety of giving him a benefit, advertising in the usual style of play-bills, as a "springe to catch woodcocks," that, between the play and farce, JOHN will MAKE A BOW—for that night only!

I am told that no pains have been spared to make the exhibitions of this season as splendid as possible. Several expert rat-catchers have been sent into different parts of the country to catch white mice for the grand pantomime of CINDERELLA. A nest full of little squab Cupids have been taken in the neighbourhood of Communipaw; they are as yet but half fledged, of the true Holland breed, and it is hoped will be able to fly about by the middle of October; otherwise they will be suspended about the stage by the waistband, like little alligators in an apothecary's shop, as the pantomime must positively be performed by that time. Great pains and expense have been incurred in the importation of one of the most portly pumpkins in New-England; and the public may be assured there is now one on board a vessel from New-Haven, which will contain Cinderella's coach and six with perfect ease, were the white mice even ten times as large.

Also several barrels of hail, rain, brimstone, and gunpowder, are in store for melo-dramas; of which a number are to be played off this winter. It is furthermore whispered me that the great thunder-drum has been new braced, and an expert performer on that instrument engaged, who will thunder in plain English, so as to be understood by the most illiterate hearer. This will be infinitely preferable to the miserable Italian thunderer employed last winter by Mr. Ciceri, who performed in such an unnatural and outlandish tongue that none but the scholars of signor Da Ponte could understand him. It will be a further gratification to the patriotic audience to know, that the present thunderer is a fellow-countryman, born at Dunderbarrack, among the echoes of the Highlands;—and that he thunders with peculiar emphasis and pompous enunciation, in the true style of a fourth of July orator.

In addition to all these additions, the manager has provided an entire new snow-storm; the very sight of which will be quite sufficient to draw a shawl over every naked bosom in the theatre; the snow is perfectly fresh, having been manufactured last August.

N. B. The outside of the theatre has been ornamented with a new chimney!!

NO. XV.—THURSDAY, OCTOBER 1, 1807.

SKETCHES FROM NATURE.

BY ANTHONY EVERGREEN, GENT.

THE brisk north-westers, which prevailed not long since, had a powerful effect in arresting the progress of belles, beaux, and wild pigeons in their fashionable northern tour, and turning them back to the more balmy region of the South. Among the rest, I was encountered, full butt, by a blast which set my teeth chattering, just as I doubled one of the frowning bluffs of the Mohawk mountains, in my route to Niagara; and facing about incontinently, I forthwith scud before the wind, and a few days since arrived at my old quarters in New-York. My first care, on returning from so long an absence, was to visit the worthy family of the Cocklofts, whom I found safe, burrowed in their country mansion. On inquiring for my highly respected coadjutor, Langstaff, I learned with great concern that he had relapsed into one of his eccentric fits of the spleen, ever since the era of a turtle dinner given by old Cockloft to some of the neighbouring squires; wherein the old gentleman had achieved a glorious victory, in laying honest Launcelot fairly under the table. Langstaff, although fond of the social board, and cheerful glass, yet abominates any excess; and has an invincible aversion to getting mellow, considering it a wilful outrage on the sanctity of imperial mind, a senseless abuse of the body, and an unpardonable, because a voluntary, prostration of both mental and personal dignity. I have heard him moralize on the subject, in a style that would have done honour to Michael Cassia himself; but I believe, if the truth were known, this antipathy rather arises from his having, as the phrase is, but a weak head, and nerves so extremely sensitive, that he is sure to suffer severely from a frolic; and will groan and make resolutions against it for a week afterwards. He therefore took this waggish exploit of old Christopher's, and the consequent quizzing which he underwent, in high dudgeon, had kept aloof from company for a fortnight, and appeared to be meditating some deep plan of retaliation upon his mischievous old crony. He had, however, for the last day or two, shown some symptoms of convalescence: had listened, without more than half a dozen twitches of impatience, to one of Christopher's unconscionable long stories; and even was seen to smile, for the one hundred and thirtieth time, at a venerable joke originally borrowed from Joe Miller: but which, by dint of long occupancy, and frequent repetition, the old gentleman now firmly believes happened to himself somewhere in New-England.

As I am well acquainted with Launcelot's haunts, I soon found him out. He was lolling on his favourite bench, rudely constructed at the foot of an old tree, which is full of fantastical twists, and with its spreading branches forms a canopy of luxuriant foliage. This tree is a kind of chronicle of the short reigns of his uncle John's mistresses; and its trunk is sorely wounded with carvings of true lovers' knots, hearts, darts, names, and inscriptions!—frail memorials of the variety of the fair dames who captivated the wandering fancy of that old cavalier in the days of his youthful romance. Launcelot holds this tree in particular regard, as he does every thing else connected with the memory of his good uncle John. He was reclining, in one of his usual brown studies, against its trunk, and gazing pensively upon the river that glided just by, washing the drooping branches of the dwarf willows that fringed its bank. My appearance roused him;—he grasped my hand with his usual warmth, and with a tremulous but close pressure, which spoke that his heart entered into the salutation. After a number of affectionate inquiries and felicitations, such as friendship, not form, dictated, he seemed to relapse into his former flow of thought, and to resume the chain of ideas my appearance had broken for a moment.

"I was reflecting," said he, "my dear Anthony, upon some observations I made in our last number; and considering whether the sight of objects once dear to the affections, or of scenes where we have passed different happy periods of early life, really occasions most enjoyment or most regret. Renewing our acquaintance with well-known but long-separated objects, revives, it is true, the recollection of former pleasures, and touches the tenderest feelings of the heart; like the flavour of a delicious beverage will remain upon the palate long after the cup has parted from the lips. But on the other hand, my friend, these same objects are too apt to awaken us to a keener recollection of what we were, when they erst delighted us; to provoke a mortifying and melancholy contrast with what we are at present. They act, in a manner, as milestones of existence, showing us how far we have travelled in the journey of life;—how much of our weary but fascinating pilgrimage is accomplished. I look round me, and my eye fondly recognizes the fields I once sported over, the river in which I once swam, and the orchard I intrepidly robbed in the halcyon days of boyhood. The fields are still green, the river still rolls unaltered and undiminished, and the orchard is still flourishing and fruitful;—it is I only am changed. The thoughtless flow of mad-cap spirits that nothing could depress;—the elasticity of nerve that enabled me to bound over the field, to stem the stream, and climb the tree;—the 'sunshine of the breast' that beamed an illusive charm over every object, and created a paradise around me!—where are they?—the thievish lapse of years has stolen them away, and left in return nothing but gray hairs, and a repining spirit." My friend Launcelot concluded his harangue with a sigh, and as I saw he was still under the influence of a whole legion of the blues, and just on the point of sinking into one of his whimsical and unreasonable fits of melancholy abstraction, I proposed a walk;—he consented, and slipping his left arm in mine, and waving in the other a gold-headed thorn cane, bequeathed him by his uncle John, we slowly rambled along the margin of the river.

Langstaff, though possessing great vivacity of temper, is most wofully subject to these "thick coming fancies:" and I do not know a man whose animal spirits do insult him with more jiltings, and coquetries, and slippery tricks. In these moods he is often visited by a whim-wham which he indulges in common with the Cocklofts. It is that of looking back with regret, conjuring up the phantoms of good old times, and decking them out in imaginary finery, with the spoils of his fancy; like a good lady widow, regretting the loss of the " poor dear man;" for whom, while living, she cared not a rush. I have seen him and Pindar, and old Cockloft, amuse themselves over a bottle with their youthful days; until by the time they had become what is termed merry, they were the most miserable beings in existence. In a similar humour was Launcelot at present, and I knew the only way was to let him moralize himself out of it.

Our ramble was soon interrupted by the appearance of a personage of no little importance at Cockloft-hall;—for, to let my readers into a family secret, friend Christopher is notoriously hen pecked by an old negro, who has whitened on the place; and is his master, almanac, and counsellor. My readers, if haply they have sojourned in the country, and become conversant in rural manners, must have observed, that there is scarce a little hamlet but has one of these old weather-beaten wiseacres of negroes, who ranks among the great characters of the place. He is always resorted to as an oracle to resolve any question about the weather, fishing, shooting, farming, and horse-doctoring: and on such occasions will slouch his remnant of a hat on one side, fold his arms, roll his white eyes, and examine the sky, with a look as knowing as Peter Pindar's magpie when peeping into a marrow-bone. Such a sage curmudgeon is Old Cæsar, who acts as friend Cockloft's prime minister or grand vizier; assumes, when abroad, his master's style and title; to wit, squire Cockloft; and is, in effect, absolute lord and ruler of the soil.

As he passed us he pulled off his hat with an air of something more than respect;—it partook, I thought, of affection. "There, now, is another memento of the kind I have been noticing," said Launcelot; "Cæsar was a bosom friend and chosen playmate of cousin Pindar and myself, when we were boys. Never were we so happy as when, stealing away on a holiday to the hall, we ranged about the fields with honest Cæsar. He was particularly adroit in making our quail-traps and fishing-rods; was always the ring-leader in all the schemes of frolicksome mischief perpetrated by the urchins of the neighbourhood; considered himself on an equality with the best of us; and many a hard battle have I had with him, about a division of the spoils of an orchard, or the title to a bird's nest. Many a summer evening do I remember when huddled together on the steps of the hall door, Cæsar, with his stories of ghosts, goblins, and witches, would put us all in a panic, and people every lane, and church-yard, and solitary wood, with imaginary beings. In process of time, he became the constant attendant and Man Friday of cousin Pindar, whenever he went a sparking among the rosy country girls of the neighbouring farms; and brought up his rear at every rustic dance, when he would mingle in the sable group that always thronged the door of merriment; and it was enough to put to the rout a host of splenetic imps to see his mouth gradually dilate from ear to ear, with pride and exultation, at seeing how neatly master Pindar footed it over the floor. Cæsar was likewise the chosen confidant and special agent of Pindar in all his love affairs, until, as his evil stars would have it, on being entrusted with the delivery of a poetic billetdoux to one of his patron's sweethearts, he took an unlucky notion to send it to his own sable dulcinea; who, not being able to read it, took it to her mistress;—and so the whole affair was blown. Pindar was universally roasted, and Cæsar discharged for ever from his confidence.

"Poor Cæsar!—he has now grown old, like his young masters, but he still remembers old times; and will, now and then, remind me of them as he lights me to my room, and lingers a little while to bid me a good-night:——believe me, my dear Evergreen, the honest, simple old creature has a warm corner in my heart;—I don't see, for my part, why a body may not like a negro as well as a white man!"

By the time these biographical anecdotes were ended we had reached the stable, into which we involuntarily strolled, and found Cæsar busily employed in rubbing down the horses; an office he would not entrust to any body else; having contracted an affection for every beast in the stable, from their being descendants of the old race of animals, his youthful contemporaries. Cæsar was very particular in giving us their pedigrees, together with a panegyric on the swiftness, bottom, blood, and spirit of their sires. From these he digressed into a variety of anecdotes, in which Launcelot bore a conspicuous part, and on which the old negro dwelt with all the garrulity of age. Honest Langstaff stood leaning with his arm over the back of his favourite steed, old Killdeer; and I could perceive he listened to Cæsar's simple details with that fond attention with which a feeling mind will hang over narratives of boyish days. His eyes sparkled with animation, a glow of youthful fire stole across his pale visage; he nodded with smiling approbation at every sentence;—chuckled at every exploit; laughed heartily at the story of his once having smoked out a country singing-school with brimstone and assafœtida;—and slipping a piece of money into old Cæsar's hand to buy himself a new tobacco-box, he seized me by the arm and hurried out of the stable brimfull of good-nature. " 'Tis a pestilent old rogue for talking, my dear fellow," cried he, "but you must not find fault with him,—the creature means well." I knew at the very moment that he made this apology, honest Cæsar could not have given him half the satisfaction had he talked like a Cicero or a Solomon.

Launcelot returned to the house with me in the best possible humour:—the whole family, who, in truth, love and honour him from their very souls, were delighted to see the sunbeams once more play in his countenance. Every one seemed to vie who should talk the most, tell the longest stories, and be most agreeable; and Will Wizard, who had accompanied me in my visit, declared, as he lighted his segar, which had gone out forty times in the course of one of his oriental tales,—that he had not passed so pleasant an evening since the birth-night ball of the beauteous empress of Hayti.

[The following essay was written by my friend Langstaff, in one of the paroxysms of his splenetic complaint; and, for aught I know, may have been effectual in restoring him to good humour.—A mental discharge of the kind has a remarkable tendency toward sweetening the temper,—and Launcelot is, at this moment, one of the best-natured men in existence.

A. EVERGREEN.]

ON GREATNESS.

BY LAUNCELOT LANGSTAFF, ESQ.

WE have more than once, in the course of our work, been most jocosely familiar with great personages; and, in truth, treated them with as little ceremony, respect, and consideration, as if they had been our most particular friends. Now, we would not suffer the mortification of having our readers even suspect us of an intimacy of the kind; assuring them we are extremely choice in our intimates, and uncommonly circumspect in avoiding connections with all doubtful characters; particularly pimps, bailiffs, lottery-brokers, chevaliers of industry, and great men. The world, in general, is pretty well aware of what is to be understood by the former classes of delinquents; but as the latter has never, I believe, been specifically defined; and as we are determined to instruct our readers to the extent of our abilities, and their limited comprehension, it may not be amiss here to let them know what we understand by a great man.

First, therefore, let us—editors and kings are always plural—premise, that there are two kinds of greatness,—one conferred by heaven—the exalted nobility of the soul;—the other, a spurious distinction, engendered by the mob and lavished upon its favourites. The former of these distinctions we have always contemplated with reverence; the latter, we will take this opportunity to strip naked before our unenlightened readers; so that if by chance any of them are held in ignominious thraldrom by this base circulation of false coin, they may forthwith emancipate themselves from such inglorious delusion.

It is a fictitious value given to individuals by public caprice, as bankers give an impression to a worthless slip of paper; thereby gaining it a currency for infinitely more than its intrinsic value. Every nation has its peculiar coin, and peculiar great men; neither of which will, for the most part, pass current out of the country where they are stamped. Your true mob-created great man, is like a note of one of the little New-England banks, and his value depreciates in proportion to the distance from home. In England a great man is he who has most ribands and gew-gaws on his coat, most horses to his carriage, most slaves in his retinue, or most toad-eaters at his table; in France, he who can most dexterously flourish his heels above his head——Duport is most incontestably the greatest man in France!—when the emperor is absent. The greatest man in China is he who can trace his ancestry up to the moon; and in this country, our great men may generally hunt down their pedigree until it burrows in the dirt like a rabbit. To be concise; our great men are those who are most expert at crawling on all fours, and have the happiest facility in dragging and winding themselves along in the dirt like very reptiles. This may seem a paradox to many of my readers, who, with great good-nature be it hinted, are too stupid to look beyond the mere surface of our invaluable writings; and often pass over the knowing allusion, and poignant meaning, that is slily couching beneath. It is for the benefit of such helpless ignorants, who have no other creed but the opinion of the mob, that I shall trace—as far as it is possible to follow him in his progress from insignificance—the rise, progress, and completion of a LITTLE GREAT MAN.

In a logocracy, to use the sage Mustapha's phrase, it is not absolutely necessary to the formation of a great man that he should be either wise or valiant, upright or honourable. On the contrary, daily experience shows that these qualities rather impede his preferment; inasmuch as they are prone to render him too inflexibly erect, and are directly at variance with that willowy suppleness which enables a man to wind and twist through all the nooks and turns and dark winding passages that lead to greatness. The grand requisite for climbing the rugged hill of popularity,—the summit of which is the seat of power,—is to be useful. And here once more, for the sake of our readers, who are, of course, not so wise as ourselves, I must explain what we understand by usefulness. The horse, in his native state, is wild, swift, impetuous, full of majesty, and of a most generous spirit. It is then the animal is noble, exalted, and useless.—But entrap him, manacle him, cudgel him, break down his lofty spirit, put the curb into his mouth, the load upon his back, and reduce him into servile obedience to the bridle and the lash, and it is then he becomes useful. Your jackass is one of the most useful animals in existence. If my readers do not now understand what I mean by usefulness, I give them all up for most absolute nincoms.

To rise in this country, a man must first descend. The aspiring politician may be compared to that indefatigable insect called the tumbler; pronounced by a distinguished personage to be the only industrious animal in Virginia, which buries itself in filth, and works ignobly in the dirt, until it forms a little ball, which it rolls laboriously along, like Diogenes in his tub; sometimes head, sometimes tail foremost, pilfering from every rut and mud-hole, and increasing its ball of greatness by the contributions of the kennel. Just so the candidate for greatness;—he plunges into that mass of obscenity, the mob; labours in dirt and oblivion, and makes unto himself the rudiments of a popular name from the admiration and praises of rogues, ignoramuses, and blackguards. His name once started, onward he goes struggling, and puffing, and pushing it before him; collecting new tributes from the dregs and offals of the land, as he proceeds, until having gathered together a mighty mass of popularity, he mounts it in triumph; is hoisted into office, and becomes a great man, and a ruler in the land;—all this will be clearly illustrated by a sketch of a worthy of the kind, who sprung up under my eye, and was hatched from pollution by the broad rays of popularity, which, like the sun, can "breed maggots in a dead dog."

TIMOTHY DABBLE was a young man of very promising talents; for he wrote a fair hand, and had thrice won the silver medal at a country academy;—he was also an orator, for he talked with emphatic volubility, and could argue a full hour, without taking either side, or advancing a single opinion;—he had still further requisites for eloquence;—for he made very handsome gestures, had dimples in his cheeks when he smiled, and enunciated most harmoniously through his nose. In short, nature had certainly marked him out for a great man; for though he was not tall, yet he added at least half an inch to his stature by elevating his head, and assumed an amazing expression of dignity by turning up his nose and curling his nostrils in a style of conscious superiority. Convinced by these unequivocal appearances, Dabble's friends, in full caucus, one and all, declared that he was undoubtedly born to be a great man; and it would be his own fault if he were not one. Dabble was tickled with an opinion which coincided so happily with his own,—for vanity, in a confidential whisper, had given him the like intimation;—and he reverenced the judgment of his friends because they thought so highly of himself;—accordingly he set out with a determination to become a great man, and to start in the scrub-race for honour and renown. How to attain the desired prizes was, however, the question. He knew by a kind of instinctive feeling, which seems peculiar to grovelling minds, that honour, and its better part—profit, would never seek him out; that they would never knock at his door and crave admittance; but must be courted, and toiled after, and earned. He therefore strutted forth into the highways, the market-places, and the assemblies of the people; ranted like a true cockerel orator about virtue, and patriotism, and liberty, and equality, and himself. Full many a political wind-mill did he battle with; and full many a time did he talk himself out of breath, and his hearers out of their patience. But Dabble found, to his vast astonishment, that there was not a notorious political pimp at a ward meeting but could out-talk him; and what was still more mortifying, there was not a notorious political pimp but was more noticed and caressed than himself. The reason was simple enough; while he harangued about principles, the others ranted about men;

where he reprobated a political error, they blasted a political character;—they were consequently, the most useful; for the great object of our political disputes is not who shall have the honor of emancipating the community from the leading strings of delusion, but who shall have the profit of holding the strings and leading the community by the nose.

Dabble was likewise very loud in his professions of integrity, incorruptibility, and disinterestedness; words which, from being filtered and refined through newspapers and election handbills, have lost their original signification; and in the political dictionary are synonymous with empty pockets, itching palms, and interested ambition. He, in addition to all this, declared that he would support none but honest men; —but unluckily as but few of these offered themselves to be supported, Dabble's services were seldom required. He pledged himself never to engage in party schemes, or party politics, but to stand up solely for the broad interests of his country;— so he stood alone; and what is the same thing, he stood still; for, in this country, he who does not side with either party, is like a body in a *vacuum* between two planets, and must for ever remain motionless.

Dabble was immeasurably surprised that a man so honest, so disinterested, and so sagacious withal,—and one too who had the good of his country so much at heart, should thus remain unnoticed and unapplauded. A little worldly advice, whispered in his ear by a shrewd old politician, at once explained the whole mystery. "He who would become great," said he, "must serve an apprenticeship to greatness; and rise by regular gradation, like the master of a vessel, who commences by being scrub and cabin-boy. He must fag in the train of great men, echo all their sentiments, become their toad-eater and parasite; —laugh at all their jokes, and above all, endeavour to make them laugh; if you only now and then make a man laugh, your fortune is made. Look but about you, youngster, and you will not see a single little great man of the day, but has his miserable herd of retainers, who yelp at his heels, come at his whistle, worry whoever he points his finger at, and think themselves fully rewarded by sometimes snapping up a crumb that falls from the great man's table. Talk of patriotism and virtue, and incorruptibility!—tut, man! they are the very qualities that scare munificence, and keep patronage at a distance. You might as well attempt to entice crows with red rags and gunpowder. Lay all these scarecrow virtues aside, and let this be your maxim, that a candidate for political eminence is like a dried herring; he never becomes luminous until he is corrupt."

Dabble caught with hungry avidity these congenial doctrines, and turned into his pre-destined channel of action with the force and rapidity of a stream which has for a while been restrained from its natural course. He became what nature had fitted him to be;—his tone softened down from arrogant self-sufficiency, to the whine of fawning solicitation. He mingled in the caucuses of the sovereign people; adapted his dress to a similitude of dirty raggedness; argued most logically with those who were of his own opinion; and slandered, with all the malice of impotence, exalted characters whose orbit he despaired ever to approach:—just as that scoundrel midnight thief, the owl, hoots at the blessed light of the sun, whose glorious lustre he dares never contemplate. He likewise applied himself to discharging, faithfully, the honourable duties of a partizan;—he poached about for private slanders and ribald anecdotes;—he folded handbills;—he even wrote one or two himself, which he carried about in his pocket and read to every body;—he became a secretary at ward-meetings, set his hand to divers resolutions of patriotic import, and even once went so far as to make a speech, in which he proved that patriotism was a virtue;—the reigning bashaw a great man;—that this was a free country, and he himself an arrant and incontestable buzzard!

Dabble was now very frequent and devout in his visits to those temples of politics, popularity, and smoke,- the ward porter-houses; those true dens of equality where all ranks, ages, and talents are brought down to the dead level of rude familiarity. 'Twas here his talents expanded, and his genius swelled up into its proper size; like the loathsome toad, which, shrinking from balmy airs and jocund sunshine, finds his congenial home in caves and dungeons, and there nourishes his venom, and bloats his deformity. 'Twas here he revelled with the swinish multitude in their debauches on patriotism and porter; and it became an even chance whether Dabble would turn out a great man or a great drunkard. But Dabble in all this kept steadily in his eye the only deity he ever worshipped—his interest. Having by this familiarity ingratiated himself with the mob, he became wonderfully potent and industrious at elections; knew all the dens and cellars of profligacy and intemperance; brought more negroes to the polls, and knew to a greater certainty where votes could be bought for beer, than any of his contemporaries. His exertions in the cause, his persevering industry, his degrading compliance, his unresisting humility, his steadfast dependence, at length caught the attention of one of the leaders of the party; who was pleased to observe that Dabble was a very useful fellow, who would go all lengths. From that moment his fortune was made;—he was hand and glove with orators and slang-whangers; basked in the sunshine of great men's smiles, and had the honour, sundry times, of shaking hands with dignitaries, and drinking out of the same pot with them at a porter-house!!

I will not fatigue myself with tracing this caterpillar in his slimy progress from worm to butterfly: suffice it that Dabble bowed and bowed, and fawned, and sneaked, and smirked, and libelled, until one would have thought perseverance itself would have settled down into despair. There was no knowing how long he might have lingered at a distance from his hopes, had he not luckily got tarred and feathered for some of his electioneering manœuvres;—this was the making of him!—Let not my readers stare;—tarring and feathering here is equal to pillory and cropped ears in English; and either of these kinds of martyrdom will ensure a patriot the sympathy and support of his faction. His partizans, for even he had his partizans, took his case into consideration;—he had been kicked and cuffed, and disgraced, and dishonoured in the cause;—he had licked the dust at the feet of the mob;—he was a faithful drudge, slow to anger, of invincible patience, of incessant assiduity;—a thorough-going tool, who could be curbed, and spurred, and directed at pleasure;—in short, he had all the important qualifications for a little great man, and he was accordingly ushered into office amid the acclamations of the party. The leading men complimented his usefulness, the multitude his republican simplicity, and the slang-whangers vouched for his patriotism. Since his elevation he has discovered indubitable signs of having been destined for a great man. His nose has acquired an additional elevation of several degrees, so that now he appears to have bidden adieu to this world and to have set his thoughts altogether on things above; and he has swelled and inflated himself to such a degree, that his friends are under apprehensions that he will one day or other explode and blow up like a torpedo.

NO. XVI.—THURSDAY, OCT. 15, 1807.

STYLE, AT BALLSTON.

BY WILLIAM WIZARD, ESQ.

NOTWITHSTANDING Evergreen has never been abroad, nor had his understanding enlightened, or his views enlarged by that marvellous sharpener of the wits, a salt-water voyage; yet he is tolerably shrewd, and correct, in the limited sphere of his observations; and now and then astounds me with a right pithy remark, which would do no discredit even to a man who had made the grand tour.

In several late conversations at Cockloft-Hall, he has amused us exceedingly by detailing sundry particulars concerning that notorious slaughter-house of time, Ballston Springs; where he spent a considerable part of the last summer. The following is a summary of his observations.

Pleasure has passed through a variety of significations at Ballston. It originally meant nothing more than a relief from pain and sickness; and the patient who had journeyed many a weary mile to the Springs, with a heavy heart and emaciated form, called it pleasure when he threw by his crutches, and danced away from them with renovated spirits and limbs jocund with vigour. In process of time pleasure underwent a refinement, and appeared in the likeness of a sober, unceremonious country-dance, to the flute of an amateur or the three-stringed fiddle of an itinerant country musician.—Still every thing bespoke that happy holiday which the spirits ever enjoy, when emancipated from the shackles of formality, ceremony, and modern politeness: things went on cheerily, and Ballston was pronounced a charming, hum-drum, careless place of resort, where every one was at his ease, and might follow unmolested the bent of his humour—provided his wife was not there;

—when, lo! all on a sudden Style made its baneful appearance in the semblance of a gig and tandem, a pair of leather breeches, a liveried footman, and a cockney!—since that fatal era pleasure has taken an entire new signification, and at present means nothing but STYLE.

The worthy, fashionable, dashing, good-for-nothing people of every state, who had rather suffer the martyrdom of a crowd than endure the monotony of their own homes and the stupid company of their own thoughts, flock to the Springs; not to enjoy the pleasures of society or benefit by the qualities of the waters, but to exhibit their equipages and wardrobes, and to excite the admiration, or what is much more satisfactory, the envy of their fashionable competitors. This, of course, awakens a spirit of noble emulation between the eastern, middle, and southern states; and every lady hereupon finding herself charged in a manner with the whole weight of her country's dignity and style, dresses and dashes and sparkles without mercy at her competitors from other parts of the Union. This kind of rivalship naturally requires a vast deal of preparation and prodigious quantities of supplies. A sober citizen's wife will break half a dozen milliners' shops, and sometimes starve her family a whole season, to enable herself to make the Springs campaign in style.—She repairs to the seat of war with a mighty force of trunks and bandboxes, like so many ammunition chests, filled with caps, hats, gowns, ribands, shawls, and all the various artillery of fashionable warfare. The lady of a southern planter will lay out the whole annual produce of a rice plantation in silver and gold muslins, lace veils, and new liveries; carry a hogshead of tobacco on her head, and trail a bale of sea-island cotton at her heels, while a lady of Boston or Salem will wrap herself up in the net proceeds of a cargo of whale-oil, and tie on her hat with a quintal of codfish.

The planters' ladies, however, have generally the advantage in this contest; for, as it is an incontestable fact, that whoever comes from the West or East Indies, or Georgia, or the Carolinas, or, in fact, any warm climate, is immensely rich, it cannot be expected that a simple cit of the north can cope with them in style. The planter, therefore, who drives four horses abroad and a thousand negroes at home, and who flourishes up to the Springs, followed by half a score of black-a-moors in gorgeous liveries, is unquestionably superior to the northern merchant, who plods on in a carriage and pair; which, being nothing more than is quite necessary, has no claim whatever to style. He, however, has his consolation in feeling superior to the honest cit who dashes about in a simple gig:—he, in return, sneers at the country squire, who jogs along with his scrubby, long-eared pony and saddle-bags; and the squire, by way of taking satisfaction, would make no scruple to run over the unobtrusive pedestrian, were it not that the last being the most independent of the whole, might chance to break his head by way of retort.

The great misfortune is, that this style is supported at such an expense as sometimes to encroach on the rights and privileges of the pocket, and occasion very awkward embarrassments to the tyro of fashion. Among a number of instances, Evergreen mentions the fate of a dashing blade from the south, who made his *entrée* with a tandem and two out-riders, by the aid of which he attracted the attention of all the ladies, and caused a coolness between several young couples, who, it was thought, before his arrival, had a considerable kindness for each other. In the course of a fortnight his tandem disappeared!—the class of good folk who seem to have nothing to do in this world but pry into other people's affairs, began to stare! —in a little time longer an outrider was missing!—this increased the alarm, and it was consequently whispered that he had eaten the horses and drank the negro.—N. B. Southern gentlemen are very apt to do this on an emergency.--Serious apprehensions were entertained about the fate of the remaining servant, which were soon verified by his actually vanishing; and, in "one little month," the dashing Carolinian modestly took his departure in the stage-coach!—universally regretted by the friends who had generously released him from his cumbrous load of style.

Evergreen, in the course of his detail, gave very melancholy accounts of an alarming famine which raged with great violence at the Springs. Whether this was owing to the incredible appetites of the company, or the scarcity which prevailed at the inns, he did not seem inclined to say; but he declares that he was for several days in imminent danger of starvation, owing to his being a little too dilatory in his attendance at the dinner-table. He relates a number of "moving accidents" which befell many of the polite company in their zeal to get a good seat at dinner; on which occasion a kind of scrub-race always took place, wherein a vast deal of jockeying and unfair play was shown, and a variety of squabbles and unseemly altercations occurred. But when arrived at the scene of action, it was truly an awful sight to behold the confusion, and to hear the tumultuous uproar of voices crying, some for one thing and some for another, to the tuneful accompaniment of knives and forks, rattling with all the energy of hungry impatience. —The feast of the Centaurs and the Lapithæ was nothing when compared with a dinner at the great house. At one time an old gentleman, whose natural irascibility was a little sharpened by the gout, had scalded his throat by gobbling down a bowl of hot soup in a vast hurry, in order to secure the first fruits of a roasted partridge before it was snapped up by some hungry rival; when, just as he was whetting his knife and fork, preparatory for a descent on the promised land, he had the mortification to see it transferred bodily to the plate of a squeamish little damsel who was taking the waters for debility and loss of appetite. This was too much for the patience of old crusty; he lodged his fork into the partridge, whipt it into his dish, and cutting off a wing of it,—"There, Miss, there's more than you can eat.—Oons! what should such a little chalky-faced puppet as you do with a whole partridge!"—At another time a mighty, sweet-disposed old dowager, who loomed most magnificently at the table, had a sauce-boat launched upon the capacious lap of a silver-sprigged muslin gown by the manœvring of a little politic Frenchman, who was dexterously attempting to make a lodgment under the covered way of a chicken-pye;—human nature could not bear it!—the lady bounced round, and, with one box on the ear, drove the luckless wight to utter annihilation.

But these little cross accidents are amply compensated by the great variety of amusements which abound at this charming resort of beauty and fashion. In the morning the company, each like a jolly Bacchanalian with glass in hand, sally forth to the Springs: where the gentlemen, who wish to make themselves agreeable, have an opportunity of dipping themselves into the good opinion of the ladies: and it is truly delectable to see with what grace and adroitness they perform this ingratiating feat. Anthony says that it is peculiarly amazing to behold the quantity of water the ladies drink on this occasion for the purpose of getting an appetite for breakfast. He assures me he has been present when a young lady of unparalleled delicacy tossed off in the space of a minute or two one and twenty tumblers and a wine-glass full. On my asking Anthony whether the solicitude of the by-standers was not greatly awakened as to what might be the effects of this debauch, he replied that the ladies at Ballston had become such great sticklers for the doctrine of evaporation, that no gentleman ever ventured to remonstrate against this excessive drinking for fear of bringing his philosophy into contempt. The most notorious water-drinkers in particular were continually holding forth on the surprising aptitude with which the Ballston waters evaporated; and several gentlemen, who had the hardihood to question this female philosophy, were held in high displeasure.

After breakfast every one chooses his amusement;—some take a ride into the pine woods and enjoy the varied and romantic scenery of burnt trees, post and rail fences, pine flats, potato patches, and log huts;—others scramble up the surrounding sand-hills, that look like the abodes of a gigantic race of ants;—take a peep at the other sand-hills beyond them;—and then—come down again: others, who are romantic, and sundry young ladies insist upon being so whenever they visit the Springs, or go any where into the country, stroll along the borders of a little swampy brook that drags itself along like an Alexandrine; and that so lazily as not to make a single murmur;—watching the little tadpoles as they frolic, right flippantly, in the muddy stream; and listening to the inspiring melody of the harmonious frogs that croak upon its borders. Some play at billiards, some play at the fiddle, and some—play the fool;—the latter being the most prevalent amusement at Ballston.

These, together with abundance of dancing, and a prodigious deal of sleeping of afternoons, make up the variety of pleasures at the Springs;—a delicious life of alternate lassitude and fatigue; of laborious dissipation and listless idleness; of sleepless nights, and days spent in that dozing insensibility which ever succeeds them. Now and then, indeed, the influenza, the fever-and-ague, or some such pale-faced intruder, may happen to throw a momentary damp on the general felicity; but on the whole, Evergreen declares that Ballston wants only six things, to wit: good air, good wine, good living, good beds, good company, and good humour, to be the most enchanting place in the world;——excepting Botany-bay, Musquito Cove, Dismal Swamp, and the Black-hole at Calcutta.

The following letter from the sage Mustapha has cost us more trouble to decypher and render into tolerable English than any hitherto published. It was full of blots and erasures, particularly the latter part, which we have no doubt was penned in a moment of great wrath and indignation. Mustapha has often a rambling mode of writing, and his thoughts take such unaccountable turns that it is difficult to tell one moment where he will lead you the next. This is particularly obvious in the commencement of his letters, which seldom bear much analogy to the subsequent parts;—he sets off with a flourish, like a dramatic hero,—assumes an air of great pomposity, and struts up to his subject mounted most loftily on stilts. L. LANGSTAFF.

LETTER FROM MUSTAPHA RUB-A-DUB KELI KHAN,

TO ASEM HACCHEM, PRINCIPAL SLAVE-DRIVER TO HIS HIGHNESS THE BASHAW OF TRIPOLI.

AMONG the variety of principles by which mankind are actuated, there is one, my dear Asem, which I scarcely know whether to consider as springing from grandeur and nobility of mind, or from a refined species of vanity and egotism. It is that singular, although almost universal, desire of living in the memory of posterity; of occupying a share of the world's attention when we shall long since have ceased to be susceptible either of its praise or censure. Most of the passions of the mind are bounded by the grave;—sometimes, indeed, an anxious hope or trembling fear will venture beyond the clouds and darkness that rest upon our mortal horizon, and expatiate in boundless futurity; but it is only this active love of fame which steadily contemplates its fruition in the applause or gratitude of future ages. Indignant at the narrow limits which circumscribe existence, ambition is for ever struggling to soar beyond them;—to triumph over space and time, and to bear a name, at least, above the inevitable oblivion in which every thing else that concerns us must be involved. It is this, my friend, which prompts the patriot to his most heroic achievements; which inspires the sublimest strains of the poet, and breathes ethereal fire into the productions of the painter and the statuary.

For this the monarch rears the lofty column; the laurelled conqueror claims the triumphal arch; while the obscure individual, who moved in an humbler sphere, asks but a plain and simple stone to mark his grave and bear to the next generation this important truth, that he was born, died—and was buried. It was this passion which once erected the vast Numidian piles, whose ruins we have so often regarded with wonder, as the shades of evening—fit emblems of oblivion—gradually stole over and enveloped them in darkness.—It was this which gave being to those sublime monuments of Saracen magnificence, which nod in mouldering desolation, as the blast sweeps over our deserted plains.——How futile are all our efforts to evade the obliterating hand of time! As I traversed the dreary wastes of Egypt, on my journey to Grand Cairo, I stopped my camel for a while and contemplated, in awful admiration, the stupendous pyramids.—An appalling silence prevailed around; such as reigns in the wilderness when the tempest is hushed and the beasts of prey have retired to their dens. The myriads that had once been employed in rearing these lofty mementoes of human vanity, whose busy hum once enlivened the solitude of the desert,—had all been swept from the earth by the irresistible arm of death;—all were mingled with their native dust;—all were forgotten! Even the mighty names which these sepulchres were designed to perpetuate had long since faded from remembrance; history and tradition afforded but vague conjectures, and the pyramids imparted a humiliating lesson to the candidate for immortality.——Alas! alas! said I to myself, how mutable are the foundations on which our proudest hopes of future fame are reposed! He who imagines he has secured to himself the meed of deathless renown, indulges in deluding visions, which only bespeak the vanity of the dreamer. The storied obelisk,—the triumphal arch,—the swelling dome, shall crumble into dust, and the names they would preserve from oblivion shall often pass away before their own duration is accomplished.

Yet this passion for fame, however ridiculous in the eye of the philosopher, deserves respect and consideration, from having been the source of so many illustrious actions; and hence it has been the practice in all enlightened governments to perpetuate, by monuments, the memory of great men, as a testimony of respect for the illustrious dead, and to awaken in the bosoms of posterity an emulation to merit the same honourable distinction. The people of the American logocracy, who pride themselves upon improving on every precept or example of ancient or modern governments, have discovered a new mode of exciting this love of glory; a mode by which they do honour to their great men, even in their lifetime!

Thou must have observed by this time that they manage every thing in a manner peculiar to themselves; and doubtless in the best possible manner, seeing they have denominated themselves "the most enlightened people under the sun." Thou wilt therefore, perhaps, be curious to know how they contrive to honour the name of a living patriot, and what unheard-of monument they erect in memory of his achievements. —By the fiery beard of the mighty Barbarossa, but I can scarcely preserve the sobriety of a true disciple of Mahomet while I tell thee!—wilt thou not smile, O Mussulman of invincible gravity, to learn that they honour their great men by eating, and that the only trophy erected to their exploits is a public dinner! But, trust me, Asem, even in this measure, whimsical as it may seem, the philosophic and considerate spirit of this people is admirably displayed. Wisely concluding that when the hero is dead he becomes insensible to the voice of fame, the song of adulation, or the splendid trophy, they have determined that he shall enjoy his quantum of celebrity while living, and revel in the full enjoyment of a ninedays' immortality. The barbarous nations of antiquity immolated human victims to the memory of their lamented dead, but the enlightened Americans offer up whole hecatombs of geese and calves, and oceans of wine, in honour of the illustrious living; and the patriot has the felicity of hearing from every quarter the vast exploits in gluttony and revelling that have been celebrated to the glory of his name.

No sooner does a citizen signalize himself in a conspicuous manner in the service of his country, than all the gormandizers assemble and discharge the national debt of gratitude—by giving him a dinner;—not that he really receives all the luxuries provided on this occasion;—no, my friend, it is ten chances to one that the great man does not taste a morsel from the table, and is, perhaps, five hundred miles distant; and, to let thee into a melancholy fact, a patriot under this economic government, may be often in want of a dinner, while dozens are devoured in his praise. Neither are these repasts spread out for the hungry and necessitous, who might otherwise be filled with food and gladness, and inspired to shout forth the illustrious name, which had been the means of their enjoyment;—far from this, Asem; it is the rich only who indulge in the banquet;—those who pay for the dainties are alone privileged to enjoy them; so that, while opening their purses in honour of the patriot, they at the same time fulfil a great maxim, which in this country comprehends all the rules of prudence, and all the duties a man owes to himself;—namely, getting the worth of their money.

In process of time this mode of testifying public applause has been found so marvellously agreeable, that they extend it to events as well as characters, and eat in triumph at the news of a treaty,—at the anniversary of any grand national era, or at the gaining of that splendid victory of the tongue—an election.—Nay, so far do they carry it, that certain days are set apart when the guzzlers, the gormandizers, and the winebibbers meet together to celebrate a grand indigestion, in memory of some great event; and every man in the zeal of patriotism gets devoutly drunk—"as the act directs."—Then, my friend, mayest thou behold the sublime spectacle of love of country, elevating itself from a sentiment into an appetite, whetted to the quick with the cheering prospect of tables loaded with the fat things of the land. On this occasion every man is anxious to fall to work, cram himself in honour of the day, and risk a surfeit in the glorious cause. Some, I have been told, actually fast for four and twenty hours preceding, that they may be enabled to do greater honour to the feast; and certainly, if eating and drinking are patriotic rites, he who eats and drinks most, and proves himself the greatest glutton, is, undoubtedly, the most distinguished patriot. Such, at any rate, seems to be the opinion here, and they act up to it so rigidly, that by the time it is dark, every kennel in the neighbourhood teams with illustrious members of the sovereign people, wallowing in their congenial element of mud and mire.

These patriotic feasts, or rather national monuments, are patronized and promoted by certain inferior cadis, called ALDERMEN, who are commonly complimented with their direction. These dignitaries, as far as I can learn, are generally appointed on account of their great talents for eating, a qualification peculiarly necessary in the discharge of their official duties. They hold frequent meetings at taverns and hotels, where they enter into solemn consultations for the benefit of lobsters and turtles;—establish wholesome regulations for the safety and preservation of fish and wild-fowl;—appoint the seasons most proper for eating oysters;—inquire into the economy of taverns, the characters of publicans, and the abilities of their cooks; and discuss, most learnedly, the merits of a bowl of soup, a chicken-pye, or a haunch of venison: in a word, the alderman has absolute control in all matters of eating, and superintends the whole police—of the belly. Having, in the prosecution of their important office, signalized themselves at so many public festivals; having gorged so often on patriotism and pudding, and entombed so many great names in their extensive maws, thou wilt easily conceive that they wax portly apace, that they fatten on the fame of mighty men, and that their rotundity, like the rivers, the lakes, and the mountains of their country, must be on a great scale! Even, so, my friend; and when I sometimes see a portly alderman, puffing along, and swelling as if he had the world under his waistcoat, I cannot help looking upon him as a walking monument, and am often ready to exclaim—"Tell me, thou majestic mortal, thou breathing catacomb!—to what illustrious character, what mighty event, does that capacious carcass of thine bear testimony?"

But though the enlightened citizens of this logocracy eat in honour of their friends, yet they drink destruction to their enemies.—Yea, Asem, wo unto those who are doomed to undergo the public vengeance, at a public dinner. No sooner are the viands removed, than they prepare for merciless and exterminating hostilities. They drink the intoxicating juice of the grape, out of little glass cups, and over each draught pronounce a short sentence or prayer;—not such a prayer as thy virtuous heart would dictate, thy pious lips give utterance to, my good Asem;—not a tribute of thanks to all bountiful Allah, nor a humble supplication for his blessing on the draught;—no, my friend, it is merely a toast, that is to say, a fulsome tribute of flattery to their demagogues;—a laboured sally of affected sentiment or national egotism; or, what is more despicable, a malediction on their enemies, an empty threat of vengeance, or a petition for their destruction; for toasts, thou must know, are another kind of missive weapon in a logocracy, and are levelled from afar, like the annoying arrows of the Tartars.

Oh, Asem! couldst thou but witness one of these patriotic, these monumental dinners: how furiously the flame of patriotism blazes forth;—how suddenly they vanquish armies, subjugate whole countries, and exterminate nations in a bumper, thou wouldst more than ever admire the force of that omnipotent weapon, the tongue. At these moments every coward becomes a hero, every ragamuffin an invincible warrior; and the most zealous votaries of peace and quiet, forget, for a while, their cherished maxims, and join in the furious attack. Toast succeeds toast;—kings, emperors, bashaws, are like chaff before the tempest; the inspired patriot vanquishes fleets with a single gun-boat, and swallows down navies at a draught, until, overpowered with victory and wine, he sinks upon the field of battle—dead drunk in his country's cause.—Sword of the puissant Khalid! what a display of valour is here!—the sons of Afric are hardy, brave, and enterprising, but they can achieve nothing like this.

Happy would it be if this mania for toasting extended no further than to the expression of national resentment. Though we might smile at the impotent vapouring and windy hyperbole, by which it is distinguished, yet we would excuse it, as the unguarded overflowings of a heart glowing with national injuries, and indignant at the insults offered to its country. But alas, my friend, private resentment, individual hatred, and the illiberal spirit of party, are let loose on these festive occasions. Even the names of individuals, of unoffending fellow-citizens, are sometimes dragged forth to undergo the slanders and execrations of a distempered herd of revellers.*— Head of Mahomet! how vindictive, how insatiably vindictive must be that spirit which can drug the mantling bowl with gall and bitterness, and indulge an angry passion in the moment of rejoicing!—"Wine," says their poet, "is like sunshine to the heart, which under its generous influence expands the good-will, and becomes the very temple of philanthropy." —Strange, that in a temple consecrated to such a divinity, there should remain a secret corner, polluted by the lurkings of malice and revenge; strange, that in the full flow of social enjoyment, these votaries of pleasure can turn aside to call down curses on the head of a fellow-creature. Despicable souls! ye

---

NOTE BY WILLIAM WIZARD, ESQ.

* It would seem that in this sentence, the Sage Mustapha had reference to a patriotic dinner, celebrated last fourth of July, by some gentlemen of Baltimore, when they righteously drank perdition to an unoffending individual, and really thought "they had done the state some service." This amiable custom of "eating and drinking damnation" to others, is not confined to any party:—for a month or two after the fourth of July, the different newspapers file off their columns of patriotic toasts against each other, and take a pride in showing how brilliantly their partizans can blackguard public characters in their cups—" they do but jest— poison in jest," as Hamlet says.

are unworthy of being citizens of this "most enlightened country under the sun:"—rather herd with the murderous savages who prowl the mountains of Tibesti; who stain their midnight orgies with the blood of the innocent wanderer, and drink their infernal potations from the skulls of the victims they have massacred.

And yet, trust me, Asem, this spirit of vindictive cowardice is not owing to any inherent depravity of soul, for, on other occasions, I have had ample proof that this nation is mild and merciful, brave and magnanimous;—neither is it owing to any defect in their political or religious precepts. The principles inculcated by their rulers, on all occasions, breathe a spirit of universal philanthropy; and as to their religion, much as I am devoted to the Koran of our divine prophet, still I cannot but acknowledge with admiration the mild forbearance, the amiable benevolence, the sublime morality bequeathed them by the founder of their faith.—Thou rememberest the doctrines of the mild Nazarine, who preached peace and good-will to all mankind; who, when he was reviled, reviled not again; who blessed those who cursed him, and prayed for those who despitefully used and persecuted him! What, then, can give rise to this uncharitable, this inhuman custom among the disciples of a master so gentle and forgiving?—It is that fiend POLITICS, Asem—that baneful fiend, which bewildereth every brain, and poisons every social feeling; which intrudes itself at the festive banquet, and, like the detestable harpy, pollutes the very viands of the table; which contaminates the refreshing draught while it is inhaled; which prompts the cowardly assassin to launch his poisoned arrows from behind the social board; and which renders the bottle, that boasted promoter of good fellowship and hilarity, an infernal engine, charged with direful combustion.

Oh, Asem! Asem! how does my heart sicken when I contemplate these cowardly barbarities? Let me, therefore, if possible, withdraw my attention from them for ever. My feelings have borne me from my subject; and from the monuments of ancient greatness, I have wandered to those of modern degradation. My warmest wishes remain with thee, thou most illustrious of slave-drivers; mayest thou ever be sensible of the mercies of our great prophet, who, in compassion to human imbecility, has prohibited his disciples from the use of the deluding beverage of the grape;—that enemy to reason—that promoter of defamation—that auxiliary of POLITICS.

Ever thine, MUSTAPHA.

NO. XVII.—WEDNESDAY, NOV. 11, 1807.

AUTUMNAL REFLECTIONS.

BY LAUNCELOT LANGSTAFF, ESQ.

When a man is quietly journeying downwards into the valley of the shadow of departed youth, and begins to contemplate, in a shortened perspective, the end of his pilgrimage, he becomes more solicitous than ever that the remainder of his wayfaring should be smooth and pleasant; and the evening of his life, like the evening of a summer's day, fade away in mild uninterrupted serenity. If haply his heart has escaped uninjured through the dangers of a seductive world, it may then administer to the purest of his felicities, and its chords vibrate more musically for the trials they have sustained;—like the viol, which yields a melody sweet in proportion to its age.

To a mind thus temperately harmonized, thus matured and mellowed by a long lapse of years, there is something truly congenial in the quiet enjoyment of our early autumn, amid the tranquillities of the country. There is a sober and chastened air of gayety diffused over the face of nature, peculiarly interesting to an old man; and when he views the surrounding landscape withering under his eye, it seems as if he and nature were taking a last farewell of each other, and parting with a melancholy smile; like a couple of old friends, who having sported away the spring and summer of life together, part at the approach of winter with a kind of prophetic fear that they are never to meet again.

It is either my good fortune or mishap to be keenly susceptible to the influence of the atmosphere; and I can feel in the morning, before I open my window, whether the wind is easterly. It will not, therefore, I presume, be considered an extravagant instance of vain-glory when I assert that there are few men who can discriminate more accurately in the different varieties of damps, fogs, Scotch-mists, and north-east storms, than myself. To the great discredit of my philosophy I confess I seldom fail to anathematize and excommunicate the weather, when it sports too rudely with my sensitive system; but then I always endeavour to atone therefor, by eulogizing it when deserving of approbation. And as most of my readers —simple folks! make but one distinction, to-wit, rain and sunshine;—living in most honest ignorance of the various nice shades which distinguish one fine day from another, I take the trouble, from time to time, of letting them into some of the secrets of nature;—so will they be the better enabled to enjoy her beauties, with the zest of connoisseurs, and derive at least as much information from my pages, as from the weather-wise bore of the almanac.

Much of my recreation since I retreated to the Hall, has consisted in making little excursions through the neighbourhood; which abounds in the variety of wild, romantic, and luxuriant landscape that generally characterizes the scenery in the vicinity of our rivers. There is not an eminence within a circuit of many miles but commands an extensive range of diversified and enchanting prospect.

Often have I rambled to the summit of some favourite hill; and thence, with feelings sweetly tranquil as the lucid expanse of the heavens that canopied me, have noted the slow and almost imperceptible changes that mark the waning year. There are many features peculiar to our autumn, and which give it an individual character. The "green and yellow melancholy" that first steals over the landscape;—the mild and steady serenity of the weather, and the transparent purity of the atmosphere, speak, not merely to the senses, but the heart; —it is the season of liberal emotions. To this suceeeds fantastic gayety, a motley dress, which the woods assume, where green and yellow, orange, purple, crimson, and scarlet, are whimsically blended together. A sickly splendour this!—like the wild and broken-hearted gayety that sometimes precedes dissolution;—or that childish sportiveness of superannuated age, proceeding, not from a vigorous flow of animal spirits,- but from the decay and imbecility of the mind. We might, perhaps, be deceived by this gaudy garb of nature, were it not for the rustling of the falling leaf, which, breaking on the stillness of the scene, seems to announce, in prophetic whispers, the dreary winter that is approaching. When I have sometimes seen a thrifty young oak changing its hue of sturdy vigour for a bright, but transient, glow of red, it has recalled to my mind the treacherous bloom that once mantled the cheek of a friend who is now no more; and which, while it seemed to promise a long life of jocund spirits, was the sure precursor of premature decay. In a little while and this ostentatious foliage disappears; the close of autumn leaves but one wide expanse of dusky brown; save where some rivulet steals along, bordered with little strips of green grass;—the woodland echoes no more to the carols of the feathered tribes that sported in the leafy covert, and its solitude and silence is uninterrupted, except by the plaintive whistle of the quail, the barking of the squirrel, or the still more melancholy wintry wind, which, rushing and swelling through the hollows of the mountains, sighs through the leafless branches of the grove, and seems to mourn the desolation of the year.

To one who, like myself, is fond of drawing comparisons between the different divisions of life, and those of the seasons, there will appear a striking analogy which connects the feelings of the aged with the decline of the year. Often as I contemplate the mild, uniform, and genial lustre with which the sun cheers and invigorates us in the month of October, and the almost imperceptible haze which, without obscuring, tempers all the asperities of the landscape, and gives to every object a character of stillness and repose, I cannot help comparing it with that portion of existence, when the spring of youthful hope, and the summer of the passions having gone by, reason assumes an undisputed sway, and lights us on with bright but undazzling lustre adown the hill of life. There is a full and mature luxuriance in the fields that fills the bosom with generous and disinterested content. It is not the thoughtless extravagance of spring, prodigal only in blossoms, nor the languid voluptuousness of summer, feverish in its enjoyments, and teeming only with immature abundance;—it is that certain fruition of the labours of the past—that prospect of comfortable realities, which those will be sure to enjoy who have improved the bounteous smiles of heaven, nor wasted away their spring and summer in empty trifling or criminal indulgence.

Cousin Pindar, who is my constant companion in these expeditions, and who still possesses much of the fire and energy of youthful sentiment, and a buxom hilarity of the spirits, often, indeed, draws me from these half-melancholy reveries, and makes me feel young again by the enthusiasm with which he contemplates, and the animation with which he eulogizes the beauties of nature displayed before him. His enthusiastic disposition never allows him to enjoy things by halves, and his feelings are continually breaking out in notes of admiration and ejaculations that sober reason might perhaps deem extravagant:—But for my part, when I see a hale, hearty old man, who has jostled through the rough path of the world, without having worn away the fine edge of his feelings, or blunted his sensibility to natural and moral beauty, I compare him to the ever-green of the forest, whose colours, instead of fading at the approach of winter, seem to assume additional lustre when contrasted with the surrounding desolation;—such a man is my friend Pindar;—yet sometimes, and particularly at the approach of evening, even he will fall in with my humour; but he soon recovers his natural tone of spirits: and, mounting on the elasticity of his mind, like Ganymede on the eagle's wing, he soars to the ethereal regions of sunshine and fancy.

One afternoon we had strolled to the top of a high hill in the neighbourhood of the Hall, which commands an almost boundless prospect; and as the shadows began to lengthen around us, and the distant mountains to fade into mists, my cousin was seized with a moralizing fit. "It seems to me," said he, laying his hand lightly on my shoulder, "that there is just at this season, and this hour, a sympathy between us and the world we are now contemplating. The evening is stealing upon nature as well as upon us;—the shadows of the opening day have given place to those of its close; and the only difference is, that in the morning they were before us, now they are behind; and that the first vanished in the splendours of noonday, the latter will be lost in the oblivion of night;—our 'May of life,' my dear Launce, has for ever fled; and our summer is over and gone:——but," continued he, suddenly recovering himself and slapping me gaily on the shoulder,—"but why should we repine?—what? though the capricious zephyrs of spring, the heats and hurricanes of summer, have given place to the sober sunshine of autumn!—and though the woods begin to assume the dappled livery of decay!—yet the prevailing colour is still green:—gay, sprightly green.

"Let us, then, comfort ourselves with this reflection; that though the shades of the morning have given place to those of the evening,—though the spring is past, the summer over, and the autumn come,—still you and I go on our way rejoicing;—

and while, like the lofty mountains of our southern America, our heads are covered with snow, still, like them, we feel the genial warmth of spring and summer playing upon our bosoms."

BY LAUNCELOT LANGSTAFF, ESQ.

In the description which I gave, some time since, of Cockloft-hall, I totally forgot to make honourable mention of the library; which I confess was a most inexcusable oversight; for in truth it would bear a comparison, in point of usefulness and eccentricity, with the motley collection of the renowned hero of La Mancha.

It was chiefly gathered together by my grandfather; who spared neither pains nor expense to procure specimens of the oldest, most quaint, and insufferable books in the whole compass of English, Scotch, and Irish literature. There is a tradition in the family that the old gentleman once gave a grand entertainment in consequence of having got possession of a copy of a philippic, by Archbishop Anselm, against the unseemly luxury of long toed shoes, as worn by the courtiers in the time of William Rufus, which he purchased of an honest brickmaker in the neighborhood, for a little less than forty times its value. He had undoubtedly a singular reverence for old authors, and his highest eulogium on his library was, that it consisted of books not to be met with in any other collection; and, as the phrase is, entirely out of print. The reason of which was, I suppose, that they were not worthy of being reprinted.

Cousin Christopher preserves these relics with great care, and has added considerably to the collection; for with the hall he has inherited almost all the whim-whams of its former possessor. He cherishes a reverential regard for ponderous tomes of Greek and Latin; though he knows about as much of these languages as a young bachelor of arts does a year or two after leaving college. A worm-eaten work in eight or ten volumes he compares to an old family, more respectable for its antiquity than its splendour;—a lumbering folio he considers as a duke;— a sturdy quarto, as an earl; and a row of gilded duodecimos, as so many gallant knights of the garter. But as to modern works of literature, they are thrust into trunks and drawers, as intruding upstarts, and regarded with as much contempt as mushroom nobility in England; who, having risen to grandeur, merely by their talents and services, are regarded as utterly unworthy to mingle their blood with those noble currents that can be traced without a single contamination through a long line of, perhaps, useless and profligate ancestors, up to William the bastard's cook, or butler, or groom, or some one of Rollo's freebooters.

Will Wizard, whose studies are of a most uncommon complexion, takes great delight in ransacking the library; and has been, during his late sojournings at the hall, very constant and devout in his visits to this receptacle of obsolete learning. He seemed particularly tickled with the contents of the great mahogany chest of drawers mentioned in the beginning of this work. This venerable piece of architecture has frowned, in sullen majesty, from a corner of the library, time out of mind; and is filled with musty manuscripts, some in my grandfather's handwriting, and others evidently written long before his day.

It was a sight, worthy of a man's seeing, to behold Will with his outlandish phiz poring over old scrawls that would puzzle a whole society of antiquarians to expound, and diving into receptacles of trumpery, which, for a century past, had been undisturbed by mortal hand. He would sit for whole hours, with a phlegmatic patience unknown in these degenerate days, except, peradventure, among the High Dutch commentators, prying into the quaint obscurity of musty parchments, until his whole face seemed to be converted into a folio leaf of black-letter; and occasionally, when the whimsical meaning of an obscure passage flashed on his mind, his countenance would curl up into an expression of gothic risibility, not unlike the physiognomy of a cabbage leaf wilting before a hot fire.

At such times there was no getting Will to join in our walks; or take any part in our usual recreations; he hardly gave us an oriental tale in a week, and would smoke so inveterately that no one else dared enter the library under pain of suffocation. This was more especially the case when he encountered any knotty piece of writing; and he honestly confessed to me that one worm-eaten manuscript, written in a pestilent crabbed hand, had cost him a box of the best Spanish segars before he could make it out; and after all, it was not worth a tobacco-stalk. Such is the turn of my knowing associate;—only let him get fairly in the track of any odd out-of-the-way whim-wham, and away he goes, whip and cut, until he either runs down his game, or runs himself out of breath;—I never in my life met with a man who rode his hobby-horse more intolerably hard than Wizard.

One of his favourite occupations for some time past, has been the hunting of black-letter, which he holds in high regard; and he often hints, that learning has been on the decline ever since the introduction of the Roman alphabet. An old book printed three hundred years ago, is a treasure; and a ragged scroll, about one-half unintelligible, fills him with rapture. Oh! with what enthusiasm will he dwell on the discovery of the Pandects of Justinian, and Livy's history: and when he relates the pious exertions of the Medici, in recovering the lost treasures of Greek and Roman literature, his eye brightens, and his face assumes all the splendour of an illuminated manuscript.

Will had vegetated for a considerable time in perfect tranquillity among dust and cobwebs, when one morning as we were gathered on the piazza, listening with exemplary patience to one of cousin Christopher's long stories about the revolutionary war, we were suddenly electrified by an explosion of laughter from the library.—My readers, unless peradventure they have heard honest Will laugh, can form no idea of the prodigious uproar he makes. To hear him in a forest, you would imagine—that is to say, if you were classical enough— that the satyrs and the dryads had just discovered a pair of rural lovers in the shade, and were deriding, with bursts of obstreperous laughter, the blushes of the nymph and the indignation of the swain;—or if it were suddenly, as in the present instance, to break upon the serene and pensive silence of an autumnal morning, it would cause a sensation something like that which arises from hearing a sudden clap of thunder in a summer's day, when not a cloud is to be seen above the horizon. In short, I recommend Will's laugh as a sovereign remedy for the spleen: and if any of our readers are troubled with that villainous complaint,—which can hardly be, if they make good use of our works,—I advise them earnestly to get introduced to him forthwith.

This outrageous merriment of Will's, as may be easily supposed, threw the whole family into a violent fit of wondering; we all, with the exception of Christopher, who took the interruption in high dudgeon, silently stole up to the library; and bolting in upon him, were fain at the first glance to join in his aspiring roar. His face,—but I despair to give an idea of his appearance!—and until his portrait, which is now in the hands of an eminent artist, is engraved, my readers must be content: —I promise them they shall one day or other have a striking likeness of Will's indescribable phiz, in all its native comeliness.

Upon my inquiring the occasion of his mirth, he thrust an old, rusty, musty, and dusty manuscript into my hand, of which I could not decypher one word out of ten, without more trouble than it was worth. This task, however, he kindly took off my hands; and, in a little more than eight and forty hours, produced a translation into fair Roman letters; though he assured me it had lost a vast deal of its humour by being modernized and degraded into plain English. In return for the great pains he had taken, I could not do less than insert it in our work. Will informs me that it is but one sheet of a stupendous bundle which still remains uninvestigated—who was the author we have not yet discovered, but a note on the back, in my grandfather's handwriting, informs us that it was presented to him as a literary curiosity by his particular friend, the illustrious RIP VAN DAM, formerly lieutenant-governor of the colony of NEW AMSTERDAM; and whose fame, if it has never reached these latter days, it is only because he was too modest a man ever to do any thing worthy of being particularly recorded.

CHAP. CIX. OF THE CHRONICLES OF THE RENOWNED AND ANTIENT CITY OF GOTHAM.

How Gotham city conquered was,
And how the folk turn'd apes—because.—Link. Fid.

ALBEIT, much about this time it did fall out that the thrice renowned and delectable city of GOTHAM did suffer great discomfiture, and was reduced to perilous extremity, by the invasion and assaults of the HOPPINGTOTS. These are a people inhabiting a far distant country, exceedingly pleasaunte and fertile; but they being withal egregiously addicted to migrations, do thence issue forth in mighty swarms, like the Scythians of old, overrunning divers countries, and commonwealths, and committing great devastations wheresoever they do go, by their horrible and dreadful feats and prowesses. They are specially noted for being right valorous in all exercises of the leg; and of them it hath been rightly affirmed that no nation in all Christendom or elsewhere, can cope with them in the adroit, dexterous, and jocund shaking of the heel.

This engaging excellence doth stand unto them a sovereign recommendation, by the which they do insinuate themselves into universal favour and good countenance; and it is a notable fact, that, let a Hoppingtot but once introduce a foot into company, and it goeth hardly if he doth not contrive to flourish his whole body in thereafter. The learned Linkum Fidelius, in his famous and unheard-of treatise on man, whom he defineth, with exceeding sagacity, to be a corn-cutting, tooth-drawing animal, is particularly minute and elaborate in treating of the nation of the Hoppingtots, and betrays a little of the Pythagorean in his theory, inasmuch as he accounteth for their being so wonderously adroit in pedestrian exercises, by supposing that they did originally acquire this unaccountable and unparalleled aptitude for huge and unmatchable feats of the leg, by having heretofore been condemned for their numerous offences against that harmless race of bipeds—or quadrupeds,—for herein the sage Linkum Fidelius appeareth to doubt and waver exceedingly—the frogs, to animate their bodies for the space of one or two generations.

He also giveth it as his opinion, that the name of Hoppingtots is manifestly derivative from this transmigration. Be this, however, as it may, the matter, albeit it hath been the subject of controversy among the learned, is but little pertinent to the subject of this history; wherefore shall we treat and consider it as naughte.

Now these people being thereto impelled by a superfluity of appetite, and a plentiful deficiency of the wherewithal to satisfy the same, did take thought that the antient and venerable city of Gotham, was, peradventure, possessed of mighty treasures, and did, moreover, abound with all manner of fish and flesh, and eatables and drinkables, and such like delightsome and wholesome excellencies withal. Whereupon calling a council of the most active heeled warriors, they did resolve forthwith to put forth a mighty array, make themselves masters of the same, and revel in the good things of the land. To this were they hotly stirred up, and wickedly incited, by two redoubtable and renowned warriors, hight PIROUET and RIGADOON; ycleped in such sort, by reason that they were two mighty, valiant, and invincible little men; utterly famous for the victories of the leg which they had, on divers illustrious occasions, right gallantly achieved.

These doughty champions did ambitiously and wickedly inflame the minds of their countrymen, with gorgeous descriptions, in the which they did cunninglie set forth the marvellous riches and luxuries of Gotham; where Hoppingtots might have garments for their bodies, shirts to their ruffles, and might riot most merrily every day in the week on beef, pudding, and such like lusty dainties.—They, Pirouet and Rigadoon, did likewise hold out hopes of an easy conquest; forasmuch as the Gothamites were as yet but little versed in the mystery and science of handling the legs; and being, moreover, like unto that notable bully of antiquity, Achilles, most vulnerable to all attacks on the heel, would doubtless surrender at the very first assault.—Whereupon, on the hearing of this inspiriting counsel, the Hoppingtots did set up a prodigious great cry of joy, shook their heels in triumph, and were all impatience to dance on to Gotham and take it by storm.

The cunning Pirouet and the arch caitiff Rigadoon, knew full well how to profit of this enthusiasm. They forthwith did order every man to arm himself with a certain pestilent little weapon, called a fiddle;—to pack up in his knapsack a pair of silk breeches, the like of ruffles, a cocked hat of the form of a half-moon, a bundle of catgut—and inasmuch as in marching to Gotham, the army might, peradventure, be smitten with scarcity of provisions, they did account it proper that each man should take especial care to carry with him a bunch of right merchantable onions. Having proclaimed these orders by sound of fiddle, they, Pirouet and Rigadoon, did accordingly put their army behind them, and striking up the right jolly and sprightful tune of *Ca Ira*, away they all capered towards the devoted city of Gotham, with a most horrible and appalling chattering of voices.

Of their first appearance before the beleaguered town, and of the various difficulties which did encounter them in their march, this history saith not; being that other matters of more weighty import require to be written. When that the army of the Hoppingtots did peregrinate within sight of Gotham, and the people of the city did behold the villainous and hitherto unseen capers, and grimaces, which they did make, a most horrific panic was stirred up among the citizens; and the sages of the town fell into great despondency and tribulation, as supposing that these invaders were of the race of the Jig-hees, who did make men into baboons when they achieved a conquest over them. The sages, therefore, called upon all the dancing men, and dancing women, and exhorted them with great vehemency of speech, to make heel against the invaders, and to put themselves upon such gallant defence, such glorious array, and such sturdy evolution, elevation, and transposition of the foot as might incontinently impester the legs of the Hoppingtots, and produce their complete discomfiture. But so it did happen, by great mischance, that divers light-heeled youth of Gotham, more especially those who are descended from three wise men, so renowned of yore for having most venturesomely voyaged over sea in a bowl, were, from time to time, captured and inveigled into the camp of the enemy; where, being foolishly cajoled and treated for a season with outlandish disports and pleasantries, they were sent back to their friends, entirely changed, degenerated, and turned topsy-turvy; insomuch that they thought thenceforth of nothing but their heels, always essaying to thrust them into the most manifest point of view;—and, in a word, as might truly be affirmed, did for ever after walk upon their heads outright.

And the Hoppingtots did day by day, and at late hours of the night, wax more and more urgent in this their investment of the city. At one time they would, in goodly procession, make an open assault by sound of fiddle in a tremendous contra dance;—and anon they would advance by little detachments and manœuvres to take the town by figuring in cotillions. But truly their most cunning and devilish craft, and subtilty, was made manifest in their strenuous endeavours to corrupt the garrison, by a most insidious and pestilent dance called the *Waltz*. This, in good truth, was a potent auxiliary; for, by it, were the heads of the simple Gothamites most villainously turned, their wits sent a wool-gathering, and themselves on the point of surrendering at discretion even unto the very arms of their invading foemen.

At length the fortifications of the town began to give manifest symptoms of decay; inasmuch as the breastwork of decency was considerably broken down, and the curtain works of propriety blown up. When that the cunning caitiff Pirouet beheld the ticklish and jeopardized state of the city—" Now, by my leg," quoth he,—he alwaya swore by his leg, being that it was an exceeding goodlie leg;—" Now, by my leg," quoth he, "but this is no great matter of recreation;—I will show these people a pretty, strange, and new way forsooth, presentlie, and will shake the dust off my pumps upon this most obstinate and uncivilized town." Whereupon he ordered, and did command his warriors, one and all, that they should put themselves in readiness, and prepare to carry the town by a GRAND BALL. They, in no wise to be daunted, do forthwith, at the word, equip themselves for the assault; and in good faith, truly, it was a gracious and glorious sight, a most triumphant and incomparable spectacle, to behold them gallantly arrayed in glossy and shining silk breeches tied with abundance of riband; with silken hose of the gorgeous colour of the salmon;—right goodlie morocco pumps decorated with clasps or buckles of a most cunninge and secret contrivance, inasmuch as they did of themselves grapple to the shoe without any aid of fluke or tongue, marvellously ensembling witchcraft and necromancy. They had, withal, exuberant chitterlings; which puffed out at the neck and bosom, after a most jolly fashion, like unto the beard of an antient he-turkey;—and cocked hats, the which they did carry not on their heads, after the fashion of the Gothamites, but under their arms, as a roasted fowl his gizzard.

Thus being equipped, and marshalled, they do attack, assault, batter and belabour the town with might and main;—most gallantly displaying the vigour of their legs, and shaking their heels at it most emphatically. And the manner of their attack was in this sort;—first, they did thunder and gallop forward in a *contre-temps;*—and anon, displayed column in a Cossack dance, a fandango, or a gavot. Whereat the Gothamites, in no wise understanding this unknown system of warfare, marvelled exceedinglie, and did open their mouths incontinently, the full distance of a bow-shot, meaning a cross-bow, in sore dismay and apprehension. Whereupon, saith Rigadoon, flourishing his left leg with great expression of valour, and most magnific carriage—"my copesmates, for what wait we here; are not the townsmen already won to our favour?—do not their women and young damsels wave to us from the walls in such sort that, albeit there is some show of defence, yet is it manifestly converted into our interests?" so saying, he made no more ado, but leaping into the air about a flight-shot, and crossing his feet six times, after the manner of the Hoppingtots, he gave a short partridge-run, and with mighty vigour and swiftness did bolt outright over the walls with a somerset. The whole army of Hoppingtots danced in after their valiant chieftain, with an enormous squeaking of fiddles, and a horrific blasting and brattling of horns; insomuch that the dogs did howl in the streets, so hideously were their ears assailed. The Gothamites made some semblance of defence, but their women having been all won over into the interest of the enemy, they were shortly reduced to make most abject submission; and delivered over to the coercion of certain professors of the Hoppingtots, who did put them under most ignominious durance, for the space of a long time, until they had learned to turn out their toes, and flourish their legs after the true manner of their conquerors. And thus, after the manner I have related, was the mighty and puissant city of Gotham circumvented, and taken by a *coup de pied:* or as it might by rendered, by force of legs.

The conquerors showed no mercy, but did put all ages, sexes, and conditions to the fiddle and the dance; and, in a word, compelled and enforced them to become absolute Hoppingtots. "Habit," as the ingenious Linkum Fidelius profoundly affirmeth, " is second nature." And this original and invaluable observation hath been most aply proved, and illustrated, by the example of the Gothamites, ever since this disastrous and unlucky mischance. In process of time, they have waxed to be most flagrant, outrageous, and abandoned dancers; they do ponder on noughte but how to gallantize it at balls, routs, and fandangoes; insomuch that the like was in no time or place ever observed before. They do, moreover, pitifully devote their nights to the jollification of the legs, and their days forsooth to the instruction and edification of the heel. And to conclude; their young folk, who whilome did bestow a modicum of leisure upon the improvement of the head, have of late utterly abandoned this hopeless task; and have quietly, as it were, settled themselves down into mere machines, wound up by a tune, and set in motion by a fiddle-stick!

NO. XVIII.—TUESDAY, NOV. 24, 1807.

THE LITTLE MAN IN BLACK.

BY LAUNCELOT LANGSTAFF, ESQ.

THE following story has been handed down by family tradition for more than a century. It is one on which my cousin Christopher dwells with more than usual prolixity; and, being in some measure connected with a personage often quoted in our work, I have thought it worthy of being laid before my readers.

Soon after my grandfather, Mr. Lemuel Cockloft, had quietly settled himself at the hall, and just about the time that the gossips of the neighbourhood, tired of prying into his affairs, were anxious for some new tea-table topic, the busy community of our little village was thrown into a grand turmoil of curiosity and conjecture—a situation very common to little gossiping villages—by the sudden and unaccountable appearance of a mysterious individual.

The object of this solicitude was a little black-looking man, of a foreign aspect, who took possession of an old building, which having long had the reputation of being haunted, was in a state of ruinous desolation, and an object of fear to all true believers in ghosts. He usually wore a high sugarloaf hat with a narrow brim; and a little black cloak, which, short as he was, scarcely reached below his knees. He sought no intimacy or acquaintance with any one; appeared to take no interest in the pleasures or the little broils of the village; nor ever talked; except sometimes to himself in an outlandish tongue. He commonly carried a large book, covered with sheepskin, under his arm; appeared always to be lost in meditation; and was often met by the peasantry, sometimes watching the dawning of day, sometimes at noon seated under a tree poring over his volume; and sometimes at evening gazing with a look of sober tranquillity at the sun as it gradually sunk below the horizon.

The good people of the vicinity beheld something prodigiously singular in all this;—a profound mystery seemed to hang about the stranger, which, with all their sagacity, they could not penetrate; and in the excess of worldly charity they pronounced it a sure sign "that he was no better than he should be;"—a phrase innocent enough in itself: but which, as applied in common, signifies nearly every thing that is bad. The young people thought him a gloomy misanthrope, because he never joined in their sports;—the old men thought still more hardly of him because he followed no trade, nor ever seemed ambitious of earning a farthing;—and as to the old gossips, baffled by the inflexible taciturnity of the stranger, they unanimously agreed that a man who could not or would not talk was no better than a dumb beast. The little man in black, careless of their opinions, seemed resolved to maintain the liberty of keeping his own secret; and the consequence was, that, in a little while, the whole village was in an uproar;—for in little communities of this description, the members have always the privilege of being thoroughly versed, and even of meddling in all the affairs of each other.

A confidential conference was held one Sunday morning after sermon, at the door of the village church, and the character of the unknown fully investigated. The schoolmaster gave as his opinion, that he was the wandering Jew;—the sexton was certain that he must be a free-mason from his silence; —a third maintained, with great obstinacy, that he was a high German doctor; and that the book which he carried about with him, contained the secrets of the black art; but the most prevailing opinion seemed to be that he was a witch;—a race of beings at that time abounding in those parts; and a sagacious old matron, from Connecticut, proposed to ascertain the fact by sousing him into a kettle of hot water.

Suspicion, when once afloat, goes with wind and tide, and soon becomes certainty. Many a stormy night was the little man in black, seen by the flashes of lightning, frisking and curveting in the air upon a broomstick; and it was always observed, that at those times the storm did more mischief than at any other. The old lady in particular, who suggested the humane ordeal of the boiling kettle, lost on one of these occasions a fine brindle cow; which accident was entirely ascribed to the vengeance of the little man in black. If ever a mischievous hireling rode his master's favourite horse to a distant frolic, and the animal was observed to be lame and jaded in the morning,—the little man in black was sure to be at the bottom of the affair; nor could a high wind howl through the village at night but the old women shrugged up their shoulders, and observed, "the little man in black was in his *tantrums.*" In short, he became the bugbear of every house; and was as effectual in frightening little children into obedience and hysterics, as the redoubtable Raw-head-and-bloody-bones himself: nor could a housewife of the village sleep in peace, except under the guardianship of a horse-shoe nailed to the door.

The object of these direful suspicions remained for some time totally ignorant of the wonderful quandary he had occasioned; but he was soon doomed to feel its effects. An individual who is once so unfortunate as to incur the odium of a village, is in a great measure outlawed and proscribed; and becomes a mark for injury and insult; particularly if he has not the power or the disposition to recriminate. The little venomous passions, which in the great world are dissipated and weakened by being widely diffused, act in the narrow limits of a country town with collected vigour, and become rancorous in proportion as they are confined in their sphere of action. The little man in black experienced the truth of this; every mischievous urchin returning from school, had full liberty to break his windows; and this was considered as a most daring exploit; for in such awe did they stand of him, that the most adventurous school boy was never seen to approach his threshold, and at night would prefer going round by the cross-roads, where a traveller had been murdered by the Indians, rather than pass by the door of his forlorn habitation.

The only living creature that seemed to have any care or affection for this deserted being was an old turnspit,—the companion of his lonely mansion and his solitary wanderings; —the sharer of his scanty meals, and, sorry am I to say it, the sharer of his persecutions. The turnspit, like his master, was peaceable and inoffensive; never known to bark at a horse, to growl at a traveller, or to quarrel with the dogs of the neighbourhood. He followed close at his master's heels when he went out, and when he returned stretched himself in the sunbeams at the door; demeaning himself in all things like a civil and well-disposed turnspit. But notwithstanding his exemplary deportment, he fell likewise under the ill report of the village;

as being the familiar of the little man in black, and the evil spirit that presided at his incantations. The old hovel was considered as the scene of their unhallowed rites, and its harmless tenants regarded with a detestation which their inoffensive conduct never merited.—Though pelted and jeered at by the brats of the village, and frequently abused by their parents, the little man in black never turned to rebuke them; and his faithful dog, when wantonly assaulted, looked up wistfully in his master's face, and there learned a lesson of patience and forbearance.

The movements of this inscrutable being had long been the subject of speculation at Cockloft-hall, for its inmates were full as much given to wondering as their descendants. The patience with which he bore his persecutions particularly surprised them; for patience is a virtue but little known in the Cockloft family. My grandmother, who it appears was rather superstitious, saw in this humility nothing but the gloomy sullenness of a wizard, who restrained himself for the present, in hopes of midnight vengeance;—the parson of the village, who was a man of some reading, pronounced it the stubborn insensibility of a stoic philosopher;—my grandfather, who, worthy soul, seldom wandered abroad in search of conclusions, took a data from his own excellent heart, and regarded it as the humble forgiveness of a Christian. But however different were their opinions as to the character of the stranger, they agreed in one particular, namely, in never intruding upon his solitude; and my grandmother, who was at that time nursing my mother, never left the room without wisely putting the large family Bible in the cradle; a sure talisman, in her opinion, against witchcraft and necromancy.

One stormy winter night, when a bleak north-east wind moaned about the cottages, and howled around the village steeple, my grandfather was returning from club, preceded by a servant with a lantern. Just as he arrived opposite the desolate abode of the little man in black, he was arrested by the piteous howling of a dog, which, heard in the pauses of the storm, was exquisitely mournful; and he fancied now and then, that he caught the low and broken groans of some one in distress.—He stopped for some minutes, hesitating between the benevolence of his heart and a sensation of genuine delicacy, which, in spite of his eccentricity, he fully possessed,—and which forbade him to pry into the concerns of his neighbours. Perhaps, too, this hesitation might have been strengthened by a little taint of superstition; for surely, if the unknown had been addicted to witchcraft, this was a most propitious night for his vagaries. At length the old gentleman's philanthropy predominated; he approached the hovel, and pushing open the door,—for poverty has no occasion for locks and keys,—beheld, by the light of the lantern, a scene that smote his generous heart to the core.

On a miserable bed, with pallid and emaciated visage, and hollow eyes;—in a room destitute of every convenience;—without fire to warm, or friend to console him, lay this helpless mortal, who had been so long the terror and wonder of the village. His dog was crouching on the scanty coverlet, and shivering with cold. My grandfather stepped softly and hesitatingly to the bed-side, and accosted the forlorn sufferer in his usual accents of kindness. The little man in black seemed recalled by the tones of compassion from the lethargy into which he had fallen; for, though his heart was almost frozen, there was yet one chord that answered to the call of the good old man who bent over him; the tones of sympathy, so novel to his ear, called back his wandering senses, and acted like a restorative to his solitary feelings.

He raised his eyes, but they were vacant and haggard;—he put forth his hand, but it was cold; he essayed to speak, but the sound died away in his throat;—he pointed to his mouth with an expression of dreadful meaning, and, sad to relate! my grandfather understood that the harmless stranger, deserted by society, was perishing with hunger!—with the quick impulse of humanity he despatched the servant to the hall for refreshment. A little warm nourishment renovated him for a short time, but not long:—it was evident his pilgrimage was drawing to a close, and he was about entering that peaceful asylum where "the wicked cease from troubling."

His tale of misery was short, and quickly told: infirmities had stolen upon him, heightened by the rigours of the season: he had taken to his bed without strength to rise and ask for assistance;—"and if I had," said he in a tone of bitter despondency, "to whom should I have applied? I have no friend that I know of in the world!—the villagers avoid me as something loathsome and dangerous; and here, in the midst of Christians, should I have perished, without a fellow-being to soothe the last moments of existence, and close my dying eyes, had not the howlings of my faithful dog excited your attention."

He seemed deeply sensible of the kindness of my grandfather; and at one time as he looked up into his old benefactor's face, a solitary tear was observed to steal adown the parched furrows of his cheek—poor outcast!—it was the last tear he shed—but I warrant it was not the first by millions! my grandfather watched by him all night. Towards morning he gradually declined; and as the rising sun gleamed through the window, he begged to be raised in his bed that he might look at it for the last time. He contemplated it for a moment with a kind of religious enthusiasm, and his lips moved as if engaged in prayer. The strange conjectures concerning him rushed on my grandfather's mind: "he is an idolater!" thought he, "and is worshipping the sun!"—He listened a moment and blushed at his own uncharitable suspicion; he was only engaged in the pious devotions of a Christian. His simple orison being finished, the little man in black withdrew his eyes from the east, and taking my grandfather's hand in one of his, and making a motion with the other towards the sun;—"I love to contemplate it," said he, "'tis an emblem of the universal benevolence of a true Christian;—and it is the most glorious work of him who is philanthropy itself!" My grandfather blushed still deeper at his ungenerous surmises; he had pitied the stranger at first, but now he revered him:—he turned once more to regard him, but his countenance had undergone a change;—the holy enthusiasm that had lighted up each feature, had given place to an expression of mysterious import;—a gleam of grandeur seemed to steal across his Gothic visage, and he appeared full of some mighty secret which he hesitated to impart. He raised the tattered nightcap that had sunk almost over his eyes, and waving his withered hand with a slow and feeble expression of dignity,—"In me," said he, with laconic solemnity,—"in me you behold the last descendant of the renowned Linkum Fidelius!" My grandfather gazed at him with reverence; for though he had never heard of the illustrious personage, thus pompously announced, yet there was a certain black-letter dignity in the name that peculiarly struck his fancy and commanded his respect.

"You have been kind to me," continued the little man in black, after a momentary pause, "and richly will I requite your kindness by making you heir to my treasures! In yonder large deal box are the volumes of my illustrious ancestor, of which I alone am the fortunate possessor. Inherit them—ponder over them, and be wise!" He grew faint with the exertion he had made, and sunk back almost breathless on his pillow. His hand, which, inspired with the importance of his subject, he had raised to my grandfather's arm, slipped from its hold and fell over the side of the bed, and his faithful dog licked it; as if anxious to soothe the last moments of his master, and testify his gratitude to the hand that had so often cherished him. The untaught caresses of the faithful animal were not lost upon his dying master;—he raised his languid eyes,—turned them on the dog, then on my grandfather; and having given this silent recommendation,—closed them for ever.

The remains of the little man in black, notwithstanding the objections of many pious people, were decently interred in the church-yard of the village; and his spirit, harmless as the body it once animated, has never been known to molest a living being. My grandfather complied, as far as possible, with his last request; he conveyed the volumes of Linkum Fidelius to his library;—he pondered over them frequently;—but whether he grew wiser, the tradition doth not mention. This much is certain, that his kindness to the poor descendant of Fidelius was amply rewarded by the approbation of his own heart and the devoted attachment of the old turnspit, who, transferring his affection from his deceased master to his benefactor, became his constant attendant, and was father to a long line of runty curs that still flourish in the family. And thus was the Cockloft library first enriched by the invaluable folios of the sage LINKUM FIDELIUS.

LETTER FROM MUSTAPHA RUB-A-DUB KELI KHAN,

TO ASEM HACCHEM, PRINCIPAL SLAVE-DRIVER TO HIS HIGHNESS THE BASHAW OF TRIPOLI.

THOUGH I am often disgusted, my good Asem, with the vices and absurdities of the men of this country, yet the women afford me a world of amusement. Their lively prattle is as diverting as the chattering of the red-tailed parrot; nor can the green-headed monkey of Timandi equal them in whim and playfulness. But, notwithstanding these valuable qualifications, I am sorry to observe they are not treated with half the attention bestowed on the before-mentioned animals. These infidels put their parrots in cages and chain their monkeys; but their women, instead of being carefully shut up in harems and seraglios, are abandoned to the direction of their own reason and suffered to run about in perfect freedom, like other domestic animals:—this comes, Asem, of treating their women as rational beings and allowing them souls. The consequence of this piteous neglect may easily be imagined:—they have degenerated into all their native wildness, are seldom to be caught at home, and, at an early age, take to the streets and highways, where they rove about in droves, giving almost as much annoyance to the peaceable people as the troops of wild dogs that infest our great cities, or the flights of locusts that sometimes spread famine and desolation over whole regions of fertility.

This propensity to relapse into pristine wildness convinces me of the untameable disposition of the sex, who may indeed be partially domesticated by a long course of confinement and restraint, but the moment they are restored to personal freedom, become wild as the young partridge of this country, which, though scarcely half hatched, will take to the fields and run about with the shell upon its back.

Notwithstanding their wildness, however, they are remarkably easy of access, and suffer themselves to be approached at certain hours of the day without any symptoms of apprehension; and I have even happily succeeded in detecting them at their domestic occupations. One of the most important of these consists in thumping vehemently on a kind of musical instrument, and producing a confused, hideous, and indefinable uproar, which they call the description of a battle;—a jest, no doubt, for they are wonderfully facetious at times, and make great practice of passing jokes upon strangers. Sometimes they employ themselves in painting little caricatures of landscapes, wherein they display their singular drollery in bantering nature fairly out of countenance; representing her tricked out in all the tawdry finery of copper skies, purple rivers, calico rocks, red grass, clouds that look like old clothes set adrift by the tempest, and foxy trees whose melancholy foliage, drooping and curling most fantastically, reminds me of an undressed perriwig that I have now and then seen hung on a stick in a barber's window. At other times they employ themselves in acquiring a smattering of languages spoken by nations on the other side of the globe, as they find their own language not sufficiently copious to supply their constant demands and express their multifarious ideas. But their most important domestic avocation is to embroider, on satin or muslin, flowers of a nondescript kind, in which the great art is to make them as unlike nature as possible;—or to fasten little bits of silver, gold, tinsel, and glass on long strips of muslin, which they drag after them with much dignity whenever they go abroad;—a fine lady, like a bird of paradise, being estimated by the length of her tail.

But do not, my friend, fall into the enormous error of supposing that the exercise of these arts is attended with any useful or profitable result—believe me, thou couldst not indulge an idea more unjust and injurious; for it appears to be an established maxim among the women of this country, that a lady loses her dignity when she condescends to be useful, and forfeits all rank in society the moment she can be convicted of earning a farthing. Their labours, therefore, are directed not towards supplying their household, but in decking their persons, and—generous souls!—they deck their persons, not so much to please themselves, as to gratify others, particularly strangers. I am confident thou wilt stare at this, my good Asem, accustomed as thou art to our eastern females, who shrink in blushing timidity even from the glance of a lover, and are so chary of their favours, that they even seem fearful of lavishing their smiles too profusely on their husbands. Here, on the contrary, the stranger has the first place in female regard, and so far do they carry their hospitality, that I have seen a fine lady slight a dozen tried friends and real admirers, who lived in her smiles and made her happiness their study, merely to allure the vague and wandering glances of a stranger, who viewed her person with indifference and treated her advances with contempt.——By the whiskers of our sublime bashaw, but this is highly flattering to a foreigner! and thou mayest judge how particularly pleasing to one who is, like myself, so ardent an admirer of the sex. Far be it from me to condemn this extraordinary manifestation of good will—let their own countrymen look to that.

Be not alarmed, I conjure thee, my dear Asem, lest I should be tempted by these beautiful barbarians to break the faith I owe to the three-and-twenty wives from whom my unhappy destiny has perhaps severed me for ever:—no, Asem, neither time nor the bitter succession of misfortunes that pursues me can shake from my heart the memory of former attachments.

I listen with tranquil heart to the strumming and prattling of these fair syrens; their whimsical paintings touch not the tender chord of my affections; and I would still defy their fascinations, though they trailed after them trains as long as the gorgeous trappings which are dragged at the heels of the holy camel of Mecca: or as the tail of the great beast in our prophet's vision, which measured three hundred and forty-nine leagues, two miles, three furlongs, and a hand's breadth in longitude.

The dress of these women is, if possible, more eccentric and whimsical than their deportment; and they take an inordinate pride in certain ornaments which are probably derived from their savage progenitors.——A woman of this country, dressed out for an exhibition, is loaded with as many ornaments as a Circassian slave when brought out for sale. Their heads are tricked out with little bits of horn or shell, cut into fantastic shapes, and they seem to emulate each other in the number of these singular baubles;—like the women we have seen in our journeys to Aleppo, who cover their heads with the entire shell of a tortoise, and, thus equipped, are the envy of all their less fortunate acquaintance. They also decorate their necks and ears with coral, gold chains, and glass beads, and load their fingers with a variety of rings; though, I must confess, I have never perceived that they wear any in their noses—as has been affirmed by many travellers. We have heard much of their painting themselves most hideously, and making use of bear's grease in great profusion; but this, I solemnly assure thee, is a misrepresentation; civilization, no doubt, having gradually extirpated these nauseous practices. It is true, I have seen two or three of these females, who had disguised their features with paint; but then it was merely to give a tinge of red to their cheeks, and did not look very frightful; and as to ointment, they rarely use any now, except occasionally a little Grecian oil for their hair, which gives it a glossy, greasy, and, they think, very comely appearance. The last-mentioned class of females, I take it for granted, have been but lately caught, and still retain strong traits of their original savage propensities.

The most flagrant and inexcusable fault, however, which I find in these lovely savages, is the shameless and abandoned exposure of their persons. Wilt not thou suspect me of exaggeration when I affirm;—wilt thou not blush for them, most discreet Mussulman, when I declare to thee, that they are so lost to all sense of modesty, as to expose the whole of their faces from their forehead to the chin, and they even go abroad with their hands uncovered!—Monstrous indelicacy!—

But what I am going to disclose, will, doubtless, appear to thee still more incredible. Though I cannot forbear paying a tribute of admiration to the beautiful faces of these fair infidels, yet I must give it as my firm opinion, that their persons are preposterously unseemly. In vain did I look around me, on my first landing, for those divine forms of redundant proportions, which answer to the true standard of eastern beauty; —not a single fat fair one could I behold among the multitudes that thronged the streets; the females that passed in review before me, tripping sportively along, resembled a procession of shadows, returning to their graves at the crowing of the cock.

This meagreness I first ascribed to their excessive volubility; for I have somewhere seen it advanced by a learned doctor, that the sex were endowed with a peculiar activity of tongue, in order that they might practise talking as a healthful exercise, necessary to their confined and sedentary mode of life. This exercise, it was natural to suppose, would be carried to great excess in a logocracy.—"Too true," thought I, "they have converted, what was undoubtedly meant as a beneficent gift, into a noxious habit, that steals the flesh from their bones and the rose from their cheeks—they absolutely talk themselves thin!" Judge then of my surprise when I was assured, not long since, that this meagreness was considered the perfection of personal beauty, and that many a lady starved herself, with all the obstinate perseverance of a pious dervise——into a fine figure!——"Nay, more," said my informer, "they will often sacrifice their healths in this eager pursuit of skeleton beauty, and drink vinegar, eat pickles, and smoke tobacco, to keep themselves within the scanty outlines of the fashions."—Faugh! Allah preserve me from such beauties, who contaminate their pure blood with noxious recipes; who impiously sacrifice the best gifts of Heaven, to a preposterous and mistaken vanity. Ere long I shall not be surprised to see them scarring their faces like the negroes of Congo, flattening their noses in imitation of the Hottentots, or like the barbarians of Ab-al Timar, distorting their lips and ears out of all natural dimensions. Since I received this information, I cannot contemplate a fine figure, without thinking of a vinegar cruet; nor look at a dashing belle, without fancying her a pot of pickled cucumbers! What a difference, my friend, between these shades and the plump beauties of Tripoli,—what a contrast between an infidel fair one and my favourite wife Fatima, whom I bought by the hundred weight, and had trundled home in a wheel-barrow!

But enough for the present; I am promised a faithful account of the arcana of a lady's toilette—a complete initiation into the arts, mysteries, spells, and potions; in short, the whole chemical process by which she reduces herself down to the most fashionable standard of insignificance; together with specimens of the strait waistcoats, the lacings, the bandages, and the various ingenious instruments with which she puts nature to the rack, and tortures herself into a proper figure to be admired.

Farewell, thou sweetest of slave-drivers! the echoes that repeat to a lover's ear the song of his mistress, are not more soothing than tidings from those we love. Let thy answer to my letters be speedy; and never, I pray thee, for a moment, cease to watch over the prosperity of my house, and the welfare of my beloved wives. Let them want for nothing, my friend; but feed them plentifully on honey, boiled rice, and water gruel; so that when I return to the blessed land of my fathers, if that can ever be! I may find them improved in size and loveliness, and sleek as the graceful elephants that range the green valley of Abimar.

Ever thine,
MUSTAPHA.

NO. XIX.—THURSDAY, DEC. 31, 1807.

FROM MY ELBOW-CHAIR.

HAVING returned to town, and once more formally taken possession of my elbow-chair, it behooves me to discard the rural feelings, and the rural sentiments, in which I have for some time past indulged, and devote myself more exclusively to the edification of the town. As I feel at this moment a chivalric spark of gallantry playing around my heart, and one of those dulcet emotions of cordiality, which an old bachelor will sometimes entertain towards the divine sex, I am determined to gratify the sentiment for once, and devote this number exclusively to the ladies. I would not, however, have our fair readers imagine that we wish to flatter ourselves into their good graces; devoutly as we adore them!—and what true cavalier does not,—and heartily as we desire to flourish in the mild sunshine of their smiles, yet we scorn to insinuate ourselves into their favour; unless it be as honest friends, sincere well-wishers, and disinterested advisers. If in the course of this number they find us rather prodigal of our encomiums, they will have the modesty to ascribe it to the excess of their own merits;—if they find us extremely indulgent to their faults, they will impute it rather to the superabundance of our good-nature, than to any servile and illiberal fear of giving offence.

The following letter of Mustapha falls in exactly with the current of my purpose. As I have before mentioned that his letters are without dates, we are obliged to give them very irregularly, without any regard to chronological order.

The present one appears to have been written not long after his arrival, and antecedent to several already published. It is more in the familiar and colloquial style than the others. Will Wizard declares he has translated it with fidelity, excepting that he has omitted several remarks on the waltz, which the honest Mussulman eulogizes with great enthusiasm; comparing it to certain voluptuous dances of the seraglio. Will regretted exceedingly that the indelicacy of several of these observations compelled their total exclusion, as he wishes to give all possible encouragement to this popular and amiable exhibition.

LETTER FROM MUSTAPHA RUB-A-DUB KELI KHAN,

TO MULEY HELIM AL RAGGI, SURNAMED THE AGREEABLE RAGAMUFFIN, CHIEF. MOUNTEBANK AND BUFFA-DANCER TO HIS HIGHNESS.

THE numerous letters which I have written to our friend the slave-driver, as well as those to thy kinsman THE SNORER, and which, doubtless, were read to thee, honest Muley, have, in all probability, awakened thy curiosity to know further particulars concerning the manners of the barbarians, who hold me in such ignominious captivity. I was lately at one of their public ceremonies, which, at first, perplexed me exceedingly as to its object; but as the explanations of a friend have let me somewhat into the secret, and as it seems to bear no small analogy to thy profession, a description of it may contribute to thy amusement, if not to thy instruction.

A few days since, just as I had finished my coffee, and was perfuming my whiskers, preparatory to a morning walk, I was waited upon by an inhabitant of this place, a gay young infidel who has of late cultivated my acquaintance. He presented me with a square bit of painted pasteboard, which, he informed me, would entitle me to admittance to the CITY ASSEMBLY. Curious to know the meaning of a phrase which was entirely new to me, I requested an explanation; when my friend informed me that the assembly was a numerous concourse of young people of both sexes, who, on certain occasions, gathered together to dance about a large room with violent gesticulation, and try to out-dress each other.—"In short," said he, "if you wish to see the natives in all their glory, there's no place like the *City Assembly;* so you must go there, and sport your whiskers." Though the matter of sporting my whiskers was considerably above my apprehension, yet I now began, as I thought, to understand him. I had heard of the war dances of the natives, which are a kind of religious institution, and had little doubt but that this must be a solemnity of the kind—upon a prodigious great scale. Anxious as I am to contemplate these strange people in every situation, I willingly acceded to his proposal, and, to be the more at ease, I determined to lay aside my Turkish dress, and appear in plain garments of the fashion of this country; as is my custom whenever I wish to mingle in a crowd without exciting the attention of the gaping multitude.

It was long after the shades of night had fallen, before my friend appeared to conduct me to the assembly. "These infidels," thought I, "shroud themselves in mystery, and seek the aid of gloom and darkness, to heighten the solemnity of their pious orgies." Resolving to conduct myself with that decent respect which every stranger owes to the customs of the land in which he sojourns, I chastised my features into an expression of sober reverence, and stretched my face into a degree of longitude suitable to the ceremony I was about to witness. Spite of myself, I felt an emotion of awe stealing over my senses as I approached the majestic pile. My imagination pictured something similar to a descent into the cave of Dom-Daniel, where the necromancers of the East are of taught their infernal arts. I entered with the same gravity demeanour that I would have approached the holy temple at Mecca, and bowed my head three times as I passed the threshold. "Head of the mighty Amrou!" thought I, on being ushered into a splendid saloon, "what a display is here! surely I am transported to the mansions of the Houris, the elysium of the faithful!"—How tame appeared all the descriptions of enchanted palaces in our Arabian poetry!—wherever I turned my eyes, the quick glances of beauty dazzled my vision and ravished my heart; lovely virgins fluttered by me, darting imperial looks of conquest, or beaming such smiles of invitation, as did Gabriel when he beckoned our holy prophet to Heaven. Shall I own the weakness of thy friend, good Muley? —while thus gazing on the enchanted scene before me, I, for a moment, forgot my country; and even the memory of my three-and-twenty wives faded from my heart; my thoughts were bewildered and led astray by the charms of these bewitching savages, and I sunk, for a while, into that delicious state of mind, where the senses, all enchanted, and all striving for mastery, produce an endless variety of tumultuous, yet pleasing emotions. Oh, Muley, never shall I again wonder that an infidel should prove a recreant to the single solitary wife allotted to him, when, even thy friend, armed with all the precepts of Mahomet, can so easily prove faithless to three-and-twenty!

"Whither have you led me?" said I, at length, to my companion, "and to whom do these beautiful creatures belong? Certainly this must be the seraglio of the grand bashaw of the city, and a most happy bashaw must he be, to possess treasures, which even his highness of Tripoli cannot parallel." "Have a care," cried my companion, "how you talk about seraglios, or you'll have all these gentle nymphs about your ears; for seraglio is a word which, beyond all others, they abhor;—most of them," continued he, "have no lord and master, but come here to catch one—they're in the market, as we term it." "Ah, hah!" said I, exultingly, "then you really have a fair, or slave-market, such as we have in the east, where the faithful are provided with the choicest virgins of Georgia and Circassia?——by our glorious sun of Afric, but I should like to select some ten or a dozen wives from so lovely an assemblage! Pray, what would you suppose they might be bought for?"——

Before I could receive an answer, my attention was attracted by two or three good-looking, middle-sized men, who, being dressed in black, a colour universally worn in this country by the muftis and dervises, I immediately concluded to be highpriests, and was confirmed in my original opinion that this was a religious ceremony. These reverend personages are entitled managers, and enjoy unlimited authority in the assemblies, being armed with swords, with which, I am told, they would infallibly put any lady to death who infringed the laws of the temple. They walked round the room with great solemnity, and, with an air of profound importance and mystery, put a little piece of folded paper in each fair hand, which I concluded were religious talismans. One of them dropped on the floor, whereupon I slily put my foot on it, and, watching an opportunity, picked it up unobserved, and found it to contain some unintelligible words and the mystic number 9. What were its virtues I know not; except that I put it in my pocket, and have hitherto been preserved from my fit of the lumbago, which I generally have about this season of the year, ever since I tumbled into the well of Zim-zim on my pilgrimage to Mecca. I enclose it to thee in this letter, presuming it to be particularly serviceable against the dangers of thy profession.

Shortly after the distribution of these talismans, one of the high-priests stalked into the middle of the room with great majesty, and clapped his hands three times; a loud explosion of music succeeded from a number of black, yellow, and white musicians, perched in a kind of cage over the grand entrance. The company were thereupon thrown into great confusion and apparent consternation.—They hurried to and fro about the room, and at length formed themselves into little groups of eight persons, half male and half female;—the music struck into something like harmony, and, in a moment, to my utter astonishment and dismay, they were all seized with what I concluded to be a paroxysm of religious phrenzy, tossing about their heads in a ludicrous style from side to side, and indulging in extravagant contortions of figure;—now throwing their heels into the air, and anon whirling round with the velocity of the eastern idolaters, who think they pay a grateful homage to the sun by imitating his motions. I expected every moment to see them fall down in convulsions, foam at the mouth, and shriek with fancied inspiration. As usual the females seemed most fervent in their religious exercises, and performed them with a melancholy expression of feature that was peculiarly touching; but I was highly gratified by the exemplary conduct of several male devotees, who, though their gesticulations would intimate a wild merriment of the feelings, maintained throughout as inflexible a gravity of countenance as so many monkeys of the island of Borneo at their anticks.

"And pray," said I, "who is the divinity that presides in this splendid mosque?"——"The divinity!—oh, I understand—you mean the *belle* of the evening; we have a new one every season: the one at present in fashion is that lady you see yonder, dressed in white, with pink ribands, and a crowd of adorers around her." "Truly," cried I, "this is the pleasantest deity I have encountered in the whole course of my travels;—so familiar, so condescending, and so merry withal;—why, her very worshippers take her by the hand, and whisper in her ear."——"My good Mussulman," replied my friend, with great gravity, "I perceive you are completely in an error concerning the intent of this ceremony. You are now in a place of public amusement, not of public worship;—and the pretty-looking young men you see making such violent and grotesque distortions, are merely indulging in our favourite amusement of dancing." "I cry your mercy," exclaimed I, "these, then, are the dancing men and women of the town, such as we have in our principal cities, who hire themselves out for the entertainment of the wealthy;—but, pray who pays them for this fatiguing exhibition?"——My friend regarded me for a moment with an air of whimsical perplexity, as if doubtful whether I was in jest or earnest.——"Sblood, man," cried he, "these are some of our greatest people, our fashionables, who are merely dancing here for amusement."——*Dancing for amusement!* think of that, Muley!—thou, whose greatest pleasure is to chew opium, smoke tobacco, loll on a couch, and doze thyself into the regions of the Houris!——Dancing for amusement!—shall I never cease having occasion to laugh at the absurdities of these barbarians, who are laborious in their recreations, and indolent only in their hours of business?——Dancing for amusement!—the very idea makes my bones ache, and I never think of it without being obliged to apply my handkerchief to my forehead, and fan myself into some degree of coolness.

"And pray," said I, when my astonishment had a little subsided, "do these musicians also toil for amusement, or are they confined to their cage, like birds, to sing for the gratification of others?—I should think the former was the case, from the animation with which they flourish their elbows."—"Not so," replied my friend, "they are well paid, which is no more than just, for I assure you they are the most important personages in the room. The fiddler puts the whole assembly in motion, and directs their movements, like the master of a puppet-show, who sets all his pasteboard gentry kicking by a jerk of his fingers:—there, now—look at that dapper little gentleman yonder, who appears to be suffering the pangs of dislocation in every limb: he is the most expert puppet in the room, and performs, not so much for his own amusement, as for that of the by-standers."—Just then the little gentleman, having finished one of his paroxysms of activity, seemed to be looking round for applause from the spectators. Feeling myself really much obliged to him for his exertions, I made him a low bow of thanks, but nobody followed my example, which I thought a singular instance of ingratitude.

Thou wilt perceive, friend Muley, that the dancing of these barbarians is totally different from the science professed by thee in Tripoli;—the country, in fact, is afflicted by numerous epidemical diseases, which travel from house to house, from city to city, with the regularity of a caravan. Among these, the most formidable is this dancing mania, which prevails chiefly throughout the winter. It at first seized on a few people of fashion, and being indulged in moderation, was a cheerful exercise; but in a little time, by quick advances, it infected all classes of the community, and became a raging epidemic. The doctors immediately, as is their usual way, instead of devising a remedy, fell together by the ears, to decide whether it was native or imported, and the sticklers for the latter opinion traced it to a cargo of trumpery from France, as they had before hunted down the yellow-fever to a bag of coffee from the West Indies. What makes this disease the more formidable is, that the patients seem infatuated with their malady, abandon themselves to its unbounded ravages, and expose their persons to wintry storms and midnight airs, more fatal, in this capricious climate, than the withering Simoom blast of the desert.

I know not whether it is a sight most whimsical or melancholy, to witness a fit of this dancing malady. The lady hops up to the gentleman, who stands at the distance of about three paces, and then capers back again to her place;—the gentleman of course does the same; then they skip one way, then they jump another;—then they turn their backs to each other;—then they seize each other and shake hands; then they whirl round, and throw themselves into a thousand grotesque and ridiculous attitudes;—sometimes on one leg, sometimes on the other, and sometimes on no leg at all;—and this they call exhibiting the graces!—By the nineteen thousand capers of the great mountebank of Damascus, but these graces must be something like the crooked-backed dwarf Shabrac, who is sometimes permitted to amuse his highness by imitating the tricks of a monkey. These fits continue at short intervals from four to five hours, till at last the lady is led off, faint, languid, exhausted, and panting, to her carriage;—rattles home;—passes a night of feverish restlessness, cold perspirations and troubled sleep;—rises late next morning, if she rises at all, is nervous, petulant, or a prey to languid indifference all day;—a mere household spectre, neither giving nor receiving enjoyment; in the evening hurries to another dance; receives an unnatural exhilaration from the lights, the music, the crowd, and the unmeaning bustle;—flutters, sparkles, and blooms for a while, until the transient delirium being past, the infatuated maid droops and languishes into apathy again;—is again led off to her carriage, and the next morning rises to go through exactly the same joyless routine.

And yet, wilt thou believe it, my dear Raggi, these are

rational beings: nay more, their countrymen would fain persuade me they have souls!—Is it not a thousand times to be lamented that beings, endowed with charms that might warm even the frigid heart of a dervise;—with social and endearing powers, that would render them the joy and pride of the harem;—should surrender themselves to a habit of heartless dissipation, which preys imperceptibly on the roses of the cheek;—which robs the eye of its lustre, the mouth of its dimpled smile, the spirits of their cheerful hilarity, and the limbs of their elastic vigour;—which hurries them off in the spring-time of existence; or, if they survive, yields to the arms of a youthful bridegroom a frame wrecked in the storms of dissipation, and struggling with premature infirmity. Alas, Muley! may I not ascribe to this cause, the number of little old women I meet with in this country, from the age of eighteen to eight-and-twenty?

In sauntering down the room, my attention was attracted by a smoky painting, which, on nearer examination, I found consisted of two female figures crowning a bust with a wreath of laurel. "This, I suppose," cried I, "was some favourite dancer in his time?"—"Oh, no," replied my friend, "he was only a general."—"Good; but then he must have been great at a cotillion, or expert at a fiddlestick—or why is his memorial here?"—"Quite the contrary," answered my companion, "history makes no mention of his ever having flourished a fiddlestick, or figured in a single dance. You have no doubt, heard of him; he was the illustrious WASHINGTON, the father and deliverer of his country; and, as our nation is remarkable for gratitude to great men, it always does honour to their memory, by placing their monuments over the doors of taverns, or in the corners of dancing-rooms."

From thence my friend and I strolled into a small apartment adjoining the grand saloon, where I beheld a number of grave-looking persons with venerable gray heads, but without beards, which I thought very unbecoming, seated around a table, studying hieroglyphics;—I approached them with reverence as so many magi, or learned men, endeavouring to expound the mysteries of Egyptian science: several of them threw down money, which I supposed was a reward proposed for some great discovery, when presently one of them spread his hieroglyphics on the table, exclaimed triumphantly, "two bullets and a bragger!" and swept all the money into his pocket. He has discovered a key to the hieroglyphics, thought

I;—happy mortal! no doubt his name will be immortalized. Willing, however, to be satisfied, I looked round on my companion with an inquiring eye—he understood me, and informed me, that these were a company of friends, who had met together to win each other's money, and be agreeable. "Is that all?" exclaimed I, "why, then, I pray you, make way, and let me escape from this temple of abominations, or who knows but these people, who meet together to toil, worry, and fatigue themselves to death, and give it the name of pleasure;—and who win each other's money by way of being agreeable;—may some one of them take a liking to me, and pick my pocket, or break my head in a paroxysm of hearty good-will!"

Thy friend,　　Mustapha.

BY ANTHONY EVERGREEN, GENT.

Nunc est bibendum, nunc pede libero
Pulsanda tellus.　　　　　*—Hor.*
Now is the tyme for wine and myrthful sportes,
For dance, and song, and disportes of syche sortes.
—Link. Fid.

The winter campaign has opened. Fashion has summoned her numerous legions at the sound of trumpet, tamborine, and drum; and all the harmonious minstrelsy of the orchestra, to hasten from the dull, silent, and insipid glades and groves, where they have vegetated during the summer; recovering from the ravages of the last winter's campaign. Our fair ones have hurried to town, eager to pay their devotions to this tutelary deity, and to make an offering at her shrine of the few pale and transient roses they gathered in their healthful retreat. The fiddler rosins his bow, the card-table devotee is shuffling her pack; the young ladies are industriously spangling muslins; and the tea-party heroes are airing their *chapeaux bras*, and pease-blossom breeches, to prepare for figuring in the gay circle of smiles, and graces, and beauty. Now the fine lady forgets her country friends in the hurry of fashionable engagements, or receives the simple intruder, who has foolishly accepted her thousand pressing invitations, with such politeness that the poor soul determines never to come again;—now the gay buck, who erst figured at Ballston, and quaffed the pure spring, exchanges the sparkling water for still more sparkling champaign; and deserts the nymph of the fountain, to enlist under the standard of jolly Bacchus. In short, now is the important time of the year in which to harangue the bon-ton reader; and, like some ancient hero in front of the battle, to spirit him up to deeds of noble daring, or still more noble suffering, in the ranks of fashionable warfare.

Such, indeed, has been my intention; but the number of cases which have lately come before me, and the variety of complaints I have received from a crowd of honest and well-meaning correspondents, call for more immediate attention. A host of appeals, petitions, and letters of advice are now before me; and I believe the shortest way to satisfy my petitioners, memorialists, and advisers, will be to publish their letters, as I suspect the object of most of them is merely to get into print.

TO ANTHONY EVERGREEN, GENT.

Sir:—As you appear to have taken to yourself the trouble of meddling in the concerns of the beau monde, I take the liberty of appealing to you on a subject which, though considered merely as a very good joke, has occasioned me great vexation and expense. You must know I pride myself on being very useful to the ladies: that is, I take boxes for them at the theatre; go shopping with them, supply them with bouquets, and furnish them with novels from the circulating library. In consequence of these attentions, I am become a great favourite, and there is seldom a party going on in the city without my having an invitation. The grievance I have to mention is the exchange of hats which takes place on these occasions; for, to speak my mind freely, there are certain young gentlemen who seem to consider fashionable parties as mere places to barter old clothes; and I am informed that a number of them manage, by this great system of exchange, to keep their crowns decently covered without their hatter suffering in the least by it.

It was but lately that I went to a private ball with a new hat, and on returning, in the latter part of the evening, and asking for it, the scoundrel of a servant, with a broad grin, informed me that the new hats had been dealt out half an hour since, and they were then on the third quality; and I was in the end obliged to borrow a young lady's beaver rather than go home with any of the ragged remnants that were left.

Now I would wish to know if there is no possibility of having these offenders punished by law; and whether it would not be advisable for ladies to mention in their cards of invitation, as a postscript, "stealing of hats and shawls positively prohibited." At any rate I would thank you, Mr. Evergreen, to discountenance the thing totally, by publishing in your paper that stealing a hat is no joke.

Your humble servant,   WALTER WITHERS.

My correspondent is informed that the police have determined to take this matter into consideration, and have set apart Saturday mornings for the cognizance of fashionable larcenies.

MR. EVERGREEN—*Sir:*—Do you think a married woman may lawfully put her husband right in a story, before strangers, when she knows him to be in the wrong; and can any thing authorize a wife in the exclamation of—"lord, my dear, how can you say so?"   MARGARET TIMSON.

DEAR ANTHONY:—Going down Broadway this morning in a great hurry, I ran full against an object which at first put me to a prodigious nonplus. Observing it to be dressed in a man's hat, a cloth overcoat and spatterdashes, I framed my apology accordingly, exclaiming, "my dear sir, I ask ten thousand pardons;—I assure you, sir, it was entirely accidental:—pray excuse me, sir," &c. At every one of these excuses the thing answered me with a downright laugh; at which I was not a little surprised, until, on resorting to my pocket-glass, I discovered that it was no other than my old acquaintance, Clarinda Trollop;—I never was more chagrined in my life; for being an old bachelor, I like to appear as young as possible, and am always boasting of the goodness of my eyes. I beg of you, Mr. Evergreen, if you have any feeling for your contemporaries, to discourage this hermaphrodite mode of dress, for really, if the fashion take, we poor bachelors will be utterly at a loss to distinguish a woman from a man. Pray let me know your opinion, sir, whether a lady who wears a man's hat and spatterdashes before marriage, may not be apt to usurp some other article of his dress afterwards.

Your humble servant,   RODERIC WORRY.

DEAR MR. EVERGREEN:—The other night, at Richard the Third, I sat behind three gentlemen, who talked very loud on the subject of Richard's wooing Lady Ann directly in the face of his crimes against that lady. One of them declared such an unnatural scene would be hooted at in China. Pray, sir, was that Mr. Wizard? SELINA BADGER.

P. S. The gentleman I allude to had a pocket-glass, and wore his hair fastened behind by a tortoise-shell comb, with two teeth wanting.

MR. EVERGRIN—*Sir:*—Being a little curious in the affairs of the toilette, I was much interested by the sage Mustapha's remarks, in your last number, concerning the art of manufacturing a modern fine lady. I would have you caution your fair readers, however, to be very careful in the management of their machinery; as a deplorable accident happened last assembly, in consequence of the architecture of a lady's figure not being sufficiently strong. In the middle of one of the cotillions, the company was suddenly alarmed by a tremendous crash at the lower end of the room, and, on crowding to the place, discovered that it was a fine figure which had unfortunately broken down from too great exertion in a pigeon wing. By great good luck I secured the corset, which I carried home in triumph; and the next morning had it publicly dissected, and a lecture read on it at Surgeon's Hall. I have since commenced a dissertation on the subject; in which I shall treat of the superiority of those figures manufactured by steel, stay-tape, and whale-bone, to those formed by dame nature. I shall show clearly that the Venus de Medicis has no pretension to beauty of form, as she never wore stays, and her waist is in exact proportion to the rest of her body. I shall inquire into the mysteries of compression, and how tight a figure can be laced without danger of fainting; and whether it would not be advisable for a lady, when dressing for a ball, to be attended by the family physician, as culprits are when tortured on the rack, to know how much more nature will endure. I shall prove that ladies have discovered the secret of that notorious juggler, who offered to squeeze himself into a quart bottle; and I shall demonstrate, to the satisfaction of every fashionable reader, that there is a degree of heroism in purchasing a preposterously slender waist at the expense of an old age of decrepitude and rheumatics. This dissertation shall be published as soon as finished, and distributed gratis among boarding-school madams and all worthy matrons who are ambitious that their daughters should sit strait, move like clock-work, and "do credit to their bringing up." In the mean time, I have hung up the skeleton of the corset in the museum, beside a dissected weazle and a stuffed alligator, where it may be inspected by all those naturalists who are fond of studying the "human form divine." Yours, &c. JULIAN COGNOUS.

P.S. By accurate calculation I find it is dangerous for a fine figure, when full dressed, to pronounce a word of more than three syllables. Fine Figure, if in love, may indulge in a gentle sigh; but a sob is hazardous. Fine Figure may smile with safety, may even venture as far as a giggle, but must never risk a loud laugh. Figure must never play the part of a confidante; as at a tea-party some fine evenings since, a young lady, whose unparalleled impalpability of waist was the envy of the drawing-room, burst with an important secret, and had three ribs—of her corset!—fractured on the spot.

MR. EVERGREEN—*Sir:*—I am one of those industrious gemmen who labour hard to obtain currency in the fashionable world. I have went to great expense in little boots, short vests, and long breeches;—my coat is regularly imported, per stage, from Philadelphia, duly insured against all risks, and my boots are smuggled from Bond-street. I have lounged in Broadway with one of the most crooked walking-sticks I could procure, and have sported a pair of salmon-coloured smallclothes, and flame-coloured stockings, at every concert and ball to which I could purchase admission. Being affeared that I might possibly appear to less advantage as a pedestrian, in consequence of my being rather short and a little bandy, I have lately hired a tall horse with cropped ears and a cocked tail, on which I have joined the cavalcade of pretty gemmen, who exhibit bright stirrups every fine morning in Broadway and take a canter of two miles per day, at the rate of three hundred dollars per annum. But, sir, all this expense has been laid out in vain, for I can scarcely get a partner at an assembly, or an invitation to a tea-party. Pray, sir, inform me what more I can do to acquire admission into the true stylish circles, and whether it would not be advisable to

charter a curricle for a month and have my cypher put on it, as is done by certain dashers of my acquaintance.
Yours to serve,   MALVOLIO DUBSTER.

TEA: A POEM.

FROM THE MILL OF PINDAR COCKLOFT, ESQ.

And earnestly recommended to the attention of all Maidens of a certain age.

OLD time, my dear girls, is a knave who in truth
From the fairest of beauties will pilfer their youth;
Who, by constant attention and wily deceit,
For ever is coaxing some grace to retreat;
And, like crafty seducer, with subtle approach,
The further indulged, will still further encroach.
Since this "thief of the world" has made off with your bloom,
And left you some score of stale years in its room—
Has depriv'd you of all those gay dreams, that would dance
In your brains at fifteen, and your bosoms entrance;
And has forc'd you almost to renounce, in despair,
The hope of a husband's affection and care—
Since such is the case, and a case rather hard!
Permit one who holds you in special regard,
To furnish such hints in your loveless estate
As may shelter your names from distraction and hate.
Too often our maidens, grown aged, I ween,
Indulge to excess in the workings of spleen;
And at times, when annoy'd by the slights of mankind,
Work off their resentment—by speaking their mind:
Assemble together in snuff-taking clan,
And hold round the tea-urn a solemn divan.
A convention of tattling—a tea party hight,
Which, like meeting of witches, is brew'd up at night:
Where each matron arrives, fraught with tales of surprise,
With knowing suspicion and doubtful surmise;
Like the broomstick whirl'd hags that appear in Macbeth,
Each bearing some relic of venom or death,
"To stir up the toil and to double the trouble,
That fire may burn, and that cauldron may bubble."

When the party commences, all starch'd and all glum,
They talk of the weather, their corns, or sit mum:
They will tell you of cambric, of ribands, of lace,
How cheap they were sold—and will name you the place.
They discourse of their colds, and they hem and they cough,
And complain of their servants to pass the time off;
Or list to the tale of some doating mamma
How her ten weeks' old baby will laugh and say taa!
    But tea, that enlivener of wit and of soul—
More loquacious by far than the draughts of the bowl,
Soon unloosens the tongue and enlivens the mind,
And enlightens their eyes to the faults of mankind.
'Twas thus with the Pythia, who served at the fount,
That flow'd near the far-famed Parnassian mount,
While the steam was inhal'd of the sulphuric spring.
Her vision expanded, her fancy took wing;—
By its aid she pronounced the oracular will
That Apollo commanded his sons to fufill.
But alas! the sad vestal, performing the rite,
Appear'd like a demon—terrific to sight.
    E'en the priests of Apollo averted their eyes,
And the temple of Delphi resounded her cries,
But quitting the nymph of the tripod of yore,
We return to the dames of the tea-pot once more.
    In harmless chit-chat an acquaintance they roast,
And serve up a friend, as they serve up a toast;
Some gentle faux pas, or some female mistake,
Is like sweetmeats delicious, or relished as cake;
A bit of broad scandal is like a dry crust,
It would stick in the throat, so they butter it first
With a little affected good-nature, and cry
"No body regrets the thing deeper than I."
Our young ladies nibble a good name in play
As for pastime they nibble a biscuit away:
While with shrugs and surmises, the toothless old dame,
As she mumbles a crust she will mumble a name.
And as the fell sisters astonished the Scot,
In predicting of Banquo's descendants the lot,
Making shadows of kings, amid flashes of light,
To appear in array and to frown in his sight,
So they conjure up spectres all hideous in hue,
Which, as shades of their neighbours, are passed in review.

The wives of our cits of inferior degree,
Will soak up repute in a little bohea;
The potion is vulgar, and vulgar the slang
With which on their neighbours' defects they harangue;
But the scandal improves, a refinement in wrong!
As our matrons are richer and rise to souchong.
With hyson—a beverage that's still more refin'd,
Our ladies of fashion enliven their mind,
And by nods, innuendoes, and hints, and what not,
Reputations and tea send together to pot.
While madam in cambrics and laces array'd,
With her plate and her liveries in splendid parade,
Will drink in imperial a friend at a sup,
Or in gunpowder blow them by dozens all up.
Ah me! how I groan when with full swelling sail
Wafted stately along by the favouring gale,
A China ship proudly arrives in our bay,
Displaying her streamers and blazing away.
Oh! more fell to our port, is the cargo she bears,
Than grenadoes, torpedoes, or warlike affairs:
Each chest is a bombshell thrown into our town
To shatter repute and bring character down.
 Ye Samquas, ye Chinquas, Chouquas, so free,
Who discharge on our coast your cursed quantums of tea,
Oh think, as ye waft the sad weed from your strand,
Of the plagues and vexations ye deal to our land.
As the Upas' dread breath, o'er the plain where it flies,
Empoisons and blasts each green blade that may rise,
So, wherever the leaves of your shrub find their way,
The social affections soon suffer decay:
Like to Java's drear waste they embarren the heart,
Till the blossoms of love and of friendship depart.
 Ah, ladies, and was it by heaven design'd,
That ye should be merciful, loving and kind!
Did it form you like angels, and send you below—
To prophesy peace—to bid charity flow!
And have ye thus left your primeval estate,
And wandered so widely—so strangely of late?
Alas! the sad cause I too plainly can see—
These evils have all come upon you through tea!
Cursed weed, that can make our fair spirits resign
The character mild of their mission divine;

That can blot from their bosoms that tenderness true,
Which from female to female for ever is due!
Oh, how nice is the texture—how fragile the frame
Of that delicate blossom, a female's fair fame!
'Tis the sensitive plant, it recoils from the breath
And shrinks from the touch as if pregnant with death.
How often, how often, has innocence sigh'd;
Has beauty been reft of its honour—its pride;
Has virtue, though pure as an angel of light,
Been painted as dark as a demon of night:
All offer'd up victims, an *auto da fe*,
At the gloomy cabals—the dark orgies of tea!

If I, in the remnant that's left me of life,
Am to suffer the torments of slanderous strife,
Let me fall, I implore, in the slang-whanger's claw,
Where the evil is open, and subject to law.
Not nibbled, and mumbled, and put to the rack,
By the sly underminings of tea party clack:
Condemn me, ye gods, to a newspaper roasting,
But spare me! oh, spare me, a tea table toasting!

NO. XX.—MONDAY JANUARY 25, 1808.

FROM MY ELBOW-CHAIR.

Extremum hunc mihi concede laborem. VIRG.
"Soft you, a word or two before we part."

IN this season of festivity, when the gate of time swings open on its hinges, and an honest rosy-faced New-Year comes waddling in, like a jolly fat-sided alderman, loaded with good wishes, good humour, and minced pies;—at this joyous era it has been the custom, from time immemorial, in this ancient and respectable city, for periodical writers, from reverend, grave, and potent essayists like ourselves! down to the humble but industrious editors of magazines, reviews, and newspapers, to tender their subscribers the compliments of the season; and when they have slily thawed their hearts with a little of the sunshine of flattery, to conclude by delicately dunning them for their arrears of subscription money. In like manner the carriers of newspapers, who undoubtedly belong to the ancient and honourable order of literati, do regularly, at the commencement of the year, salute their patrons with abundance of excellent advice, conveyed in exceeding good poetry, for which the aforesaid good-natured patrons are well pleased to pay them exactly twenty-five cents. In walking the streets I am every day saluted with good wishes from old gray-headed negroes, whom I never recollect to have seen before; and it was but a few days ago, that I was called to receive the compliments of an ugly old woman, who last spring was employed by Mrs. Cockloft to whitewash my room and put things in order; a phrase which, if rightly understood, means little else than huddling every thing into holes and corners, so that if I want to find any particular article, it is, in the language of an humble but expressive saying,—"looking for a needle in a haystack." Not recognizing my visitor, I demanded by what authority she wished me a "Happy New-Year?" Her claim was one of the weakest she could have urged, for I have an innate and mortal antipathy to this custom of putting things to rights;—so giving the old witch a pistereen, I desired her forthwith to mount her broomstick, and ride off as fast as possible.

Of all the various ranks of society, the bakers alone, to their immortal honour be it recorded, depart from this practice of making a market of congratulations; and, in addition to always allowing thirteen to the dozen, do with great liberality, instead of drawing on the purses of their customers at the New-Year, present them with divers large, fair, spiced cakes; which, like the shield of Achilles, or an Egyptian obelisk, are adorned with figures of a variety of strange animals, that, in their conformation, out-marvel all the wild wonders of nature.

This honest gray-beard custom of setting apart a certain portion of this good-for-nothing existence for the purposes of cordiality, social merriment, and good cheer, is one of the inestimable relics handed down to us from our worthy Dutch ancestors. In perusing one of the manuscripts from my worthy grandfather's mahogany chest of drawers, I find the new year was celebrated with great festivity during that golden age of our city, when the reins of government were held by the renowned Rip Van Dam, who always did honour to the season by seeing out the old year; a ceremony which consisted in plying his guests with bumpers, until not one of them was capable of seeing. "Truly," observes my grandfather, who was generally of these parties—"Truly, he was a most stately and magnificent burgomaster! inasmuch as he did right lustily carouse it with his friends about New-Year; roasting huge quantities of turkeys; baking innumerable minced pies; and smacking the lips of all fair ladies the which he did meet, with such sturdy emphasis that the same might have been heard the distance of a stone's throw." In his days, according to my grandfather, were first invented these notable cakes, hight new-year-cookies, which originally were impressed on one side with the honest, burly countenance of the illustrious Rip; and on the other with that of the noted St. Nicholas, vulgarly called Santaclaus;—of all the saints in the kalendar the most venerated by true Hollanders, and their unsophisticated descendants. These cakes are to this time given on the first of January to all visitors, together with a glass of cherry-bounce, or raspberry-brandy. It is with great regret, however, I observe that the simplicity of this venerable usage has been much violated by modern pretenders to style! and our respectable new-year-cookies, and cherry-bounce, elbowed aside by plum-cake and outlandish liqueurs, in the same way that our worthy old Dutch families are out-dazzled by modern upstarts, and mushroom cockneys.

In addition to this divine origin of new-year festivity; there is something exquisitely grateful, to a good-natured mind, in seeing every face dressed in smiles;—in hearing the oft-repeated salutations that flow spontaneously from the heart to the lips;—in beholding the poor, for once, enjoying the smiles of plenty, and forgetting the cares which press hard upon them, in the jovial revelry of the feelings;—the young children decked out in their Sunday clothes and freed from their only cares, the cares of the school, tripping through the streets on errands of pleasure;—and even the very negroes, those holiday-loving rogues, gorgeously arrayed in cast-off finery, collected in juntos, at corners, displaying their white teeth, and making the welkin ring with bursts of laughter,—loud enough to crack even the icy cheek of old winter. There is something so pleasant in all this, that I confess it would give me real pain to behold the frigid influence of modern style cheating us of this jubilee of the heart; and converting it, as it does every other article of social intercourse, into an idle and unmeaning ceremony. 'Tis the annual festival of good-humour;—it comes in the dead of winter, when nature is without a charm, when our pleasures are contracted to the fireside, and when every thing that unlocks the icy fetters of the heart, and sets the genial current flowing, should be cherished, as a stray lamb found in the wilderness; or a flower blooming among thorns and briers.

Animated by these sentiments, it is with peculiar satisfaction I perceived that the last New-Year was kept with more than ordinary enthusiasm. It seemed as if the good old times had rolled back again and brought with them all the honest, unceremonious intercourse of those golden days, when people were more open and sincere, more moral, and more hospitable than now;—when every object carried about it a charm which the hand of time has stolen away, or turned to a deformity; when the women were more simple, more domestic, more lovely, and more true; and when even the sun, like a hearty old blade as he is, shone with a genial lustre unknown in these degenerate days:—in short, those fairy times, when I was a mad-cap boy, crowding every enjoyment into the present moment;—making of the past an oblivion;—of the future a heaven; and careless of all that was "over the hills and far away." Only one thing was wanting to make every part of the celebration accord with its ancient simplicity. The ladies, who—I write it with the most piercing regret—are generally at the head of all domestic innovations, most fastidiously refused that mark of good will, that chaste and holy salute which was so fashionable in the happy days of governor Rip and the patriarchs. Even the Miss Cocklofts, who belong to a family that is the last intrenchment behind which the manners of the good old school have retired, made violent opposition;—and whenever a gentleman entered the room, immediately put themselves in a posture of defence;—this Will Wizard, with his usual shrewdness, insists was only to give the visitor a hint that they expected an attack; and declares, he has uniformly observed, that the resistance of those ladies who make the greatest noise and bustle, is most easily overcome. This sad innovation originated with my good aunt Charity, who was as arrant a tabby as ever wore whiskers; and I am not a little afflicted to find that she has found so many followers, even among the young and beautiful.

In compliance with an ancient and venerable custom, sanctioned by time and our ancestors, and more especially by my own inclinations, I will take this opportunity to salute my readers with as many good wishes as I can possibly spare; for, in truth, I have been so prodigal of late, that I have but few remaining. I should have offered my congratulations sooner; but, to be candid, having made the last new-year's campaign, according to custom, under cousin Christopher, in which I have seen some pretty hard service, my head has been somewhat out of order of late, and my intellects rather cloudy for clear writing. Besides, I may allege as another reason, that I have deferred my greetings until this day, which is exactly one year since we introduced ourselves to the public; and surely periodical writers have the same right of dating from the commencement of their works that monarchs have from the time of their coronation; or our most puissant republic from the declaration of its independence.

These good wishes are warmed into more than usual benevolence by the thought that I am now, perhaps, addressing my old friends for the last time. That we should thus cut off our work in the very vigour of its existence may excite some little matter of wonder in this enlightened community.—Now, though we could give a variety of good reasons for so doing, yet it would be an ill-natured act to deprive the public of such an admirable opportunity to indulge in their favourite amusement of conjecture: so we generously leave them to flounder in the smooth ocean of glorious uncertainty. Besides, we have ever considered it as beneath persons of our dignity to account for our movements or caprices;—thank heaven, we are not like the unhappy rulers of this enlightened land, accountable to the mob for our actions, or dependent on their smiles for support!—this much, however, we will say, it is not for want of subjects that we stop our career. We are not in the situation of poor Alexander the Great, who wept, as well indeed he might, because there were no more worlds to conquer; for, to do justice to this queer, odd, rantipole city and this whimsical country, there is matter enough in them to keep our risible muscles and our pens going until doomsday.

Most people, in taking a farewell which may, perhaps, be for ever, are anxious to part on good terms; and it is usual, on such melancholy occasions, for even enemies to shake hands, forget their previous quarrels, and bury all former animosities in parting regrets. Now, because most people do this, I am determined to act in quite a different way; for, as I have lived, so I should wish to die in my own way, without imitating any person, whatever may be his rank, talents, or reputation. Besides, if I know our trio, we have no enmities to obliterate, no hatchet to bury, and as to all injuries—those we have long since forgiven. At this moment there is not an individual in the world, not even the Pope himself, to whom we have any personal hostility. But if, shutting their eyes to the many striking proofs of good-nature displayed through the whole course of this work, there should be any persons so singularly ridiculous as to take offence at our strictures, we heartily forgive their stupidity; earnestly entreating them to desist from all manifestations of ill-humour, lest they should, peradventure, be classed under some one of the denominations of recreants we have felt it our duty to hold up to public ridicule. Even at this moment we feel a glow of parting philanthrophy stealing upon us;—a sentiment of cordial good-will towards the numerous host of readers that have jogged on at our heels during the last year; and, in justice to ourselves, must seriously protest, that if at any time we have treated them a little ungently, it was purely in that spirit of hearty affection with which a schoolmaster drubs an unlucky urchin, or a humane muleteer his recreant animal, at the very moment when his heart is brim-full of loving-kindness. If this is not considered an ample justification, so much the worse; for in that case I fear we shall remain for ever unjustified;—a most desperate extremity, and worthy of every man's commiseration!

One circumstance in particular has tickled us mightily as we jogged along, and that is the astonishing secrecy with which we have been able to carry on our lucubrations! Fully aware of the profound sagacity of the public of Gotham, and their wonderful faculty of distinguishing a writer by his style, it is with great self-congratulation we find that suspicion has never pointed to us as the authors of Salmagundi. Our gray-beard speculations have been most bountifully attributed to sundry smart young gentlemen, who, for aught we know, have no beards at all; and we have often been highly amused, when they were charged with the sin of writing what their harmless minds never conceived, to see them affect all the blushing modesty and beautiful embarrassment of detected virgin authors. The profound and penetrating public, having so long been led away from truth and nature by a constant perusal of those delectable histories and romances from beyond seas, in which human nature is for the most part wickedly mangled and debauched, have never once imagined this work was a genuine and most authentic history; that the

Cocklofts were a real family, dwelling in the city;—paying scot and lot, entitled to the right of suffrage, and holding several respectable offices in the corporation.—As little do they suspect that there is a knot of merry old bachelors seated snugly in the old-fashioned parlour of an old-fashioned Dutch house, with a weathercock on the top that came from Holland, who amuse themselves of an evening by laughing at their neighbours in an honest way, and who manage to jog on through the streets of our ancient and venerable city without elbowing or being elbowed by a living soul.

When we first adopted the idea of discontinuing this work, we determined, in order to give the critics a fair opportunity for dissection, to declare ourselves, one and all, absolutely defunct; for, it is one of the rare and invaluable privileges of a periodical writer, that by an act of innocent suicide he may lawfully consign himself to the grave and cheat the world of posthumous renown. But we abandoned this scheme for many substantial reasons. In the first place, we care but little for the opinion of critics, who we consider a kind of free-booters in the republic of letters; who, like deer, goats, and divers other graminivorous animals, gain subsistence by gorging upon the buds and leaves of the young shrubs of the forest, thereby robbing them of their verdure and retarding their progress to maturity. It also occurred to us, that though an author might lawfully in all countries kill himself outright, yet this privilege did not extend to the raising himself from the dead, if he was ever so anxious; and all that is left him in such a case is to take the benefit of the metempsychosis act and revive under a new name and form.

Far be it, therefore, from us to condemn ourselves to useless embarrassments, should we ever be disposed to resume the guardianship of this learned city of Gotham, and finish this invaluable work, which is yet but half completed. We hereby openly and seriously declare, that we are not dead, but intend, if it pleases Providence, to live for many years to come;—to enjoy life with the genuine relish of honest souls; careless of riches, honours, and every thing but a good name, among good fellows; and with the full expectation of shuffling off the remnant of existence, after the excellent fashion of that merry Grecian who died laughing.

TO THE LADIES.

BY ANTHONY EVERGREEN, GENT.

NEXT to our being a knot of independent old bachelors, there is nothing on which we pride ourselves more highly than upon possessing that true chivalric spirit of gallantry, which distinguished the days of king Arthur, and his valiant knights of the Round-table. We cannot, therefore, leave the lists where we have so long been tilting at folly, without giving a farewell salutation to those noble dames and beauteous damsels who have honoured us with their presence at the tourney. Like true knights, the only recompense we crave is the smile of beauty; and the approbation of those gentle fair ones, whose smile and whose approbation far excels all the trophies of honour, and all the rewards of successful ambition. True it is, that we have suffered infinite perils in standing forth as their champions, from the sly attacks of sundry arch caitiffs, who, in the overflowings of their malignity, have even accused us of entering the lists as defenders of the very foibles and faults of the sex.—Would that we could meet with these recreants hand to hand;—they should receive no more quarter than giants and enchanters in romance.

Had we a spark of vanity in our natures, here is a glorious occasion to show our skill in refuting these illiberal insinuations;—but there is something manly, and ingenuous, in making an honest confession of one's offences when about retiring from the world;—and so, without any more ado, we doff our helmets and thus publicly plead guilty to the deadly sin of GOOD NATURE; hoping and expecting forgiveness from our good-natured readers,—yet careless whether they bestow it or not. And in this we do but imitate sundry condemned criminals, who, finding themselves convicted of a capital crime, with great openness and candour do generally in their last dying speech make a confession of all their previous offences, which confession is always read with great delight by all true lovers of biography.

Still, however, notwithstanding our notorious devotion to the gentle sex, and our indulgent partiality, we have endeavoured, on divers occasions, with all the polite and becoming delicacy of true respect, to reclaim them from many of those delusive follies and unseemly peccadilloes in which they are unhappily too prone to indulge. We have warned them against the sad consequences of encountering our midnight damps and withering wintry blasts;—we have endeavoured, with pious hand, to snatch them from the wildering mazes of the waltz, and thus rescuing them from the arms of strangers, to restore them to the bosoms of their friends; to preserve them from the nakedness, the famine, the cobweb muslins, the vinegar cruet, the corset, the stay-tape, the buckram, and all the other miseries and racks of a fine figure. But, above all, we have endeavoured to lure them from the mazes of a dissipated world, where they wander about, careless of their value, until they lose their original worth;—and to restore them, before it is too late, to the sacred asylum of home, the soil most congenial to the opening blossom of female loveliness; where it blooms and expands in safety, in the fostering sunshine of maternal affection, and where its heavenly sweets are best known and appreciated.

Modern philosophers may determine the proper destination of the sex;—they may assign to them an extensive and brilliant orbit, in which to revolve, to the delight of the million and the confusion of man's superior intellect; but when on this subject we disclaim philosophy, and appeal to the higher tribunal of the heart;—and what heart that had not lost its better feelings, would ever seek to repose its happiness on the bosom of one whose pleasures all lay without the threshold of home;—who snatched enjoyment only in the whirlpool of dissipation, and amid the thoughtless and evanescent gayety of a ballroom. The fair one who is for ever in the career of amusement, may for a while dazzle, astonish, and entertain; but we are content with coldly admiring; and fondly turn from glitter and noise, to seek the happy fire-side of social life, there to confide our dearest and best affections.

Yet some there are, and we delight to mention them, who mingle freely with the world, unsullied by its contaminations; whose brilliant minds, like the stars of the firmament, are destined to shed their light abroad and gladden every beholder with their radiance;—to withhold them from the world, would be doing it injustice;—they are inestimable gems, which were never formed to be shut up in caskets; but to be the pride and ornament of elegant society.

We have endeavoured always to discriminate between a female of this superior order, and the thoughtless votary of pleasure; who, destitute of intellectual resources, is servilely dependent on others for every little pittance of enjoyment; who exhibits herself incessantly amid the noise, the giddy frolic, and capricious vanity of fashionable assemblages; dissipating her languid affections on a crowd; lavishing her ready smiles with indiscriminate prodigality on the worthy, or the undeserving; and listening, with equal vacancy of mind, to the conversation of the enlightened, the frivolity of the coxcomb, and the flourish of the fiddle-stick.

There is a certain artificial polish, a commonplace vivacity acquired by perpetually mingling in the *beau monde;* which, in the commerce of the world, supplies the place of natural suavity of good humour; but is purchased at the expense of all original and sterling traits of character. By a kind of fashionable discipline, the eye is taught to brighten, the lip to smile, and the whole countenance to irradiate with the semblance of friendly welcome, while the bosom is unwarmed by a single spark of genuine kindness or good-will.—This elegant simulation may be admired by the connoisseur of human character, as a perfection of art; but the heart is not to be deceived by the superficial illusion; it turns with delight to the timid retiring fair one, whose smile is the smile of nature; whose blush is the soft suffusion of delicate sensibility; and whose affections, unblighted by the chilling effects of dissipation, glow with all the tenderness and purity of artless youth. Hers is a singleness of mind, a native innocence of manners, and a sweet timidity, that steal insensibly upon the heart, and lead it a willing captive; though venturing occasionally among the fairy haunts of pleasure, she shrinks from the broad glare of notoriety, and seems to seek refuge among her friends, even from the admiration of the world.

These observations bring to mind a little allegory in one of the manuscripts of the sage Mustapha; which, being in some measure applicable to the subject of this essay, we transcribe for the benefit of our fair readers.

Among the numerous race of the Bedouins, who people the vast tracts of Arabia Deserta, is a small tribe, remarkable for their habits of solitude and love of independence. They are of a rambling disposition, roving from waste to waste, slaking their thirst at such scanty pools as are found in those cheerless plains, and glory in the unenvied liberty they enjoy. A youthful Arab of this tribe, a simple son of nature, at length growing weary of his precarious and unsettled mode of life, determined to set out in search of some permanent abode. "I will seek," said he, "some happy region, some generous clime, where the dews of heaven diffuse fertility;—I will find out some unfailing stream; and, forsaking the joyless life of my forefathers, settle on its borders, dispose my mind to gentle pleasures and tranquil enjoyments, and never wander more."

Enchanted with this picture of pastoral felicity, he departed from the tents of his companions; and having journeyed during five days, on the sixth, as the sun was just rising in all the splendours of the east, he lifted up his eyes and beheld extended before him, in smiling luxuriance, the fertile regions of Arabia the Happy. Gently swelling hills, tufted with blooming groves, swept down into luxuriant vales, enameled with flowers of never-withering beauty. The sun, no longer darting his rays with torrid fervour, beamed with a genial warmth that gladdened and enriched the landscape. A pure and temperate serenity, an air of voluptuous repose, a smile of contented abundance, pervaded the face of nature; and every zephyr breathed a thousand delicious odours. The soul of the youthful wanderer expanded with delight;—he raised his eyes to heaven, and almost mingled with his tribute of gratitude a sigh of regret that he had lingered so long amid the sterile solitudes of the desert.

With fond impatience he hastened to make choice of a stream where he might fix his habitation, and taste the promised sweets of this land of delight. But here commenced an unforeseen perplexity; for, though he beheld innumerable streams on every side, yet not one could he find which completely answered his high-raised expectations. One abounded with wild and picturesque beauty, but it was capricious and unsteady in its course; sometimes dashing its angry billows against the rocks, and often raging and overflowing its banks. Another flowed smoothly along, without even a ripple or a murmur; but its bottom was soft and muddy, and its current dull and sluggish. A third was pure and transparent, but its waters were of a chilling coldness, and it had rocks and flints in its bosom. A fourth was dulcet in its tinklings, and graceful in its meanderings; but it had a cloying sweetness that palled upon the taste; while a fifth possessed a sparkling vivacity, and a pungency of flavour, that deterred the wanderer from repeating his draught.

The youthful Bedouin began to weary with fruitless trials and repeated disappointments, when his attention was suddenly attracted by a lively brook, whose dancing waves glittered in the sunbeams, and whose prattling current communicated an air of bewitching gayety to the surrounding landscape. The heart of the wayworn traveller beat with expectation; but on regarding it attentively in its course, he found that it constantly avoided the embowering shade; loitering with equal fondness, whether gliding through the rich valley, or over the barren sand;—that the fragrant flower, the fruitful shrub, and worthless bramble were alike fostered by its waves, and that its current was often interrupted by unprofitable weeds. With idle ambition, it expanded itself beyond its proper bounds, and spread into a shallow waste of water, destitute of beauty or utility, and babbling along with uninteresting vivacity and vapid turbulence.

The wandering son of the desert turned away with a sigh of regret, and pitied a stream which, if content within its natural limits, might have been the pride of the valley, and the object of all his wishes. Pensive, musing, and disappointed, he slowly pursued his now almost hopeless pilgrimage, and had rambled for some time along the margin of a gentle rivulet, before he became sensible of its beauties. It was a simple pastoral stream, which, shunning the noonday glare, pursued its unobtrusive course through retired and tranquil vales;—now dimpling among flowery banks and tufted shrubbery; now winding among spicy groves, whose aromatic foliage fondly bent down to meet the limpid wave. Sometimes, but not often, it would venture from its covert to stray through a flowery meadow; but quickly, as if fearful of being seen, stole back again into its more congenial shade, and there lingered with sweet delay. Wherever it bent its course, the face of nature brightened into smiles, and a perennial spring reigned upon its borders.—The warblers of the woodland delighted to quit their recesses and carol among its bowers: while the turtle-dove, the timid fawn, the soft-eyed gazelle, and all the rural populace, who joy in the sequestered haunts of nature, resorted to its vicinity.—Its pure, transparent waters rolled over snow-white sands, and heaven itself was reflected in its tranquil bosom.

The simple Arab threw himself upon its verdant margin;—he tasted the silver tide, and it was like nectar to his lips;—he bounded with transport, for he had found the object of his wayfaring. "Here," cried he, "will I pitch my tent:—here will I pass my days; for pure, oh, fair stream, is thy gentle current; beauteous are thy borders; and the grove must be a paradise that is refreshed by thy meanderings!"

Pendant opera interrupta. —Virg.
The work's all aback. —*Link. Fid.*

"How hard it is," exclaimed the divine Con-futsé, better known among the illiterate by the name of Confucius, "for a man to bite off his own nose!" At this moment I, William Wizard, Esq., feel the full force of this remark, and cannot but give vent to my tribulation at being obliged, through the whim of friend Langstaff, to stop short in my literary career, when at the very point of astonishing my country, and reaping the brightest laurels of literature. We daily hear of shipwrecks, of failures and bankruptcies; they are trifling mishaps which, from their frequency, excite but little astonishment or sympathy; but it is not often that we hear of a man's letting immortality slip through his fingers; and when he does meet with such a misfortune, who would deny him the comfort of bewailing his calamity?

Next to embargo, laid upon our commerce, the greatest public annoyance is the embargo laid upon our work; in consequence of which the produce of my wits, like that of my country, must remain at home; and my ideas like so many merchantmen in port, or redoubtable frigates in the Potomac, moulder away in the mud of my own brain. I know of few things in this world more annoying than to be interrupted in the middle of a favourite story, at the most interesting part, where one expects to shine; or to have a conversation broken off just when you are about coming out with a score of excellent jokes, not one of which but was good enough to make every fine figure in corsets split her sides with laughter. In some such predicament am I placed at present; and I do protest to you, my good-looking and well-beloved readers, by the chop-sticks of the immortal Josh, I was on the very brink of treating you with a full broadside of the most ingenious and instructive essays that your precious noddles were ever bothered with.

In the first place, I had, with infinite labour and pains, and by consulting the divine Plato, Sanconiathon, Apollonius, Rhodius, Sir John Harrington, Noah Webster, Linkum Fidelius, and others, fully refuted all those wild theories respecting the first settlement of our venerable country; and proved, beyond contradiction, that America, so far from being, as the writers of upstart Europe denominate it, the new world, is at least as old as any country in existence, not excepting Egypt, China, or even the land of the Assiniboins; which, according to the traditions of that ancient people, has already assisted at the funerals of thirteen suns and four hundred and seventy thousand moons!

I had likewise written a long dissertation on certain hieroglyphics discovered on these fragments of the moon, which have lately fallen, with singular propriety, in a neighbouring state;—and have thrown considerable light on the state of literature and the arts in that planet;—showing that the universal language which prevails there is High Dutch; thereby proving it to be the most ancient and original tongue, and corroborating the opinion of a celebrated poet, that it is the language in which the serpent tempted our grandmother Eve.

To support the theatric department, I had several very judicious critiques, ready written, wherein no quarter was shown either to authors or actors; and I was only waiting to determine at what plays or performances they should be levelled. As to the grand spectacle of Cinderella, which is to be represented this season, I had given it a most unmerciful handling: showing that it was neither tragedy, comedy, nor farce; that the incidents were highly improbable, that the prince played like a perfect harlequin, that the white mice were merely powdered for the occasion, and that the new moon had a most outrageous copper nose.

But my most profound and erudite essay in embryo is an analytical, hypercritical review of these Salmagundi lucubrations; which I had written partly in revenge for the many waggish jokes played off against me by my confederates, and partly for the purpose of saving much invaluable labour to the Zoiluses and Dennises of the age, by detecting and exposing all the similarities, resemblances, synonymies, analogies, coincidences, &c., which occur in this work.

I hold it downright plagiarism for any author to write, or even to think, in the same manner with any other writer that either did, doth, or may exist. It is a sage maxim of law—

"*Ignorantia neminem excusat*"—and the same has been extended to literature: so that if an author shall publish an idea that has been ever hinted by another, it shall be no exculpation for him to plead ignorance of the fact. All, therefore, that I had to do was to take a good pair of spectacles, or a magnifying glass, and with Salmagundi in hand, and a table full of books before me, to muse over them alternately, in a corner of Cockloft library: carefully comparing and contrasting all odd ends and fragments of sentences. Little did honest Launce suspect, when he sat lounging and scribbling in his elbow-chair, with no other stock to draw upon than his own brain, and no other authority to consult than the sage Linkum Fidelius!—little did he think that his careless, unstudied effusions would receive such scrupulous investigation.

By laborious researches, and patiently collating words, where sentences and ideas did not correspond, I have detected sundry sly disguises and metamorphoses of which, I'll be bound, Langstaff himself is ignorant. Thus, for instance— The little man in black is evidently no less a personage than old Goody Blake, or goody something, filched from the Spectator, who confessedly filched her from Otway's "wrinkled hag with age grown double." My friend Launce has taken the honest old woman, dressed her up in the cast-off suit worn by Twaits, in Lampedo, and endeavoured to palm the imposture upon the enlightened inhabitants of Gotham. No further proof of the fact need be given, than that Goody Blake was taken for a witch; and the little man in black for a conjuror; and that they both lived in villages, the inhabitants of which were distinguished by a most respectful abhorrence of hobgoblins and broomsticks;—to be sure the astonishing similarity ends here, but surely that is enough to prove that the little man in black is no other than Goody Blake in the disguise of a white witch.

Thus, also, the sage Mustapha in mistaking a brag party for a convention of magi studying hieroglyphics, may pretend to originality of idea, and to a familiar acquaintance with the black-letter literati of the east;—but this Tripolitan trick will not pass here;—I refer those who wish to detect this larceny to one of those wholesale jumbles or hodge podge collections of science, which, like a tailor's pandemonium, or a giblet-pie, are receptacles for scientific fragments of all sorts and sizes.— The reader, learned in dictionary studies, will at once perceive I mean an encyclopædia. There, under the title of magi,

Egypt, cards, or hieroglyphics, I forget which, will be discovered an idea similar to that of Mustapha, as snugly concealed as truth at the bottom of a well, or the mistletoe amid the shady branches of an oak: and it may at any time be drawn from its lurking place, by those hewers of wood and drawers of water, who labour in humbler walks of criticism. This is assuredly a most unpardonable error of the sage Mustapha, who had been the captain of a ketch, and, of course, as your nautical men are for the most part very learned, ought to have known better.—But this is not the only blunder of the grave Mussulman, who swears by the head of Amrou, the beard of Barbarossa, and the sword of Khalid, as glibly as our good Christian soldiers anathematize body and soul, or a sailor his eyes and odd limbs. Now I solemnly pledge myself to the world, that in all my travels through the east, in Persia, Arabia, China, and Egypt, I never heard man, woman, or child utter any of those preposterous and new-fangled asseverations; and that, so far from swearing by any man's head, it is considered, throughout the east, the greatest insult that can be offered to either the living or dead to meddle in any shape even with his beard. These are but two or three specimens of the exposures I would have made; but I should have descended still lower; nor would have spared the most insignificant; and, or but, or nevertheless, provided I could have found a ditto in the Spectator or the dictionary;—but all these minutiæ I bequeath to the Lilliputian literati of this sagacious community, who are fond of hunting "such small deer," and I earnestly pray they may find full employment for a twelvemonth to come.

But the most outrageous plagiarisms of friend Launcelot are those made on sundry living personages. Thus: Tom Straddle has been evidently stolen from a distinguished Brummagem emigrant, since they both ride on horseback;—Dabble, the little great man, has his origin in a certain aspiring counsellor, who is rising in the world as rapidly as the heaviness of his head will permit; mine uncle John will bear a tolerable comparison, particularly as it respects the sterling qualities of his heart, with a worthy yeoman of Westchester county;—and to deck out Aunt Charity, and the amiable Miss Cocklofts, he has rifled the charms of half the ancient vestals in this city. Nay, he has taken unpardonable liberties with my own person! —elevating me on the substantial pedestals of a worthy gentleman from China, and tricking me out with claret coats, tight breeches, and silver-sprigged dickeys, in such sort that I can scarcely recognize my own resemblance;—whereas I absolutely declare that I am an exceeding good-looking man, neither too tall nor too short, too old nor too young, with a person indifferently robust, a head rather inclining to be large, an easy swing in my walk; and that I wear my own hair, neither queued, nor cropped, nor turned up, but in a fair, pendulous oscillating club, tied with a yard of nine-penny black riband.

And now, having said all that occurs to me on the present pathetic occasion,—having made my speech, wrote my eulogy, and drawn my portrait, I bid my readers an affectionate farewell; exhorting them to live honestly and soberly;—paying their taxes, and reverencing the state, the church, and the corporation;—reading diligently the Bible and the almanac, the newspaper, and Salmagundi;—which is all the reading an honest citizen has occasion for;—and eschewing all spirit of faction, discontent, irreligion, and criticism.

Which is all at present,
From their departed friend,
WILLIAM WIZARD.

THE END.

www.ingramcontent.com/pod-product-compliance
Lightning Source LLC
Chambersburg PA
CBHW021623250426
43672CB00037B/1918